Turkey's Economy from different perspectives after 1980

Ebru Gül Yılmaz / H. Neyir Tekeli (eds)

Turkey's Economy from different perspectives after 1980

The past, present and the future

PETER LANG

Bibliographic Information published by the Deutsche Nationalbibliothek
The Deutsche Nationalbibliothek lists this publication in the Deutsche Nationalbibliografie; detailed bibliographic data is available online at http://dnb.d-nb.de.

Library of Congress Cataloging-in-Publication Data
A CIP catalog record for this book has been applied for at the Library of Congress.

Colour Illustration: @iStock.com /courtneyk

Printed by CPI books GmbH, Leck

ISBN 978-3-631-81175-7 (Print)
E-ISBN 978-3-631-81601-1 (E-PDF)
E-ISBN 978-3-631-81602-8 (EPUB)
E-ISBN 978-3-631-81603-5 (MOBI)
DOI 10.3726/b16695

Peter Lang – Berlin · Bern · Bruxelles · New York · Oxford · Warszawa · Wien

This publication has been peer reviewed.

www.peterlang.com

This collection of assets aims to review Turkey's economy from different perspectives by focusing on the period after the 1980s, today and the future. Each section focuses on different parts of the full economic picture; such as innovation on economy, deindustrialization, circular economy, tourism, monetary policies, financial sector effects on economy, foreign trade, digitalization effects on economy, labor force, income inequality, and insurance sector effects.

The Editors

Ebru Gül Yılmaz is Assistant Prof. in the Department of International Trade at Istanbul Gelisim University, Turkey. She is also vice dean of Faculty of Economics, Administrative and Social Sciences. Her areas of research are digitalization, international trade, and macroeconomics. She also has 22 years of experience in banking sector as senior auditor, branch manager, senior department manager, and head of banking operations.

H. Neyir Tekeli is Assistant Prof. Dr. in the Istanbul Kültür University, Turkey. She is also head of Ground Handling Services Management Department. Her areas of research are tourism, tourism management, and tourism economics.

Preface

Turkey has a crucial change in terms of economic infrastructure after the decision of opening up the economy at 1980. Following import substituting industrialization strategy ended with an economic crisis at the end of the 1970s. With the beginning of the 1980s in January, a very radical economic program was announced that brought economic liberalization. After economic liberalization each economic dynamic has changed and is never going to be the same again especially after opening up the capital account completely at 1989. The aim of this book is to share the academic research outputs and the field experiences on Turkey's economy for the related period with contributors from different backgrounds and different perspectives.

The contributors to this book with their both academic and field experience provide a broad understanding of Turkey's economy after the 1980s and also expand the readers' horizon on having a better understanding of expectations for the future. We appreciate them for becoming a team, and we sincerely thank each of them for sharing their experience and expertise.

Ebru Gül Yılmaz Editor

Contents

Notes on Contributors

Cengiz Doğru is Assistant Prof. in the Department of Finance and Banking at Nişantaşı University, Turkey. He also gives lectures at İstanbul Bilgi University as a part-time lecturer. He was a former Sworn in-Banks Auditor at the Turkish Treasury and former Bank Board Member at various banks in Turkey, Cyprus, and the Netherlands. His research and interest areas are financial markets, risk management, financialization, and corporate governance.

Çiğdem Boz, born in 1978, is Associate Professor of macroeconomics in the Department of International Trade at Istanbul Gelisim University, Turkey. She is also interested in history of economic thought and political economy. As a founder of the theater of economic thought, she has recently directed a documentary about the Turkish economy.

Damla Özekan is Assistant Prof. in the Department of International Trade at Istanbul Gelisim University, Turkey. She also gives lectures in MBA at Isik University. Her studying areas include international economics, international trade, sustainable development, circular economy, and economical and political aspects of energy and environment. She is working as a consultant and trainer to the municipalities and companies in the field of climate action planning and sustainability leadership.

Ebru Gül Yılmaz is Assistant Prof. in the Department of International Trade at Istanbul Gelisim University, Turkey. She is also vice dean of Faculty of Economics, Administrative and Social Sciences. Her areas of research are digitalization, international trade, and macroeconomics. She also has 22 years of experience in banking sector as senior auditor, branch manager, senior department manager, and head of banking operations.

Evrim Ildem Develi is a part-time Assistant Prof. in the Institute of Social Sciences of Işık University. She is also giving consultancy to firms and teaching at training programmes for SMEs. Her studying areas include marketing, e-commerce, business administration, international marketing, and innovation management in firms.

Furkan Evranos is Assistant Prof. in the Department of Banking and Finance at Beykent University, Turkey. He is one of the founders of Cogito Park & Co

Investments Group and currently a Board Member and General Manager at Cogito Park & Co FT Institute and Cogito Park & Co Technology Development.

Hakan Özcan is Assistant Prof. in the Department of International Finance at Istanbul Okan University, Turkey. His areas of research are digitalization, international finance, and insurance.

Hazar Dördüncü is Assistant Prof. in the Department of International Trade and Logistics at Nişantaşı University, Turkey. He is also Vice Dean of Faculty of Economics, Administrative and Social Sciences and director of the School Applied Sciences. His areas of research are international trade, logistics, and aviation management.

H. Neyir Tekeli is Assistant Prof. Dr. in Istanbul Kültür University, Turkey. She is also head of Ground Handling Services Management Department. Her areas of research are tourism, tourism management, and tourism economics.

Onur Özdemir is Assistant Prof. in the Department of International Trade (English) at Istanbul Gelisim University, Turkey. He is currently working on income distribution, inequality, financialization, economic growth, and heterodox economics.

Sezgi Gedik is a research assistant in the Department of Tourism and Hotel Management at Istanbul University-Cerrahpasa, Turkey. Her areas of research are tourism economy, environment, and cultural heritage.

Suna Muğan Ertuğral is Assistant Prof. in the Department of Economic Development and International Economics at Istanbul University, Turkey. Her areas of research are tourism economics, sustainable tourism, employment relations, and macroeconomics.

Yeliz Sevimli Saitoğlu, PhD, is the head of Banking and Insurance Department at Istanbul Kültür University, Turkey. Her research and interest areas are statistics, biostatistics, decision trees, probability, and quantitative methods.

Assist. Prof. Dr. Cengiz Doğru

Monetary Policy in Turkey from 1980 to Present "Maintaining Price Stability and Financial Stability"

Abstract: In this chapter, Turkey's monetary policy applications as well as the results of these policies between 1980 and 2018 will be analyzed. These periods will be examined according to the alignment with monetary policy conversions about implementations, tactics, and strategies. Since the monetary policy instruments, mostly focused on solving the existing problems and responding to crises, both problems and monetary policies applied for precautionary measures are chronologically evaluated together. In addition the recent monetary policies have been studied as a separate in subheadings.

Keywords: Monetary Policy, Financial Stability, Financial Crises, Inflation Targeting, Monetary Transmission Mechanism

1 Introduction

Keynesian thought has become popular and very dominant all over the World since the Bretton Woods Conference in 1944. However, it was softened and then mostly abandoned in the late 1970s. During this period, a number of governments designed their economic policies according to the Keynesian thought and principles.

After the 1980s, ideas of globalization, financial liberalization, and privatization have risen. It was unprecedented that many governments have adopted detailed and strict privatization programs in their countries such as the USA, the UK, France, Germany, Mexico, and Turkey.

Moreover, financialization has begun to threaten national economy policies as well as economic actors of the whole economy. Financialization has forced governments, legal entities, and other members of the society to use more financial instruments. Not only governmental institutions and companies but also households become important customers of banks by using various financial products from basic payment instruments such as credit cards to complex synthetic financial derivatives and securities.

It is obvious that Turkey was affected by the mentioned changes in specified periods. Furthermore, Turkey was one of the countries hit hard by the various crises. Thus the country has faced a large number of financial crises which were called time to time as currency crises, debt crises, liquidity crises, and banking crises between 1980 and 2018.

The Central Bank of Turkey has designed and implemented such monetary policies appropriate to the economical needs and change of the World under the concepts of globalization, financial liberalization, financial deepening, and financialization concepts in accordance with the Turkish Government's monetary and fiscal policy.

Monetary policy tools used by central banks are open market operations, discount lending, and reserve requirements. Many central banks design and implement their monetary policies around these instruments.

2 Decisive Monetary Policy Periods of Turkey

In this section, important developments affecting the monetary policy will be classified and explained in chronological order in order to cover the significant changes and developments in which they are involved.

2.1 Pre-1980 Period Monetary Policies

Although the subject of this book is defined as post-1980 economic developments, in order to evaluate the post-1980 developments and the macroeconomic framework, the analysis of the previous periods is important at this stage. Therefore, the key developments affecting the monetary policy in the pre-1980 period are summarized below.

2.1.1 Establishment of the Republic Central Bank of Turkey

The Central Bank of Turkey (hereinafter referred to as the Central Bank) started to operate as the national Central Bank of the young Turkish Republic in 1930. The Central Bank has been defined as an independent and autonomous body, and these peculiarities were emphasized on its establishment law and its shareholders' agreement. Besides, Central Bank's primary objective is defined to support the economic development of the country. According to the founding act, Central Bank is granted with the exclusive privilege of issuing banknotes in Turkey.

Furthermore, the Bank was also authorized to set rediscount rates, to regulate the money market transactions and the circulation of TL, to execute Treasury operations, and to take all necessary measures for the sake of safeguarding the value of the Turkish currency. Central Bank also was assigned as the treasurer of the Government (CBRT, 2018a).

In the 1930s, the Government was the unique authority to set exchange rates under the fixed exchange rate regime in force at that time. Since the main payment instruments in the country were checks and promissory notes other than money, the Central Bank used the rediscount rates mechanism effectively as the main monetary policy tool. In contrast to developments in the World, the 1930s were a period of low inflation in the country.

2.1.2 World War II and Its Implications

Despite not participating in the war, Turkey was affected by the negative conditions of World War II in the 1940s. Under these adverse conditions, the Government used the Central Bank resources for financing budget deficits and other public finance needs instead of using these resources for implementing independent monetary policy. For this reason, economic and fiscal conditions deteriorated between 1938 and 1948.

The Central Bank implemented a monetary policy for achieving growth and rapid development as a target in the 1950s. Hence the Government began to finance economic growth with Central Bank resources. In line with these targets, the Central Bank provided short-term advances to the Treasury for the first time in its history.

2.1.3 The Importance of the State Planning Organization on Monetary Policies

Turkey adopted the planned economy in the 1960s. In the same year, the Undersecretariat of State Planning Organization (SPO) was founded and started to prepare five-year development plans for the country. These plans were covering all aspects of the economical targets such as monetary policy, fiscal policy, growth, employment, inflation rates, etc.

Besides, these plans were mandatory to be implemented for the public sector. However, plans were encouraging for the private sector with its special stimulation and bolstering programs. The Government carried out economic and industrial developments in the country with the help of these plans. Under these circumstances, the Central Bank implemented expansionary monetary policies and perpetually continued to bolster the Government budget's financing needs as the Government's sole treasurer in order to reach planned targets.

Meanwhile, the control mechanisms of the fixed exchange rate regime were gradually transferred to the Central Bank. It was started to regulate this subject with its circulars and communiques such as Communique on the Protection of the Value of Turkish Money and Capital Movements Circular.

The new Central Bank Act (No: 1211) was accepted in 1970 by the Parliament with introducing new concepts for efficient central banking. With this new act, the Central Bank increased its power on monetary policy instruments. In addition, the new law brought a compulsory rule that the Government should ask the opinion of the bank about money and credit-related applications and implementations.

Moreover, the Central Bank was authorized to conduct open market operations to regulate money supply and liquidity according to financial markets' needs like the other pioneer central banks such as Federal Reserve Bank of the United States and the Bank of England of the UK. The Central Bank also was permitted to grant medium-term loans for the purpose of supporting investments and economic development. The amount of advances available to the Treasury was raised to 15 percent of the budget appropriation for the related year. During these years, the collaboration of the Central Bank and the State Planning Organization was a very important element for achieving targets of the monetary policy.

2.2 Monetary Policies of the 1980–1990 Period

In this specified decade, there have been important changes in monetary policy practices in Turkey due to experiencing some significant development such as 24 January 1980 Decisions, September 12 Military Coup, and bankers' bankruptcy scandal. In this case, the Government and the Central Bank responded to these negative developments with new monetary policy practices.

2.2.1 Decisions of 24 January 1980

In the early 1980s, the financial liberalization thoughts were becoming more significant throughout the World. Simultaneously, there were unprecedented changes in the Turkish economy in the 1980s.

The Government announced the structural conversion decisions on the economy which was called the Decisions of 24 January 1980. The impact of these decisions affected the whole national economy for almost four decades, still continuing to do so.

The Government has decided to adopt free market economy in light of these decisions. Therefore, floor and ceiling price applications were abandoned for achieving financial liberalization process under the concept of free market conditions. Besides, foreign trade regulations were amended to provide more liberal and competitive currency and investment environment.

The 24 January 1980 Decisions were taken by the Ministers' Council dated 24 January 1980 and entered into force. The outlines of these decisions are briefly as follows (Tuleykan and Bayramoğlu, 2016):

- TL was devalued, and simultaneously the foreign exchange regime was rearranged according to new policies.
- The flexible foreign exchange regime was accepted instead of fixed exchange regime and then the Turkish lira was allowed to fluctuate against foreign currencies.
- The Central Bank was authorized to manage national gold and foreign exchange reserves of the country.
- The Central Bank was also authorized to use all policy tools in order to get price stability. Therefore price stability became the main target for the Central Bank.
- Some certain precautions were taken to reduce the share of the state in the economy and support purchases of agricultural products in parallel with the implementation in State Economic Enterprises (SEEs) were restricted.
- Subsidies, except on fertilizers, energy, and transport, have been abolished.
- Foreign trade has been liberalized, and foreign capital investments have been encouraged.
- Overseas contracting services has been bolstered.
- Import is gradually liberalized, and exports have been encouraged with tax rebate, low interest rate loan, import exemption for exporters, and customs exemption.

With these decisions taken on 24 January 1980, the main objectives that are aimed to be realized can be listed as follows:

- Decreasing inflation rapidly and taking it down,
- Increasing foreign exchange revenues through realistic exchange rate policy implementation and improving the balance of payments by exceeding the foreign exchange bottleneck,
- To increase exports rapidly with various incentive decisions and to focus on exportation of industrial products following the industrialization policy towards exportation,
- To empower the SEEs to freely determine the prices of the products that they produce and to mitigate the burden on the Treasury by making these damaging organizations profitable,
- Release of interest rates and increase savings by ensuring that the money of the individuals under the pillow is transferred to the financial sector,
- Increasing foreign investment by attracting the country with various incentives,
- Ending the controls on prices and determining the prices according to the supply and demand in the market,

- Minimize the role of the State in economic activities and its intervention in the economy,
- Decreasing unemployment by turning to investments that increase employment,
- Tax reform, increasing tax revenues, and ensuring justice in taxation,
- Reducing the privileges in favor of the public sector between the public and private sectors.

All these changes gave to the Central Bank the opportunity to implement a more comfortable and steerable monetary and exchange rate policies. In accordance with these decisions, national banks were more comfortable on determining the loan and deposit interest rates under market conditions without the Government's intervention. The Central Bank was authorized to monitor and report these deposit and loan interest rates for regulating the financial markets.

2.2.2 Military Coup, Bankers' Bankruptcy, and Its Implications

After announcing the 24 January Decisions, a military coup occurred in the same year. Hence the implementation of these decisions in a determined manner was interrupted by the military government.

Due to the insufficiently regulated financial and investment environment and the absence of the capital markets law, nonbank financial institutions, called banker, began to implement an interest rate race in the country. Therefore, the bankers' crisis erupted in Turkey in 1982. At the end of the crisis, more than 10 bankers collapsed with unpaid debts of their capital markets instruments to their customers who mostly have no financial literacy. In the same year, the capital markets were starting to regulate truly, and the Capital Market Board was founded in Turkey for the first time.

In 1984, with the amendment in the Protection of the Value of Turkish Currency Act, the limitations and prohibitions of purchasing, selling, and possessing foreign currencies were removed. In a sense, it meant to transmit of the convertibility (Kazgan et al., 2000).

2.2.3 Improvement of Monetary Policy Instruments Between 1985 and 1990

In the second half of the 1980s, new market instruments were developed to implement its monetary policy by the Central Bank. These were interbank money market transactions, foreign exchange, and effective market transactions. In addition, open market transactions were also put into operation. With the establishment of the interbank money market on April 2, 1986, the Central Bank was no longer the only source for meeting the interbank liquidity needs.

With the establishment of the foreign exchange market, the Central Bank allowed banks to regulate their foreign exchange reserves by mediating the determination of exchange rates in the market. As a result of these regulations, the Central Bank began to implement a monetary policy to manage total money and credit supply by controlling total reserves. In addition, the Central Bank was authorized to determine the interest rates by the Government in 1987 (Bakır 2007).

In 1989, the Law of the Protection of the Value of Turkish Money (Decree No. 32) was amended and was further liberalized. Hence, local residents were allowed to conduct operations directly in foreign currency without any limitation or prohibition, and also it announced the Turkish lira as a convertible currency. Furthermore, the signals of more flexible exchange regime were introduced to the financial markets.

In the late 1980s, the instruments used to manage monetary policy were mandatory reserves (deposit reserve requirements), open market operations, and disponobilty mechanisms. Reserve requirement rates for deposit accounts, especially in economies where capital markets are undeveloped mostly used as an powerful monetary policy tool. This tool, which is used frequently in the Turkish financial system, was referred for protection and not changed very often (Akçay, 1997).

The Central Bank without informing the public has made monetary programming in itself in the period from 1986 to 1989. However, the period in which the targets of monetary size were committed in a planned manner and financial and price stability were selected as the objective of the period is after 1990. Although not announced to the public, the targets for 1986 were achieved to a great extent. In 1987, there was a serious deviation in the inflation rate, but other variables were in line with the targets (Doğru and Savrul, 2012).

2.3 Monetary Policies of the 1990–2000 Period

Innovations in financial markets in the World started in the 1980s and then gained speed in the 1990s. In parallel, it was difficult for predicting a monetary relationship that could be the basis for setting a policy in advance. In this context, the effects of monetary programming policies started to decrease, in line with financial and technical innovations (Çetin, 2016).

2.3.1 Using Monetary Targeting as a Main Monetary Policy Tool in 1990

2.3.1.1 Monetary Targeting in General

In a situation where monetary targeting strategy is followed, the Central Bank explains that the annual growth target of monetary size will be of a certain value. For example, the growth rate of M1 will be 5 % or M2 growth rate will be 6 %. The Central Bank is then responsible for achieving this target. In the 1970s, many countries adopted monetary targeting. The most important of these countries are Germany, Switzerland, Canada, the UK, Japan, and the USA.

One advantage of monetary targeting is to know immediately whether the Central Bank has reached its goal or not. For this reason, monetary targets may send rapid signals to the public and financial markets about the intentions of policy makers to control the monetary policy situation and control inflation. However, the success of monetary targeting depends to a large extent on the strong and reliable relationship between the objective variable and the targeted monetary aggregate. If this relationship is weak, the monetary size target does not work correctly (Mishkin, 2010).

Moreover, since the studies conducted after the 1990s, it has been found that there is no high level of correlation between the money base and prices. Central banks find it increasingly difficult to meet the monetary targets that they envisaged. Innovations and new methods of application, such as the widespread use of electronic money in the form of paper money, the increasing availability of technology in shopping, have made the circulation rate of money quite volatile. Therefore, central banks started to experience high rates of deviations in monetary targeting. In addition, in stabilization programs where the money supply was used as a nominal anchor, fluctuations and sudden shocks continued to be seen in the economy, even though inflation was under control. For all these reasons, nominal anchor regimes based on monetary targeting or money supply were abandoned in the early 1990s (Doğru and Savrul, 2012).

2.3.1.2 Implementation of Monetary Targeting in Turkey

On January 16, 1990, the Central Bank announced the first monetary targeting program to the public, immediately after the agreement on the restriction of advances between the Treasury and the Central Bank as a result of the completion of internal and external financial liberalizations in 1989.

In this program, it was stated that the target of the program was to meet the liquidity of the market needs together with the target of stability of exchange rates and interest rates. The program is based on setting targets on the Central Bank balance sheet. Hence, some targets have been identified such as total balance sheet size, domestic liabilities, domestic assets, and central bank money as the monetary aggregates instead of M1 (demand deposits and money in circulation), M2 (M1 + Term Deposit), and M2Y (M2 + Foreign Currency Deposits in banks resident in Turkey) (Bakır 2007).

The program has three purposes in the medium term. Firstly, to curb the growth of the balance sheet by keeping the domestic credit expansion under control; secondly, by lowering the Central Bank's foreign exchange liability, increasing the ratio of Central Bank money within the total liabilities; and thirdly, to increase its international reserves due to the rising Central Bank's foreign exchange risk position.

Although the Program initially gave positive results at the beginning, the Gulf War in 1990 affected the financial markets as well as the Government's monetary and fiscal policy. The economy deteriorated further together with public budget deficits, current account deficits, political instability, early general elections, and weak capital structures of national banks.

2.3.2 The 1994 Financial Crisis and Increasing Importance of Monetary Policies

In the first quarter of 1994, the Government announced a change that the public borrowing instruments' interest rates would be decreased and adversely their maturities would be increased both in Turkish Lira and the other convertible foreign currencies side. Whereas almost all of the potential buyers and holders of these instruments were local Turkish banks due to financial dominance effect.

These banks would not have carried such a long-term bond portfolios with its lower yields and bearing huge FX risk due to these banks' weak asset qualities, low level capital adequacies, and lack of risk management standards. Therefore the public borrowing program failed. Both inflation rates and exchange rates were skyrocketed.

During the 1994 financial crisis, all public and private domestic banks were affected adversely. As a result, operating licenses of three private banks (Marmara Bank, Impexbank, and TYT Bank) were canceled and their managements and surveillances were taken over to Savings Deposit Insurance Fund (SDIF) by the Government.

In April 1994, the Government announced the New Economy Program, which included a number of certain precautions for financial markets. In the context of the program, Turkish lira was devalued while the tax rates of fuel oil and public monopoly products (cigarettes and alcohol) increased considerably.

Besides, the use of Central Bank resources by the Treasury was restricted, and this advance facility was terminated in 1998.

In July 1994, Turkey signed a 14-month stand-by agreement with the International Monetary Fund (IMF). Although it was agreed to allocate 897 Million US$ loan facility in terms of the agreement, only 682 million US$ of this amount could be received by the Turkish Government (Erdinç, 2007).

Between 1995 and 1999, the Central Bank focused on preventing speculative movements in the FX markets and reducing fluctuations in exchange rates and implemented policies towards establishing stability in financial markets (CBRT, 2018a).

2.4 Monetary Policies of the 2000–2010 Period

This period was very painful and difficult times for the Turkish economy. The political and financial crises in 2000 and 2001 turned into a banking crisis. On the other hand, the USA Mortgage Crisis in 2008 and European Union Debt Crisis in 2010 had affected the Turkish economy very negatively. In this section, evaluations will be made about the monetary policies implemented during the mentioned crisis periods.

2.4.1 The 2000–2001 Financial Crisis and Implemented Monetary Policy Tools

2.4.1.1 Earthquake in the Marmara Region and Political Instability

Turkey suffered from a major earthquake in the Marmara Region in August 1999. As a matter of fact, deteriorated public finance has worsened even more due to the earthquake's financial burden. The Government has decided to collect a new additional tax on government bonds returns which was called as Fiscal Balance Tax for compensating earthquake's expenditures.

On the other hand, the political instability created by the three-party coalition government and the nonconformity of the Government with the President were delaying the measures to be taken and further fueling the coming crisis. Since economic conditions further deteriorated as a result of exogenous shocks, a new economic program based on exchange rates was introduced in 2000. The proposed applications and implementations on the stabilization program could not prevent the economy going bad in accordance with a result of failure to execute. The failure to complete the structural reforms envisaged in the stabilization program. It also led to a weakening of confidence in the program, and in February 2001, Turkey's economy faced a serious economic crisis.

2.4.1.2 Implementation of the Stabilization Program

The main objective in nominal anchor-based stabilization programs is to take inflation down with a fixed exchange rate to eliminate macroeconomic imbalances and to make reforms by benefiting from the partial relief of the economy. The lack of necessary reforms within the prescribed period brought a deep financial crisis.

Monetary base expansion was based on foreign assets in the monetary policy program. Leaving the monetary base entirely in foreign currency inflows has laid the ground for short-term speculative monetary inflows. The lack of initiatives to prevent these movements adversely affected the program. In economies where liquidity is entirely based on foreign assets, the structure and resilience of the banking system is of great importance. In the case of a capital outflow in an economy with a banking sector that has a high interest rate risk and no foreign exchange surplus, it is inevitable that the economy will encounter liquidity risk and foreign exchange attack (Kepenek and Yenturk, 2010).

Despite of the plan started in 2000, implementation of proposed structural reforms in the program started 11 months after the initiation of the program. International Monetary Fund and the other international investors have created ideas that political power did not bolster the program. Apart from the structural reforms, the recommendations for the program were fulfilled. For instance, due to the increase in public revenues through earthquake tax and indirect taxes and contraction of noninterest public expenditures, it reached the goal of the noninterest surplus in the consolidated budget.

2.4.2 Financial Crisis Turns to Banking Crisis

As it is known, the most important reasons for the crises are the increase in interest rates, the problems in the banking sector, and the financial imbalance of the public. These three factors in Turkey have always maintained its existence and its importance during crises. If there is excessive deterioration in the balance sheets of banks, bank bankruptcies will begin and the whole system will be damaged by the contagion effect. The decrease in bank loans during the financial crisis period will reduce the supply of funds to the borrowers, and this will also increase the interest rates. Thus, the current debt crisis will turn into a banking crisis (Mishkin, 2010).

In parallel with the above findings, financial debt crisis turned into a banking crisis in 2000. The regulations required by the stabilization program in the Turkish banking sector could not be made. As per the new banking law adopted in 1999, it was decided to establish the Banking Regulation and Supervision

Authority (BRSA) and it started to work in 2000. However, as soon as the new institution was established, it had to deal with a number of urgent structural banking problems which will turn into a banking crisis.

Meanwhile, Turkish Banking Sector was bearing a number of financial and structural weaknesses and fragilities. At the beginning of the 2000–2001 crisis, Turkish Banking Sector was small in terms of scale compared with equivalent economies, supporting public finance rather than real sector, had weak deposit to credit transformation, low concentration with new entries into the sector, and also weak risk management culture. Global capital took a very small interest in this sector (BRSA, 2010).

These weaknesses and fragilities can be summarized as follows:

- The number of banks has increased quickly following financial liberalization.
- The negative effects of state-owned banks within the system have become clear.
- Losses from duties given to state-owned banks, which contradicts economic rationale and the weaknesses in management.
- The Turkish Banking Sector did not make a stable progress within the period of 1990–2000.
- The sector receded from its essential function which is intermediation.
- The public sector had crowded out private investments with high real interest, and at the same time it had consumed a big amount of banking sector's resources.
- Banking sector has also placed its own resources on government bonds having high interest and nominal yield, and a securities-weighted placement structure with 0 % risk in terms of capital adequacy has appeared.
- The sector was operating with very low capital adequacy.
- Dollarization has affected the resource structure and especially deposits negatively.
- Maturity mismatch which is the most fundamental problem of the banking sector.
- The insufficiency of the scope and effectiveness of the regulations in banking.
- The weaknesses in risk management and corporate governance applications have made the banking system become oversensitive to liquidity, interest, and exchange rate risks.
- Postponing the resolution of problems of the banks under close monitoring has augmented the difficulties.
- The deficiencies in the implementation of financial reporting and international accounting standards.
- Inadequacies and delays in complying with international standards.
- The exploitation of banks' resources by the shareholders.

These fragilities and weaknesses would turn the financial crisis into a banking crisis (BRSA, 2010). During the crisis, 22 banks were taken over by the SDIF. Most of them were subject to liquidation, but only a small number of banks could be sold such as Sumerbank (Oyakbank), Demirbank (HSBC), and Sitebank (Nova Bank) by the SDIF.

2.4.3 November 2000 Crisis

Until the crisis, the Central Bank did not increase net domestic assets as suggested in the program. As a result of the lack of corrective devaluation in the beginning, there was a current deficit which was much higher than the one specified in the program. The lack of necessary reforms in the banking sector, the high current account deficit and consumption level, the delay of the political power in making reforms, led to the widespread belief that the program could not be carried out in November 2000.

In this period, the ratio of short-term debt to international reserves increased, with capital outflows in the second half of November. As of November 22, a liquidity demand emerged in the banking sector. The Central Bank did not maintain liquidity due to the November 2000 program. Graph 1 illustrates the time deposit interest rates between 2000 and 2005.

As a result, interest rates increased to 2000 percent (some state-owned banks applied 5000 percent), which led to a devaluation expectation. After these developments, the Central Bank had to raise its net domestic assets to give liquidity to the market. The limitation on the net domestic assets rule has been abandoned. The liquidity shortage in the economy resulted in contraction in the real sector and that speculative turmoil could not be foreseen.

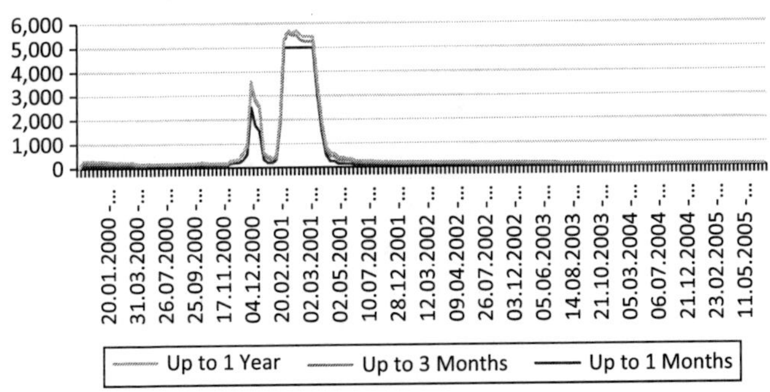

Graph 1: Commercial Banks Time Deposit Interest Rates. **Source:** CBRT (EVDS), 2019

Furthermore, the urgent measures to be taken against these situations were not planned. All of these things became an important deficiency of the program. On December 4, 2000, the IMF requested the Government to abandon the program. The reason for this was the concern about the depletion of reserves due to the currency attack. The Government of the period did not give up the program.

2.4.4 February 2001 Crisis

On February 19, 2001, after a political dispute between the prime minister and the president, a second crisis took place and a large amount of capital in the economy went abroad. As a result of the willingness of banks to close their short FX positions, demand for foreign currency increased and liquidity squeezed. Therefore, interest rates immediately increased.

As a result of the rapid capital outflows in February, both foreign exchange prices and interest rates climbed. The fluctuating exchange rate regime also triggered the exchange rate increases considerably. This situation caused the Central Bank's foreign exchange reserves to become critical.

The Central Bank reserves were $ 24.8 billion at the beginning of the year 2001, whereas it decreased to USD 18.5 billion in March. The decline in the reserves to this level limited the Central Bank's power to intervene in the foreign exchange market. The fact that banks and companies increased their foreign exchange demand in order to close their short foreign exchange positions made the increase in foreign exchange prices permanent.

On the other hand, due to the speculative purchases of foreign banks, the increasing demand for Turkish Lira (TL) also led to an increase in interest rates. In the said period, the indicators related to the public sector also deteriorated and inflation rose to 88.6 percent. There have also been significant deteriorations in macroeconomic variables such as GDP and unemployment rates.

2.4.5 The 2000–2001 Crisis Remediation Program: "Transition to Strong Economy Program"

Following these developments, "Transition to Strong Economy Program" which was announced in two sections on April 14 and May 15, 2001, was put into operation. This Program addressed issues such as transparency and accountability in the public sector, restructuring of banks, establishing strong relations in the real sector, reaching the financial balance of the public sector, and restructuring the financial sector.

In these difficult times in Turkey's economic conditions, it was inevitable to change the Central Bank's Act. As a result of the long-standing problems in monetary policy and the deepening crises in the recent period, a new act was adopted on April 25, 2001, by the Parliament.

In this context, the new Law stipulates that the Bank shall determine, at its own discretion, the monetary policy that it will implement and the monetary policy tools that it is going to use. Hence, the Bank has gained instrument independence like in many advanced economies. The new law also states that the Bank shall support growth and employment policies of the Government, provided that they are not in conflict with the objective of maintaining price stability (CBRT, 2018a).

Another important amendment made to the Law was that the Central Bank was prohibited from granting advances and extending credits to the Treasury or other public institutions, and from purchasing debt instruments issued by the Treasury and public establishments and institutions in the primary market. Thus, the practice of using Central Bank resources in financing public sector deficits was terminated. This amendment is important as it ended the monetization of public deficits, one of the primary causes of inflation.

2.4.6 *Switching to Inflation Targeting*

2.4.6.1 *Inflation Targeting in General*

As a matter of fact, the development of financial markets and the acceleration of international capital movements have made it difficult to implement monetary targeting and exchange rate targeting strategies. In the previous years, the implementation of interest rate and nominal income targeting strategies, which were used as intermediate target variables, were not fully achieved. This has made inflation targeting a popular alternative policy strategy in recent years.

The implementation of inflation targeting was initiated and succeeded for the first time in New Zealand in 1990. New Zealand's success in implementing this policy has led to the adoption of this approach by other countries such as the United Kingdom and Canada.

Another important element of the aforementioned program is the floating exchange rate regime. Under this regime, the level of exchange rates is determined in the free market under supply and demand conditions. With the abandonment of the exchange rate anchor following the economic crisis in February 2001, a search for new monetary policy regimes began. Under the new Central Bank Law, while the concept of price stability was highlighted, legal regulations were made to facilitate the transition to inflation targeting. The new law stipulates that the primary duty of the Central Bank is price stability, which has been an important step in the transition to the inflation targeting regime. The inflation targeting regime was described as giving the Central Bank the task of ensuring price stability (Çetin, 2016).

In the light of these developments and successful country experiences with an amendment to the Central Bank Law in 2001, maintaining *financial stability* was defined as the supporting objective of the Bank. In this restructuring process, it was decided to change the monetary policy strategy as well. In line with the primary objective of price stability, the "inflation targeting regime" was adopted in 2002. Accordingly, the Central Bank started to use short-term interest rates as the main policy instrument.

2.4.6.2 Taylor Rule in Inflation Targeting

The Taylor Rule was developed by the American economist John Taylor. A rule that requires central banks to change their policy rates in the same direction as the difference between the actual and targeted inflation rates and the actual and potential output level. This rule can be written as follows:

$$r = \widehat{r} + \pi + h(\pi - \tilde{\pi}) + g\left(y - \widehat{y}\right) \tag{1}$$

This rule indicates that the policy rate (r) should be set equal to the inflation rate (π) plus an equilibrium real interest rate determined by the monetary authority ($\hat{r}$) plus a weighted average of two gaps: (1) an inflation gap, current inflation (π) minus a target inflation rate ($\tilde{\pi}$), and (2) an output gap, the percentage deviation of real GDP (y) from an estimate of its potential full employment level ($\hat{y}$). In the formula, (h) is the inflation response coefficient of the Central Bank, which brings the difference between the actual inflation and the target inflation to the nominal discount rate (Mishkin, 2010).

Nowadays, central banks have not adopted monetary policy according to the Taylor Rule. However, this rule is used only as a guide. Because, while there is undesired tendencies in the inflation or economic conjuncture, the Taylor Rule systematically allows to be known the attitude of the monetary authority in advance (CBRT, 2018b).

2.4.6.3 Implicit Inflation Targeting

Under the National Program set out in May 2001, the main objective of monetary policy was to reduce the inflation to single digits in the medium term and to achieve price stability. To this end, the Central Bank has adopted the *Implicit Inflation Targeting* in monetary policy strategy.

The new regime has been named implicit inflation targeting because of the fact that the Monetary Policy Committee did not make an interest rate decision. Besides, the forward inflation forecasts and the Central Bank's possible policy responses were not published.

Implicit inflation targeting was applied between 2002 and 2005. It was thought that the problems in the banking sector were not yet fully resolved: there was a habit of pricing based on past inflation rates, the movements in exchange rates were effective in determining the inflation, and the fact that the financial dominance was effective so it was too early for the transition to inflation targeting. Therefore, implicit inflation targeting was preferred.

In addition to setting targets consistent with inflation target and growth forecast for the monetary base in specified periods, the Central Bank follows a monetary policy focusing on future inflation. In this context, short-term interest rates, which are the main policy instruments, are taken into consideration only by taking into consideration the values that inflation can take in the future and are used effectively only in order to reach the inflation target. When the necessary conditions are met, the Central Bank plans to adopt the Inflation Targeting monetary policy strategy.

In 2002, the Central Bank made significant changes to its monetary policy operational structure in preparation for the inflation targeting strategy and within the framework of modern central banking and strengthened these practices in 2003. In this context, no significant change was expected in the liquidity management strategy in 2004. Excess liquidity in the market continued to be withdrawn by reverse repo transactions carried out at the ISE Repo-Reverse Repo Market within the framework of Turkish lira deposit transactions and open market operations in the Interbank Money Market (Erkan, 2003).

In spite of the fact that the policy rate was not changed and the negative developments in the global level during the 2002–2004 period (the Iraq War, expectations that the FED could go ahead and increase the rates aggressively), the program gave successful results. As a result of the inflation developments and their prediction to be in line with the targets, the Central Bank has repeatedly decreased its interest rates (Özatay, 2011).

2.4.6.4 *Maintaining Price Stability*

The new regime introduced, the *price stability*, is the main objective of the Central Bank. The inflation target was shared with the public at the beginning of the year. The overnight interest rates as the Central Bank's main policy instrument was started to determine according to the Central Bank's inflation forecasts.

In 2003, as in 2002, the Central Bank would make limited interventions, not only directed to the level of exchange rates, to avoid excessive fluctuations in both directions in exchange rates, but also to increase foreign exchange reserves in line with favorable developments in the balance of reverse currency substitution and payments. It was announced that the auctions will do.

In this context, on May 6, 2003, daily foreign exchange buying auctions were resumed in line with the objective of strengthening the international reserve position as a result of the foreign exchange supply surplus in the markets due to the reverse currency substitution and developments in the balance of payments. In order to reduce the excessive volatility in the exchange rate, the markets were intervened in a transparent and limited manner.

In the first half of 2003, the Central Bank met all monetary performance criteria and indicative targets set by the International Monetary Fund. In addition, the resumption of the aforementioned program and floating exchange rate regime sent positive signals to the markets and contributed to a significant improvement in inflation expectations.

In line with these developments, the Central Bank reduced policy rate (short-term interest rates) five times from April and reduced the overnight borrowing interest rate from 44 percent to 29 percent. The Central Bank, together with the Government, set the inflation target for 2003 as 20 percent. However, the 2003 inflation rate was even lower than the targeted level.

All these developments, which paved the way for the realization of these favorable conditions and supported the decline in inflation, emerged as the product of the monetary and fiscal policies implemented in accordance with the economic program.

2.4.6.5 Positive Effects and Results of the Stability Program

The effect of an independent monetary policy that focused on budget discipline and inflation on economic stability has been clearly observed in 2003 by a number of elements:

Firstly, the fact that a consistent income and budget policy has been applied to the target has been the most important signal to be sincere about the fight against inflation. This approach has led to a downward trend in inflation expectations for the next 12-month period, even in periods of rapid inflation.

Secondly, the monetary and fiscal policies implemented in line with the program targets contributed to the establishment of a safe environment and reduced the risk premium by reducing concerns about the sustainability of borrowing. These developments contribute to the reduction of long-term interest rates, strengthen the Turkish lira, and thus support the fight against inflation in terms of costs.

Thirdly, fiscal and monetary discipline also enables the revival of domestic demand to be realized in a controlled manner and thus contributes to preventing a demand-side pressure on inflation.

As a result, 2002–2003 was a period in which the fight against inflation was not a miraculous formula, and it was observed that monitoring monetary and fiscal policies consistent with the target with a high level of reliability would bring great gains in a short time (Dünya Gazetesi, 2004).

In 2004, the Central Bank continued to implement implicit inflation targeting under the floating exchange rate regime. In this context, monetary aggregates was also to be taken into consideration, but the priority would be the convergence of inflation to the targeted level. In other words, many times, as stated in the Central Bank reports and presentations, the developments in the monetary base will be evaluated in terms of the information contained regarding the future inflation, rather than a definite target, taking into account the difficulties in estimating the money demand during the downward trend in inflation.

Although no liquidity shortage is expected in 2004, standard and intraday repo auctions will be actively used in case of any liquidity squeeze, and short-term interest rates were created within the framework of the Central Bank interest rates.

The floating exchange rate regime continued in 2004, and the exchange rate was based on market conditions. In 2004, the Central Bank intervened in the direction of buying or selling, when the exchange rates fluctuated. Moreover, the Central Bank continued to strengthen its foreign exchange reserves if the developments in the balance of payments and reverse dollarization were appropriate. The form of strengthening the foreign exchange reserves will be transparent, through the exchange of auctions, based on the mechanisms established by consultation with market participants.

2.4.6.6 Transition to Explicit Inflation Targeting Regime

In 2005, as a result of a number of positive improvements, the idea of the transition to inflation targeting regime thought occurred. These improvements can be listed as getting successful results of implicit inflation targeting, the historically low level coming of Turkey's credit risk in the international market, the disappearance of the public sector borrowing requirement, and having fallen significantly in the public debt, as a result of finding a healthy structure of the banking sector in 2005.

The fact that the Monetary Policy Committee is now at the center of the interest rate decisions and the Central Bank would issue quarterly inflation reports has been effective in deciding to switch from the *implicit* inflation targeting regime to the *explicit* inflation targeting regime. The Central Bank decided to set a point target and explain a range around this target.

In May 2006, Turkey's credit risk increased as a result of the reduction in global risk appetite in financial markets, and inflation rates began to deviate from the target. The Central Bank responded to these developments by increasing interest rates. Although global risk perception declined, presidential elections increased political tensions in 2007. There were also loosening tendencies in fiscal policy. Turkey's economy has been affected negatively by increase in the World's energy and food prices.

2.4.7 Implications of 2008 Mortgage Crisis and 2010 European Union Debt Crisis

In 2008, the global financial crisis that started in the United States further increased uncertainties. The volatility of exchange rates and interest rates has increased Turkey's credit risk. Starting from October, energy and commodity prices declined in parallel with global demand. This environment has caused significant fluctuations in both inflation rates and forecasts. While the policy rate followed a volatile course in the period of 2006–2008, the Central Bank started to reduce the policy interest rate as of November 2008 as a result of the economic downturn.

As the economic downturn continued in the first nine months of 2009, the Central Bank continued to lower the policy rate. The most recent discount was made in November 2009 and the Central Bank cut the policy rate from 16.75 percent to 6.5 percent in this period. The inflation rate remained above the target in 2006–2008 period. The deviations from the target were reflected in expectations. The inflation expectations for the end of 2007 were also raised.

In 2009, inflation remained below the target for the first time since inflation targeting was explicitly implemented. In this context, 2009 and 2010 year-end targets were updated to 7.5 percent and 6.5 percent, respectively. These two objectives were previously explained as 4 percent (Özatay, 2011).

The success of the Central Bank increased the effectiveness of monetary policy on financial variables and expectations. Result in a large change in the risk perception towards Turkey, the Turkish Lira's durability increased. The downward slope of market rates also reduced real interest rates. Parallel to these developments, loan rates declined in the second half of 2009. In the same year, inflation developments were in line with the targets.

The inflation targeting regime allows for timely response to economic shocks. The Central Bank may also focus on sudden weaknesses due to external factors in growth and employment, provided they do not conflict with the price stability target. Monetary policy in Turkey, with sound banking and prudent fiscal policy, has become more resistant. It is thought that the monetary policy will become stronger with the fiscal policy as the Government's Medium Term Program and the EU harmonization process. In the medium term, the Central Bank must monitor the developments in public finance in determining monetary policy strategies. In the light of all developments and evaluations, the inflation target was determined as 6.5, 5.5, and 5 percent in 2010, 2011, and 2012, respectively (TCMB, 2009).

2.4.8 Responsive Implementations to the Crises by the Central Bank

The Central Bank's practices in 2010 were mostly for the purpose of responding to the Mortgage Crisis and the debt crisis in the EU. In April 2010, the Central Bank announced that it would begin to reduce liquidity measures by adopting a new strategy called take-off strategy and that the required reserve ratios would be reduced to the previous level. Within the scope of the take-off strategy, the Central Bank terminated the application of interest payments to required reserves, increased required reserve ratios, and differentiated them according to their maturities.

In order to control the rate of credit growth, the reserve requirement ratios were chosen as a tool. It aims to extend the maturity of the banking system's liabilities by applying low and high provision rates for short maturities. The interest corridor was expanded. Interest rates are kept low to slow down short-term capital inflows that make the economy fragile. The overnight borrowing rate was reduced by 500 basis points to 1.50 percent and the policy rate by 75 basis points to 6.25 percent.

According to the seasonally adjusted data, policies implemented as of the end of 2010 respond to two quarter delayed and the current account deficit improved gradually. Similarly, it was concluded that the Central Bank's monetary policies affected the real economy and the growth process after approximately two quarters (Süslü and Dişbudak, 2012).

With the weakening of the impact of the global crisis on financial markets in 2010, the Central Bank announced on April 14, 2010, the withdrawal of liquidity measures taken during the crisis and the take-off strategy including normalization of the operational framework of monetary policy.

Accordingly, the Central Bank withdrew the temporary liquidity support that was introduced during the crisis period. In this context, it increased the required liquidity gradually while increasing the required reserve ratios. In order to contribute to the financial stability as well as the monetary policy take-off strategy, the Central Bank has designed a more flexible method for foreign exchange buying auctions in order to adapt to the volatility of capital flows while accelerating reserve accumulation and introduced this method starting from October 2010 (TCMB, 2010).

In the postcrisis period, the Central Bank's policy rate was the main determinant of the interest rates in the money and credit markets. The interest rate decline continued in 2010 as well. Due to the positive developments in the economy, credit rating agencies have increased Turkey's credit rating in 2010. As a result of the effects of the crisis, the divergence in the growth rates of domestic and foreign demand and rapid credit expansion increased the current account deficit.

3 Monetary Policies After 2011 and Beyond

In this section, the Central Bank's monetary policy implementations and engagement of new policy instruments will be evaluated between 2011 and 2018. Rising of global risks will be mentioned shortly and then new monetary policy instruments developed by the Central Bank under the current economic outlook will be evaluated in detail.

3.1 Rationale for Converting Monetary Policies

Developments in Europe and the United States and the decisions taken have led to the expansion of the current account deficit in the Government's Medium Term Program which was prepared for 2011–2013 period. In addition to the Central Bank's objective of price stability, the aim of financial stability has been the necessity to implement policies to adapt to the new conjuncture.

In the new conjuncture, the main policy instrument requires the use of alternative instruments such as liquidity management and reserve requirements along with short-term interest rates (one-week repo auction interest). The step to protect financial stability has been to extend the maturity of the banking sector's liabilities. With the measures to be taken, it is aimed to spread both deposit and foreign capital inflows to a longer term. The differentiation of the reserve requirements according to the maturities and the fact that certain liability items which are not subject to the required reserve before are included in the required reserve can be evaluated within this scope.

In order to limit the risks related to the current account deficit, increasing public savings and maintaining fiscal discipline are also important. In particular, the deterioration in the public debt dynamics in the peripheral countries in Europe caused the public debt indicators to become increasingly important. Under the aforementioned economic conditions and international improvements, the Central Bank introduced a number of new monetary policy instruments.

3.2 Monetary Transmission Mechanism's Theoretical Framework

3.2.1 Monetary Transmission Mechanism in General

The policy decisions of the central banks affect economic activity and inflation mainly through four channels. It is not possible to separate the channels of monetary transmission mechanism with precise lines, and it is assumed that the channels affect or complement each other. These channels are interest channel, asset prices channel (including bank lending channel and stock channel), expectations channel, and exchange rate channel. These are illustrated in Fig. 1 (TCMB, 2012).

Figure 1 basically illustrates channels of the monetary transmission mechanism and explains the relationship between each other. Within the framework of this new monetary policy implemented since April 2010, the Central Bank determined credit growth, exchange rates, and expectations as transfer channels between tools and targets (Fig. 2). (Mishkin 2010).

3.2.1.1 Interest Channel

The interest channel, which is the most traditional transmission channel in monetary transmission mechanisms, is also referred to as the Keynesian standard monetary transmission channel. Considering this channel, the monetary authority is changing the marginal cost of the debt; it affects the cash flow and consumption decisions of consumers, and investment and spending decisions of the producers and changes the total demand in the economy.

The functioning of the interest channel starts with a change in the short-term interest rate and results in the reflection of this change to medium- and long-term interest rates through the supply and demand mechanisms in the financial markets. The change in short-term nominal interest rates of the monetary authority affects the short- and long-term real interest rates under the assumption that prices are solid.

The effect of monetary policy changes on long-term real interest rates may be different than expected. According to the expectations theory, long-term interest rates will depend on the effect of the change in the policy rate on the expectations of interest rates.

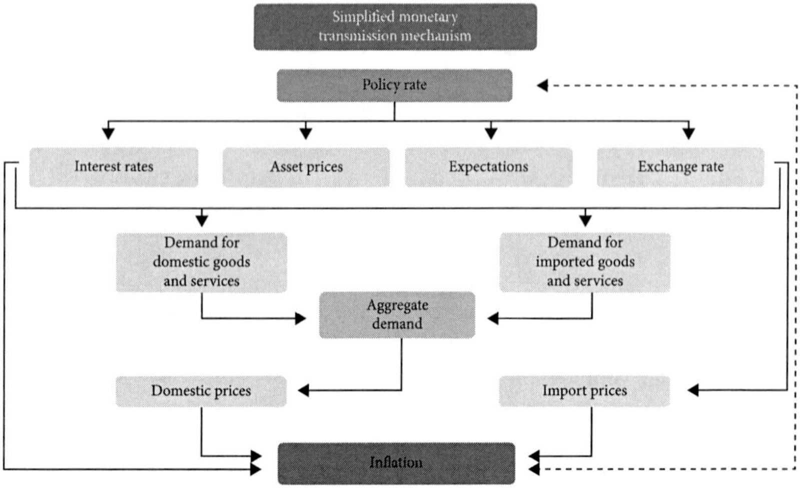

Fig. 1: Simplified Monetary Transmission Mechanism. **Source:** The Central Bank of Turkey

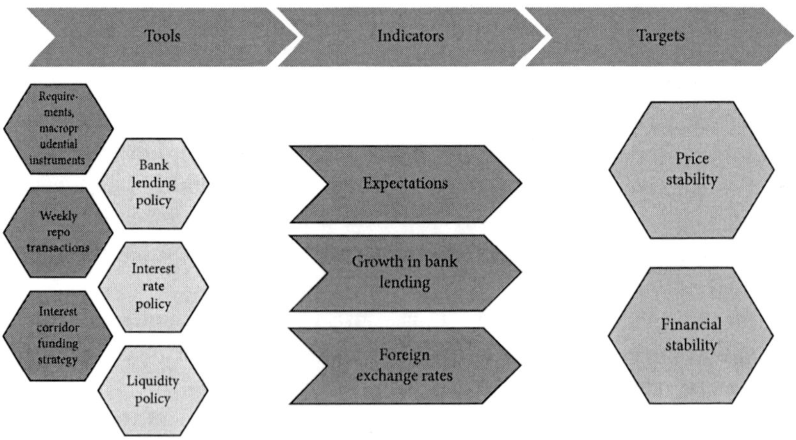

Fig. 2: Monetary Policy Tools, Indicators, and Targets. **Source:** Yörükoğlu

3.2.1.2 *Asset Prices Channel*

Changes in nominal interest rates or money supply of central banks also have an impact on asset prices. This effect can be monitored over bank lending channel and stock prices channel.

Bank Lending Channel

As a result of the expansionary monetary policy, the banks will increase their deposits and the amount of loans they can give. This increase in the amount of loans will lead to an increase in the investment expenditures of the firms and will have an expansionary effect on the total demand. Moreover, it is expected that the expansionary monetary policy will increase the value of the firms, decrease the perceived debt risk, increase the cash flow and reduce the nominal debt burden, and decrease the moral hazard and adverse selection effect resulting from the information asymmetry.

Stock Prices Channel

When central banks lower interest rates, demand for stocks will increase as bond yields will decrease. This will increase the price of the stocks. As a result of these developments, the market value of the firms will increase compared to the cost of the company, and the investment and production will increase. An alternative channel to the stock channel also includes changes in consumption expenditures as a result of the influence of stock prices on the wealth level of individuals.

3.2.1.3 *Expectations Channel*

Expectations channel is the transfer channel of the economic units through the changes that they expect to be experienced in economic conditions, particularly inflation. A central bank with a high credibility can create a sense of confidence in the economy in order to achieve price stability and influence the developments in prices as long as it can give an idea about future inflation to economic units. In order for the central bank to explain its future policies in line with the principle of transparency, it is necessary for the economic units to believe that the policies implemented by the bank will be successful.

3.2.1.4 *Exchange Rate Channel*

The exchange rate channel affects both the total demand and the total supply. In an economy where there is monetary expansion, investment in that country will be less profitable and capital outflows will be seen for the investors of the country as the domestic real interest rates will decrease. This process, which will continue with the decline of the value of the national currency, will cause the value of goods produced in the country to become cheaper than foreign goods. The increase in net exports and aggregate demand in the nominal exchange rates will be realized at the rate of real exchange rate changes.

In general terms, the effect of the exchange rate channel on the transmission mechanism is directly proportional to the degree of openness of the countries. The more open a country is, the more effective the exchange rate channel will be.

Factors affecting the Monetary Transfer Mechanism are government's interventions to the markets, pricing mechanism in the economy, structure of financial system, maturity structure of financial contracts, financial situation of banking system, capital movements, sources of finance, households, and firms.

3.2.2 Composition of the New Monetary Policy

The Central Bank introduced a new monetary policy in the 2010 composition by expanding the framework of the inflation targeting regime that it has implemented since 2006 in order to limit macrofinancial risks. In addition to its primary objective of price stability, the Central Bank increased the importance of financial stability.

In this context, by designing a policy framework that aims to reduce macrofinancial risks arising from external balances and capital flows, it established the indicator foot of the new policy on credit growth and exchange rate. In addition to the short-term interest rates used by the Central Bank as a policy instrument, it has started to use different complementary policy instruments such as reserve requirements, interest rate corridor, liquidity management, and reserve option mechanism.

Table 1 depicts a comparison of previous and new monetary policy practices implemented by the Central Bank (TCMB, 2013).

The use of these tools, especially in the monetary transmission mechanism and the prominence of credit and exchange rate channel, has led to some changes in the functioning of these channels. The following section shows how the functioning of credit and exchange rate channels changes in the context of the new policy.

As it is shown in Tab. 2, these tools can be divided into two parts as structural tools and conjunctural tools (TCMB, 2013).

Within the scope of the new monetary policy, the targets were tried to be reached with the help of the channels shown in the figure. Bank lendings and exchange rate as transmission channels serve as a bridge between the tools and

Tab. 1: Comparison of Monetary Policy Framework. **Source:** The Central Bank of Turkey

Tools & Targets	**Previous Framework**	**New Framework**
Tools	Policy Interest Rate	Policy Interest Rate Liquidity Management Interest Rate Corridor Reserve Requirements Reserve Option Mechanism
Targets	Price Stability	Price Stability Financial Stability

Tab. 2: Monetary Policy Tools. **Source:** The Central Bank of Turkey

Structural Tools			**Conjunctural Tools**	
Maturity-Based Reserve Requirements	Leverage-Based Reserve Requirements	Reserve Option Mechanism	Policy Interest Rate and Interest Rate Corridor	Liquidity Management

the targets. Interest rates, required reserve ratios, bank lending, and exchange rate channels as monetary transmission mechanism channels aim to influence price stability and financial stability.

In order to facilitate communication, the Central Bank featured bank lending and exchange rate variables as transmission channels. It has enabled the policy to be implemented in a healthier manner due to the reason that the two variables are explained without delay and it is easy to observe and the direct interaction with the policy tools can be established. Thus, the process from the policy tools to its targets is made more understandable and observable (Kara, 2012).

3.2.3 The Central Bank's New Monetary Policy Framework and Tools

As the risk appetite increased and the volatility in short-term capital movements increased, the awareness of financial stability led the central banks to seek new policies after the global financial crisis. Within this framework, the Central Bank has gradually adopted a new monetary policy design including financial stability without compromising on price stability since the end of 2010. While the aim of the old monetary policy approach was only price stability, price stability and financial stability in the new monetary policy have been considered as an objective. While the policy instrument is the policy rate in the old monetary policy, structural instruments (policy rate, liquidity management, and interest rate corridor) are used in the implementation of the new monetary policy (TCMB, 2011).

3.2.3.1 *Maturity-Based Reserve Requirements*

The reserve requirement ratio is the amount that the statutory rate of banks' deposits and other liabilities must be kept within the central bank. The reserve requirement ratios are high for short-term liabilities and adversely low for long-term liabilities. The reserve requirement ratios of the banks at the central bank may vary depending on the maturity of their liabilities.

3.2.3.2 *Leverage-Based Reserve Requirements*

The leverage ratio was introduced into the Turkish Banking System by Basel III regulations. Accordingly, the ratio will be calculated by dividing the core capital of a bank by the sum of on-balance sheet and off-balance sheet risks, and it should not be less than 3 %. In other words, a bank may take on-balance sheet and off-balance sheet risk 33.3 times of its core capital. This international definition was totally accepted by the Central Bank, and it was exactly reflected to the Central Bank's Reserve Requirements' Communique in 2013.

According to this regulation, Banks have leverage ratios calculated as;

- Less than 3 percent are additionally 2 points,
- Three percent (3 inclusive) to 4 percent, additionally 1.5 points,
- Four percent (4 inclusive) to 5 percent in addition to 1 point,

compulsory reserve should be established following the calculation period. As can be seen from the abovementioned regulation, the use of the leverage ratio by the central bank as a financial stability tool is carried out by applying additional required reserve ratios to the banks with high leverage ratio (TCMB, 2013).

3.2.3.3 *Reserve Option Mechanism*

The Reserve Option Mechanism (ROM) is a tool designed by the Central Bank that allows TL-denominated reserve requirements to be paid in foreign currency and gold. Central banks require that reserve requirements calculated on liabilities subject to required reserves in foreign currencies are generally kept either in domestic currency or in foreign currencies with high international validity, such as the US dollar. The ROM provided a different dimension to the reserve requirement policy by giving banks the opportunity to keep their TL liabilities as FX. As far as it is known, ROM application of the Central Bank is a first in the World (Böcütoğlu, 2015).

At first glance, this opportunity brought to the banks with the ROM can be seen as contrasting with the Central Bank's sovereignty, but it is clear that ROM has a goal of benefiting from money substitution, considering the years of money substitution in our country and the capital flows that might create instability after the global crisis. However, it is emphasized that the most important objective of the ROM is to limit the negative effects of excessive volatility in capital movements on macroeconomic and financial stability (Binici et al., 2016).

On the other hand, due to the fact that the liability structure of the Turkish banking system is largely based on foreign currency, banks are experiencing difficulty in converting the foreign currency from these sources into Turkish lira. In addition, they are subject to maturity and interest rate mismatch. Therefore, they apply to London Money Market for conducting cross-currency swap transactions to eliminate this mismatch. ROM acts as the function of cross-currency swaps and saves banks from paying large amount of swap costs. Therefore, almost all of Turkish banks use and utilize the ROM facility to the full extent. The ROM as an automatic stabilizer reduces the exchange rate volatility of the capital flows on domestic markets and partially reduces the need for the interest rate corridor (TCMB, 2013).

3.2.3.4 Policy Interest Rate

Central banks have the ability to control money supply and short-term interest rates through official interest rates. Central banks determine the interest rates of the short-term debts to banks in order to provide the liquidity required by the banks and the borrowing to withdraw excess liquidity. Central banks aim to influence the general level of economic activity and prices by determining this interest rate. Therefore, this interest rate is called the policy interest rate.

Decisions on policy rates are taken by the Monetary Policy Committee (MPC). In the interest rate decisions, a medium-term perspective focuses on the future inflation outlook. In addition, the principle of non-response to the transient effects of external shocks on inflation and the policy response to the medium-term targets are adopted. In this context, when the MPC makes a decision on interest, it considers a wide range of information such as total supply-demand balance, fiscal policy indicators, monetary indicators and loan size, wage, employment, unit cost, productivity developments, public and private sector pricing behaviors, inflation expectations, and exchange rates. Today, the Central Bank uses the one-week repo auction interest rate as the policy rate (CBRT, 2018b).

3.2.3.5 Interest Rate Corridor and Active Liquidity Policy

The interest rate corridor is the remaining area between the overnight borrowing and overnight lending rates of the Central Bank, and the market interest rates are formed within this corridor. The Central Bank may fund the banks through a one-week repo with quantity auction.

In this system, the amount of funding made in one-week term can be changed on a daily basis and the market interest can be at the desired level within the corridor. The width of the interest rate corridor determines the fluctuations in the Central Bank's liquidity operations and short-term market rates. In May 2010, the CBRT started a one-week repo auction within the scope of its new monetary policy and became the main funding tool of the Bank (Fig. 3). (CBRT, 2013).

In order to increase the predictability of monetary policy and strengthen the transmission mechanism, it was decided to determine the overnight borrowing and lending rates of the Central Bank with a margin of +/- 150 basis points around the one-week repo auction rate. Thus, overnight borrowing and lending rates formed a symmetrical corridor around the one-week repo auction rate (CBRT, 2018c).

In case of a liquidity shortage, banks may borrow overnight at certain limits from the central bank, and may lend to the central bank in case of excess liquidity.

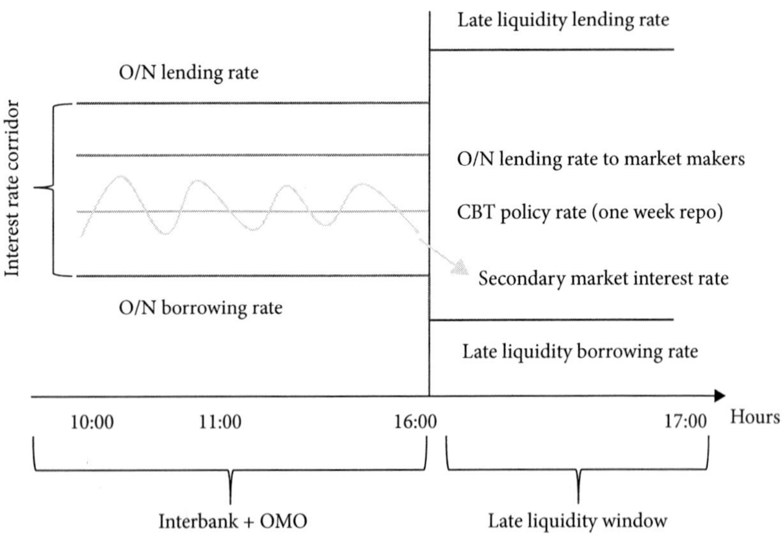

Fig. 3: Implementation on Interest Rate Corridor. **Source:** The Central Bank of Turkey

The interest rate corridor refers to the interest rate with a lower and upper limit. The upper limit is the interest rate to be used by the central bank in the loans to be provided to banks, while the lower limit is the interest rate to be applied in the debts to be received from the banks.

When the central bank wants to influence the credit volume of banks, it can use the interest rate corridor tool. By holding the interest rate corridor broadly, the central bank may reduce the predictability of short-term interest rates, increase uncertainty, and reduce credit. In addition, the wide corridor provides the power to make flexible decisions against global changes without waiting for the Monetary Policy Committee one month later. Since the central bank will raise the upper limit of the interest rate corridor, banks may have a higher interest cost against a possible fund demand, and banks may also tend to raise interest rates on their loans (Kara, 2012).

Graph 2 illustrates interest rate corridor, CBRT average funding rate, and one-week repo rates.

3.3 Recent Developments on Monetary Policy

Graph 3 shows improvements of the inflation rates between 2006 and 2018 as annual percentage change.

As it can be seen from Graph 3, inflation rates continued to decrease after the adoption of inflation targeting and maintained their horizontal trend until September 2016. However, since September 2016, both the producer price index

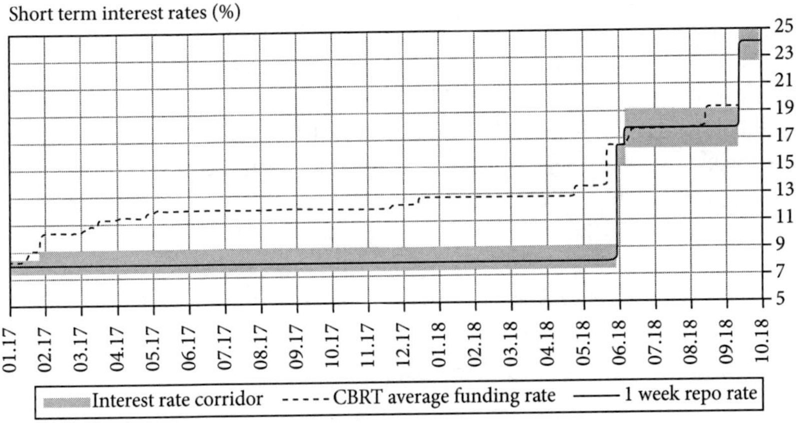

Graph 2: Interest Rate Corridor Realization. **Source:** The Central Bank of Turkey

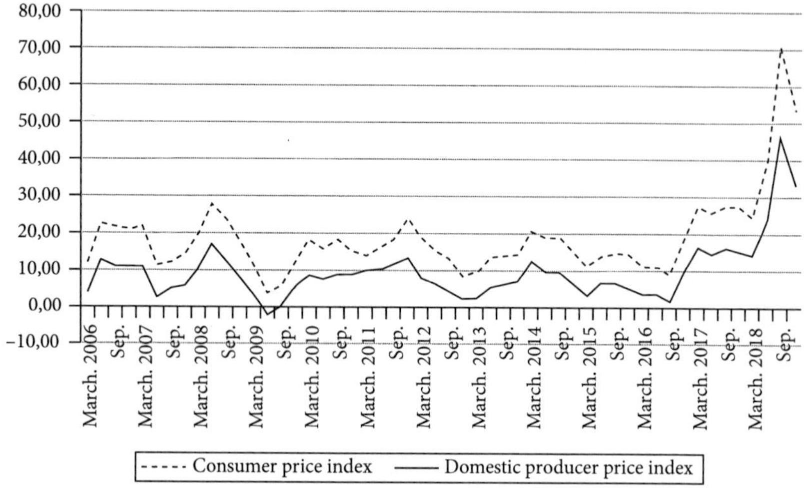

Graph 3: Implications of Inflation Targeting Regime to Price Indexes. **Source:** TUİK (2019), Temel İstatistikler, Enflasyon ve Fiyat

and the consumer price index have entered a rapid upward trend and inflation targeting has not been achieved.

According to the Central Bank Law No. 1211, if the inflation target is not attained, the Central Bank is accountable for reporting to the Government and announcing to the public the reasons for the deviation from the inflation target and the necessary measures to be taken.

Due to the inflation target not being achieved, the Central Bank published an open letter to the Government. In this letter, it was emphasized that the inflation target for 2018 was set jointly with the Government at 5 percent. It was also indicated that the Central Bank would write an open letter to the Government should the year-end inflation deviate from the target range (by more than two percentage points from the target in either direction). Besides, the year-end inflation stood above the target range in 2018. With this open letter, the Central Bank put across on the reasons for the deviation of inflation from the target and explains the measures already taken – and to be taken – to bring inflation back to the target (TCMB, 2019).

4 Conclusion and Final Remarks

There have been important changes in monetary policy practices in Turkey between 1980 and 1990 due to the experiencing of some significant developments such as 24 January 1980 Decisions, September 12 Military Coup, and bankers' bankruptcy scandal. In this case, the Government and the Central Bank responded to these negative developments with new monetary policy practices.

In the 1994 financial crisis, all public and private domestic banks were affected adversely. After the 1994 crisis, the Government announced *The Transition to Strong Economy Program* which included a number of certain precautions for financial markets. Between 1995 and 1999, the Central Bank focused on preventing speculative movements in the FX markets and reducing fluctuations in exchange rates and implemented policies towards establishing stability in financial markets.

The political and financial crises in 2000 and 2001 have turned into a banking crisis. On the other hand, the USA Mortgage Crisis in 2008 and European Union Debt Crisis in 2010 have affected Turkish economy very negatively. The Central Bank has adopted the *Implicit Inflation Targeting* in monetary policy strategy in 2001, and it was applied between 2002 and 2005. The new regime introduced, the *price stability*, is the main objective of the Central Bank. In 2005, as a result of a number of positive improvements, the idea of the transition to inflation targeting regime thought occurred and decided to switch from the *implicit* inflation targeting regime to the *explicit* inflation targeting regime in 2006.

In 2008, the global financial crisis that started in the United States further increased uncertainties. The volatility of exchange rates and interest rates has increased Turkey's credit risk. This environment has caused significant fluctuations in both inflation rates and forecasts.

The Central Bank introduced a new monetary policy in 2010 composition by expanding the framework of the inflation targeting regime that it has implemented since 2006 in order to limit macrofinancial risks. In addition to its primary objective of price stability, the Central Bank increased the importance of financial stability. Within the framework of this new monetary policy implemented since April 2010, the Central Bank determined credit growth, exchange rates, and expectations as transfer channels between tools and targets under the concept of Monetary Transmission Mechanism. In this context, by designing a policy framework that aims to reduce macrofinancial risks arising from external balances and capital flows, it established the indicator foot of the new policy on credit growth and exchange rate. In addition to the short-term interest rates used by the Central Bank as a policy instrument, it has started to use different complementary policy instruments such as reserve requirements, interest rate corridor, liquidity management, and reserve option mechanism.

In conclusion, Turkey was one of the hardest hit countries by the various crises. The Central Bank of Turkey has designed and implemented such monetary policies appropriate to the economical needs and change of the World under the concepts of globalization, financial liberalization, and financialization in accordance with the Government. The policies implemented by the Central Bank were, on the one hand, a response to economic developments and crises and, on the other hand, these policies developed in a similar way to the leading central banks.

Bibliography

Akçay, M.A. (1997), **Para Politikası Araçları Türkiye ve Çeşitli Ülkelerdeki Uygulamalar** (Uzmanlık Tezi), Ankara: DPT.

Bakır, C. (2007), **Merkezdeki Banka, Türkiye Cumhuriyet Merkez Bankası ve Uluslararası Bir Karşılaştırma**, İstanbul: İstanbul Bilgi Üniversitesi.

Binici, M., Kara, H. and Özlü, P. (2016), "Unconventional Interest Rate Corridor and the Monetary Transmission: Evidence From Turkey", **CBRT Working,** Paper No: 16/08, Retrieved from www.tcmb.gov.tr.

Böcütoğlu, M.E. (2015), **Rezerv Opsiyon Mekanizmasının Banka Davranışlarına Etkisi** (Uzmanlık Yeterlik Tezi), Ankara: TCMB.

BRSA. (2010), "From Crisis to Financial Stability (Turkey Experience)", **Working Paper**, Revised Third Edition, Retrieved from www.bddk.org.tr.

CBRT. (2018a), **The Central Bank of the Turkish Republic of Turkey History and Duties, General**, Retrieved from www.tcmb.gov.tr.

CBRT. (2018b), **100 Soruda Merkez Bankacılığı**, ISBN: 978-605-4911-74-5, Retrieved from www.tcmb.gov.tr.

CBRT. (2013), Monetary Transmission Mechanism, Ankara, Retrieved from www.tcmb.gov.tr.

CBRT. (2019), Commercial Banks Time Deposit Interest Rates, CBRT- EVDS, https://evds2.tcmb.gov.tr/index.php?/evds/dashboard/990.

CBRT. (2018c), **2019 Yılı Para ve Kur Politikası,** Retrieved from www.tcmb.gov.tr.

Çetin, M.Y. (2016), "Türkiye Cumhuriyet Merkez Bankası (TCMB) Para Politikası Uygula malarının Gelişimi", **Finansal Araştırmalar ve Çalışmalar Dergisi**, Vol.8, N.14, pp. 67–101.

Doğru, B. and Savrul, B.K. (2012), "Nominal Çapalar ve Türkiye'deki Uygulama Sonuçları", **Sosyal Bilimler Dergisi**, N.1, pp. 1–36.

Dünya Gazetesi. (2004), **MB:2004 Yılında da Düşük Enflasyon Hedefli Para Politikamızı Sürdüreceğiz** (02.01.2004).

Erdinç, Z. (2007), "Uluslararası Para Fonu – Türkiye İlişkilerinin Gelişimi ve 19.Stand-By Anlaşması", **Dumlupınar Üniversitesi Sosyal Bilimler Dergisi,** N.18.

Erkan, B. (2003), **Türkiye'de 1980 Sonrası Merkez Bankası Politikaları**, Retrieved from http://www.geocities.com/ceteris_paribus_tr/b_erkan.doc.

Kara, H.A. (2012), "Küresel Kriz Sonrası Para Politikası", **TCMB Çalışma Tebliği**, No.12/17, Retrieved from www.tcm.gov.tr.

Kara, H., Alper, K. and Yörükoğlu, M. (2013), "Alternative Tools to Manage Capital Flow Volatility", **BIS Working**, Papers No: 73.

Kazgan, H., Öztürk, M. and Koraltürk, M. (2000), **Türkiye Cumhuriyet Merkez Bankası**, İstanbul: Creative Yayıncılık.

Kepenek, Y. and Yenturk, N. (2010), **Türkiye Ekonomisi**, İstanbul: Remzi Kitabevi.

Mishkin, F.S. (2010), **The Economics of Money, Banking and Financial Markets**, Ninth and Global Edition, Pearson.

24 Ocak Kararları. **TR Offical Gazette (1980)** (16591, 5 April 1980).

Özatay, F. (2011), **Parasal İktisat Kuram ve Politika**, 2. Baskı, Ankara: Efil Yayınevi.

Süslü, B. and Dişbudak, C. (2012), "TCMB'nin Para Politikası Duruşunun Alternatif Açıklaması: Parasal Durum Endeksi (MCI)", **Yönetim ve Ekonomi**, Vol.19, N.2, pp. 67–85.

TCMB. (2009), **2010 Yılında Para ve Kur Politikası**, Ankara.

TCMB. (2010), **2011 Yılında Para ve Kur Politikası**, Ankara.

TCMB. (2011), **2012 Yılında Para ve Kur Politikası**, Ankara.

TCMB. (2012), **2013 Yılı Para ve Kur Politikası**, Ankara.

TCMB. (2019), **Open Letter to the Government**, Retrieved from www.tcmb.gov.tr.

TUİK. (2019), **Temel İstatistikler**, Enflasyon ve Fiyat www.tuik.gov.tr.

Tuleykan, H. and Bayramoğlu, S. (2016), "Türkiye'de 24 Ocak Kararları İle Başlayan Finansal Serbestleşmenin Günümüz İktisadi ve Mali Yapısına Yansımaları", **International Journal of Social Science**, N.44, pp. 401–420.

Assoc. Prof. Çiğdem Boz

De-industrialization in Turkey

Abstract: The study of deindustrialization, understood as the relative decline in the share of manufacturing in total national employment and output, really took off in the 1980s as the scale and consequences of economic restructuring and job losses in manufacturing became much more apparent and tangible. The deindustrialization wave that came to the fore after the 1980s is closely related to the neoliberal transformation that dominated the entire world in that era. The cost of applying neoliberal policies were thus the crises faced as a result of the economy becoming gradually more fragile, and drifting away from industrialization as a societal target.When we analyze industrialization policies of Turkey, one can see that Turkey implemented two main strategies from 1960s until today. The first is import substitution industrialization strategies, which were implemented between 1963 and 1980, and the second is export-oriented industrialization strategies, which were implemented 1980 onwards. Albeit somewhat differently, these strategies were implemented by many developing countries around the same periods in the same order for the same purposes. However, the period between the 1980s and today should be analyzed in two subcategories as 1980–2000 and post-2000. This is due to the fact that industrialization and policies related to this, although to a lesser extent than the 1960s, kept their important places between 1980 and 2000. We can describe the period between 2000 and today as "deindustrialization" period since the industrialization target fell off the agenda even further after 2000.

Keywords: de-industrialization, Turkey, Neo-liberal policies

1 Introduction

In the last 40 years, the developing countries have been through different growth and industrialization paths. It can be determined that "industrialization" was essentially limited to East and Southeast Asia under very similar external world conditions and global economic conjuncture in case of late industrialization possibilities. These economies both made great industrialization moves and maintained their industrialization processes under the most fluctuating and inhibitive conditions of global economic order (Taymaz and Voyvoda, 2017). Other developing countries, on the other hand, entered a process of "deindustrialization."

The concept of deindustrialization first emerged in the United Kingdom. It came into focus with the slowing industrial growth in the 1970s (Tregenna, 2011). Singh (1977) was one of the first to describe the connection between deindustrialization and the structural imbalance. In his interpretation, deindustrialization means that the processing industry is unable to satisfy domestic demand or conduct a level of export that could increase the level of employment. A key process in the spatial economic restructuring that is sweeping through the advanced capitalist countries during the 1980s is the deindustrialization of manufacturing (Cheshire, 1991). Tertiarization happens parallel to deindustrialization; in other words, the service sector becomes stronger (Barta et al., 2008).

In general, deindustrialization can be discussed under two different economic settings formed under two different economic policies: structural change and globalization. However, Hegyi-Keri (2016) argues that structural change is often identified with deindustrialization. Deindustrialization is a narrower term and often what is meant by it is either decreases in the number of people employed in the industry (Kiss, 2010; Cheshire 1991) or a decline in industrial production. Before the 1990s, particularly the industrial policies and national of the developing countries could affect the speed and extent of deindustrialization arising from structural change. However, national policies started to be considered as international competition, preventing interventions when globalization became deeper. As a result of globalization in Turkey, as with many other countries, it was observed that production industry's share in GDP declined and production sector composition changed with regards to technology.

Yet the term "deindustrialization" definitively fell into current language with the publication of Bluestone and Harrison's (1982) famous and seminal book entitled *The Deindustrialization of America*. Defining "deindustrialization" as the "widespread and systematic disinvestment in a nation's basic productive capacity" (1982:6), the authors expressed great concern about the wave of plant closings that swept through the northern USA during the 1970s and the ongoing erosion of America's industrial base, a phenomenon supposedly caused in part by a "globalization gambit" linking international capital flows and industrial investment decisions with both local and personal troubles (Leif van Neuss, 2016).

Verley (1997:420) also employs the term "deindustrialization" to describe the economic decline of some European proto-industrial regions, notably in France and Britain, which failed their transition to modern industry at times of the industrial revolution. The term "deindustrialization" has also been largely used to refer to regions that industrialized over the 19th and 20th century based on some comparative advantage, like the presence of economically valuable natural resources (coal, iron, etc.), and finally experienced a decline in the performance of their traditional sectors because of some competitiveness loss that could result, for instance, from the emergence of a new "technical system," as it was called by Gille (1978), or growing trade (Neuss; 2016).

The study of deindustrialization, understood as the relative decline in the share of manufacturing in total national employment and output, really took off in the 1980s as the scale and consequences of economic restructuring and job losses in manufacturing became much more apparent and tangible. Deindustrialization, which came to the fore after 1980, has two main reasons. First is the structural change, which is a change in sector composition as a result of moving from relatively less beneficial sectors to more beneficial sectors. The other reason is trade affecting these changes. Investigating the deindustrialization phenomenon in developed countries, Rowthorn and Ramasway (1997) state that North-South trade plays little role in these changes and they attribute the deindustrialization to internal factors of the country. Doğruel and Doğruel (2019) claim that this evaluation cannot show the effects of globalization to the fullest as this evaluation covers the period between 1970 and 1994, since the real effect of increased trade started in the 1990s when globalization intensified. It is argued that the trade relations that are improved due to globalization may cause deindustrialization in industrialized countries as well as developing countries (Neuss; 2016, Paolera et al., 2018). Thus, while deindustrialization was a result of structural changes before the 1990s, it was the result of the meshing of global and financial relations after the 1990s (Doğruel and Doğruel, 2019).

Previously thought to only affect developed countries, academic research on deindustrialization only focused on those countries. Dani Rodrik's essay titled "Early Deindustrialization" claimed that this phenomenon is observed in middle-income and even low-income countries since the 1980s, and that deindustrialization that starts before the industry sector had developed to a certain point is more dangerous for the economy (Öz, 2018:1).

When Van Neuss (2016) summarizes the key economic forces behind deindustrialization, he says that the theoretical literature has thus identified various channels through which structural change, and deindustrialization, can occur. They range from demand-side factors and also include elements about the intersectoral division of labor (outsourcing) and international trade. According to Van Neuss (2016: 4), despite the growing literature devoted to structural change, the causes of deindustrialization are, however, still not fully understood; and he suggests:

> *In their course of economic development, virtually all advanced countries have followed a broadly similar trajectory. Up until the 18th century, agriculture was the most important sector in all national economies around the globe, absorbing most of the labor force and contributing most of the production. As from the second half of the 18th century, a number of countries, especially those that are nowadays viewed as the most economically successful countries, have experienced a successful wave of industrialization. According to traditional*

historiography, the industrial revolution began in Britain then swept through Europe and North America, before reaching Japan and Russia by the end of the 19th century. While the causes of the industrial revolution are still heatedly debated in the literature, it is nevertheless widely recognized that the industrial revolution, a period that witnessed an unprecedented rise in the rates of efficiency advance, marked the starting point of modern economic growth, defined as the sustainable increase in GDP per capita, and accelerated the process of structural change. The growth of GDP per capita in successful countries has been accompanied with a fall in the agricultural share of employment and output, and a rise in the share of services. Manufacturing has moved on a different trajectory as its share in national output and employment follows a hump shape, that is, it is increasing for lower levels of economic development and decreasing for higher levels of economic development. The decreasing part of this trajectory refers to the process of "deindustrialization", a phenomenon which has particularly affected the most advanced economies since the last third of the 20th century.

There is an important body of literature defining deindustrialization processes and characterizing the underlying reasons for both developed and developing countries (Palma, 2008; Rowthorn and Ramaswamy, 1997, 1999). According to this literature, "early deindustrialization" definition is used to assert the deindustrialization tendency of developing countries especially after the 1980s, as opposed to "positive" deindustrialization definition, which feeds on productivity increase and Kuznetsian notions of demand shift, and which is used to define the processes developed countries have undergone in general. Accordingly, apart from exceptions (that are almost all Asian countries), the per capita income level that corresponds to the decline in industry (employment/added value) ratios in developing countries is too low compared to developed countries that went through the same process. Based on the assertion that the industry is the most important sector in creating the connections of production, learning, and income in economy, and thereby providing sustainable growth and dynamic productivity increase in economy; deindustrialization can be seen as a pathology that halts the economy's potential growth, labor, and resource utilization (Singh, 1977). Basing it on the determination that indicates production industry is the most dynamic sector in cases of innovation and progression, Rodrik (2013) claims that the "unconditional convergence" between developing and developed countries only works for the industry; and emphasizes that the growth potential of early deindustrialized economies would also be negatively affected (Taymaz and Voyvoda, 2017).

The deindustrialization wave that came to the fore after the 1980s is closely related to the neoliberal transformation that dominated the entire world in that era. The 1970s were very tough for the world economy. Due to the consequences of the Vietnam War, Bretton Woods' gold and dollar-based fixed exchange rate order had fallen apart, and Keynesian policies could not provide a sufficient response to the inflation and depression that occurred after the increase in petrol prices. First the Thatcher government in England and then the Reagan government in the USA made the case that Keynesian intervention methods should be abandoned and policies that focus more on market mechanisms should be adopted both in domestic and international financial policies in order to end the depression. Decreasing public expenditures, abandoning welfare state policies, and privatizing public financial enterprises constituted the main articles of this agenda. The reflections of the neoliberal economy policies on the international scale were the alleviation of trade barriers and reduced supervision on the movement of capital. In the following years, Bretton Woods' fixed exchange rate regime left its place to floating exchange rate regime, while capital movements with increasing volumes started to become a source of instability for the world economy.

After World War II, import substitution industrialization strategy was adopted in the developing countries parallel to Keynesian policies. However, a change in policies became a growing issue for developing countries when market-oriented policies began to gain importance in developed countries and world economy. International institutions such as IMF and World Bank played an important role in abandoning import substitution policies and adopting market-oriented policies, which would be referred to as Washington Consensus later on. These institutions began to recommend developing countries to abandon protectionism of import substitution and of government interventionism, and to adopt market mechanisms and open their economies to foreign countries. Even though developing countries were reluctant to do so, it was getting harder for them to resist IMF's pressure of market-oriented policies especially in the times of crisis during which they need external support (Akyüz, 2007). The cost of applying neoliberal policies were thus the crises faced as a result of economy becoming gradually more fragile, and drifting away from industrialization as a societal target.

Yet, not every developing country adopted neoliberal policies. A few developing countries had started to maintain policies regarding manufactured goods exportation in East Asia since the 1960s. Following the Japanese example, these countries were using government intervention strongly in industrialization process. Starting from the 1970s and 1980s, China and India too joined among countries who combined export-oriented industrialization and government intervention. First China, then India reached very high growth rates thanks to very high saving and investment rates. Thus, the center of economy started shifting from the two ends of Atlantic Ocean towards East Asia (Pamuk, 2014).

If we take a look at historical development within the Turkish context; while the long-term growth speed of Turkey in the 1960s was around 5.5 %, the amount had slightly gone down in the 1970s, and then settled around 4–4.5 % from the 1980s until today. This proportion did not show significant increase in the 2000s. Industrial growth speed of Turkey was higher than GDP growth speed during the examined period. But this difference gradually declined and decreased to 0.3–0.4 points in the 2000s. In other words, industry lost its rapidly growing, leading sector qualification. In order to understand the changing role of industry in the economy better, industrial employment rate within total employment should be considered as well. This portion has been decreasing in Turkey ever since the 2000s. This decrease is higher in registered employment. The most important reasons for this difference are that informal employment rate is higher in nonindustrial employment and that informal employment rate the in abovementioned period went down. Following 2002, finance and construction sectors got the highest increase in employment rates. In sum, the industry's tendency to increase its ratio within production and employment since the 1960s paused in mid-1990s and began to decrease in the early 2000s (Taymaz and Voyvoda, 2017).

When we analyze industrialization policies of Turkey, one can see that Turkey implemented two main strategies from the 1960s until today. The first is import substitution industrialization strategies, which were implemented between 1963 and 1980, and the second is export-oriented industrialization strategies which were implemented 1980 onwards. Albeit somewhat differently, these strategies were implemented by many developing countries around the same periods in the same order for the same purposes. As can be observed, both of these strategies are in accordance with the global conjuncture (Kepenek and Yentürk, 2013:361). However, the period between the 1980s and today should be analyzed in two subcategories as 1980–2000 and post-2000. This is due to the fact that industrialization and policies related to this, although to a lesser extent than the 1960s, kept their important places between 1980 and 2000. We can describe the period between 2000 and today as the "deindustrialization" period since the industrialization target fell off the agenda even further after 2000.

2 Industrialization in Planned Period Before 1980 (1963–1980)

Rapid spread of industrialization as a development strategy and of industry policies to poor environmental economies as the main tool of this strategy took place in the post-World War II period. Şenses (1989) emphasizes that the development economy that emerged in this period views industrialization as a prerequisite in order to close the development gap. In other words, the dominant opinion is one that states important systematic changes will occur between 1946 and 1973 in production, foreign trade, and employment structures of the countries in industrialization process, and that these changes are crucial to understand the sources of long-term economic growth (Taymaz and Voyvoda, 2017).

While evaluating the matters that make the industry sector special, Tregenna (2009) in a way summarizes the Kaldor Laws. According to that, back and forth production links are stronger in the industry sector compared to other sectors. As such, the effect of the increase in unit demand on a whole economy can be higher in the industry sector compared to other sectors. Therefore, there is a strong and positive correlation between the growth of industry sector and total economy growth. That is why industry sector can be deemed the motor of growth. Besides, industry sector is relatively an important sector thanks to the possibilities it provides in developing and using new technology. Moreover, technological innovations that increase the productivity in industry sector find fields of application in other economic sectors (agriculture and tertiary) and create positive externality. When evaluated within this framework, the industry becomes a crucial sector in making economic growth sustainable not only because of the production/technological innovations within it, but also because of the connections it creates with the entire economy through these elements (Taymaz and Voyvoda, 2017).

Thereby industry in general, and production industry in particular, is special since it is the (1) driving force of growth periods involving other sectors of economy, (2) main source of total productivity increase both intra- and cross-sectorally. Consequently, Turkey has chosen its leading sector as production industry when it adopted planned development as a model with the Constitution of 1961, and development plans were attempted to be made through production industry (Türel, 2007).

According to Eğilmez (2015), this choice was correct, because Turkey needed to produce machines, tools, and equipment to be used in production to catch up with developed economies. It either had to import abovementioned machines, tools, and equipment and do production with them or produce those machines, tools, and equipment here and create a two-stage growth effect. Turkey chose the latter and adopted "production industry will be the locomotive of our development" slogan.

In this very direction, during the planned period (63–80), private sector mainly focused on consumer and consumer durable goods, while public sector started to focus on intermediate goods production via state economic enterprises. Implemented policies in this period can be summarized as following: a) protecting the domestic market from possible external competitions, b) endorsing industry investments, c) strengthening internal demand by income and wages policies, and d) overvalued exchange rate policy.

An industrialization move took place in Turkey with import substitution industrialization strategy, extending from consumer durable goods to intermediate goods. In many sectors, a learning effect that came to be through using imported technology appeared, a body of knowledge was accumulated, and the industrial worker class came into existence. In private sector, even though it was based on installation at first, production of simple technology began. However, this production is far from meeting requirement of investment goods of domestic industry. Obtaining these products from outside continually increased the foreign trade deficit. Another factor that increases foreign trade deficit is that the exportation economy is punished due to the implementation of the overvalued exchange rate policy. Indeed, a great proportion of exportation consisted of agricultural products instead of industry goods throughout the period. Thus, while a resource shift from agriculture sector towards industry sector was happening, the country faced a heavy foreign debt problem due to the gradually increasing foreign trade deficit. It resulted in a crucial foreign currency bottleneck during 1978–1979. This accelerated the search for a new industrialization strategy in Turkey; and combined with innovations in global conjuncture, it caused a transition to export-oriented industrialization strategies that many developing countries adopted to gain foreign exchange. These policies are actually a part of the transformation that started in the 1980s.

3 (De)Industrialization After 1980

Extensively and to an unexpected extent, Turkey put a radical stabilization and liberalization program into force on January 24, 1980, in the wake of the deep economic depression on which the political instability of the 1970s also had effect. Main purposes of these decisions were, in the short term, to provide stability by improving balance of payments and by reducing inflation; and in the long term, to create an economy more concentrated on market and going outwards – export in particular. Domestic goods markets were joined to world markets with the decisions of January 24; and with Decree No. 32 in 1989, the country proceeded to the second and final stage of "deregulation" by liberalizing all capital movements.

A traditional goal since the establishment of the republic, industrialization was abandoned after 1980, and it became impossible to talk about policy implementations regarding industrial development. There were some assumptions that the results of implemented policies after 1980 would create a friendly environment in industry. This new approach in the development process was the adoption of a new approach in terms of industrialization, namely "passive policies." In reality, economic policies from 1980 onwards were a repetition of the policies recommended by international economic establishments to overcome the crisis towards the end of the 1970s. These policies did not directly have a goal for accelerating economic growth and industrialization, nor were designed for these purposes. Nonetheless, they directly or indirectly had effects on industry and production sector in particular (Doğruel and Doğruel, 2019). With the 1980 transformation, Turkey was joined to the world economy without going through a preparation period, and thus, agriculture and industry sectors took a heavy blow. Industry structure, created during the import substitution period, was gradually opened to foreign competition. In the beginning, the private sector was highly reluctant towards import liberalization. Companies and groups focusing on export supported the new implementations, while groups focusing on import substitution and big holdings that produce consumer-durable goods and automotive insisted on maintaining protective policies. But in the following years, selective encouragement and support implementations of import substitution period were largely wiped out. The industry leaned towards exportation while importation was more and more liberalized. Between the years 1980 and 1990, Turkey became the country with the highest increase in export in the world. Textile, clothing, iron, and steel products were some of the product groups that were among the top. One reason for the increase was the Iran-Iraq War, which increased the exportation of Turkey to Middle East; and other reasons were the reduction of real foreign currency values and the support for export. This strong support also had influence on illegal fictitious export (Barlow and Şenses, 1995).

We can say that there was an important increase in export with export-oriented industrialization strategy implemented after 1980, and that this increase occurred mostly in production industry goods. Yet, export increase in Turkey after 1980 did not bring a significant industrialization leap mainly in production capacity increase. Such a fast increase in export, without a doubt, was possible due to the production capacity and skill accumulation created during the import substitution period. In the first 10 years of the implementation, exportation increase was made possible by using the industry capacity taken over from pre-1980s more actively and by reducing exportation prices rather than production costs via various policies. Thus, it would be more accurate to name these policies as "export-increasing policies" instead of "export-oriented industrialization" (Kepenek and Yentürk, 2013:363).

Therefore, the increases in the added value of production industry in the 1980s were made possible by increasing the capacity usage ratio of the industry and suppressing domestic demand. Real devaluations and low prices helped suppress domestic demand, and export increased by way of intensive export incentives. Despite these successes in export, new policies could not motivate private investments. The most important factors in production industry investments being low were: high interest rates, failure to maintain political and institutional stability, and failure to ensure that new policies would be persistent and stable. Even in export-oriented industries, producers preferred focusing on directing the current capacity towards export rather than creating new capacity due to limited domestic demand.

Neoliberal economy policies caused the structural transformations that were executed in the 1960s and particularly 1970s in production industry to halt, and even to revert to the early 1960s' structure. Instead of an industrialization approach based on technologic maturpoation, qualified manpower, and dynamic comparative supremacies, they implemented incentive policies and policies which are aimed to unite with international economy via current comparative supremacies. As a result of these implemented policies, the sectors such as textile labor-intensive iron and steel whose price elasticity are high, gained a competitive supremacy on the base of low cost and price. So, exportation structure were gradually concentrated on those sectors. It can be argued that the decreasing role of the government also affected this change.

According to Şenses and Taymaz (2015), one of the most important problems regarding industrialization and economic growth of Turkey is not having carried out economic structural change. Agriculture sector still has a significant proportion in total employment. Natural resource and labor-intensive sectors also have a great place in production industry. Partial success in industrial structure change was achieved in the 1960s and 1970s, and proportion of labor intensive sectors in production industry employment was lowered to 28 % in 1977 from 47 % in 1963. However, because of the policies after the 1980s, it went back to around 40 % in the late 1990s. After the 1980s, an industry structure that concentrates on low-cost industries appeared. Moreover, these sectors (clothing, basic chemical industry goods, carpets and rug, readymade textile, and canned vegetable and fruits) have limited growth potential since they produce low income–elasticity goods. Moreover there was a competition pressure of South and East Asian countries. The reason why growth and income increase speed could not reach high numbers after the 1980s was low technology and added value contents of manufactured goods. Since the 1960s, industry in Turkey, as observed in successful examples of East Asia, followed a strategy that goes after short-term interests instead of switching to production in higher-technology branches. Instead of reinforcing research activities and increasing new technology production capacity, Turkey collaborated with multinational companies in high technology sectors, such as in automotive sector, and technology was imported. That is why, in its globalization period, Turkey went towards labor-intensive branches in which low production costs provides an important advantage regarding domestic production and particularly export-oriented production. Progressing to higher technology production branches took place slowly (Pamuk, 2014:306).

It is also observed that Turkey sold off public investments and pricing of goods and services which are produced by currency rate, interest, foreign trade policy, and state economic enterprises which play an important role in the industrialization period. The government made important investments in communication and transportation in order to increase exportation and left the other fields to private investors. Domestic and foreign private investments that are expected to fill this gap could not show the expected development (Şenses and Taymaz, 2015). Compound of investments conspicuously went on against industry, and this sector's investment rate whose total capital stock was 29 % in 1978–1979 was reduced to 16 % in 1988 (Boratav, 2003).

As how it was in many other countries, employment did not significantly increase in Turkey as manufacturing increases in production industry after the 1980s. Much of the increase of employment occurred in service industry. This was because rapid increase in industrial labor efficiency restricts employment opportunities.

The implementations which form a basis for exportation increasing policies of Turkey which were implemented after 1980 can be collected under four titles: a) lowering the value of the money via devaluation, b) lowering domestic demand and labor force costs, c) reducing customs walls and protectionism, and d) direct financial assistance to exportation.

Yet, providing financial incentive to exportation creates an artificial competitive power, while long-term competitive power is contingent upon removing the structural causes of domestic and foreign price differences. Turkey could not implement required policies until the mid-1990s in order for gaining a structural competitive power and insisted on financial incentives that produce results in short term. It had become extremely difficult to have resort to such financial assistances due to international agreements which were signed especially after the year 1987.

Turkey could not meet the foreign trade deficit throughout the period, and exportation increasing policies which were implemented after 1980 lost their effects, while in the 1990s, in this very case, the idea of creating new industrialization strategies was brought to agenda in order for Turkish industry to have a long-term structural competitive power increase. But at the same time, the 1990s were the transition years due to foreign financial freedom. The financial freedom that the Turkey started to implement in this period had negative effects on production industry for different reasons. The most important ones of those reasons are: cease of public infrastructural investments due to deterioration in public accounts, negative effects of rapidly rising interest rates on possible production industry sectors investments, appearance of inconsistencies which result in high inflation, and reduction of production industry competitive power due to the value increase of Turkish lira.

Capital inflows, which occurs in the wake of liberalization of every kind of capital movement in 1989 with decision number 32, results in abrasion of national savings. National currency value rises before foreign currencies during the years in which capital inflows were high. Thereby, foreign trade deficit rises and current account deficit increases. Financial crises that occur due to increased current account deficit and economy becoming more fragile affects real sector over time. Rise of national currency value before foreign currency results in favor of goods which are not subject to trade, with regard to relative prices of the goods which are and are not subject to trade; and this status brings up profitability, production, and investment increase in sectors which are not subject to trade. Import and agricultural liberalization policies result in the agriculture sector clearly becoming importer as the economy gradually relies on construction, and Turkey encounters with early deindustrialization (Eşiyok, 2018).

The Turkish industry was preserved against foreign competition from the day it was established until the 1980s, and it was developed in an environment where domestic competition was lacking and where only a few companies were present in a few sectors. The main pursuit of the post-80s economy in which the export was tried to be increased via great assistances in import substitution period when domestic demand was kept high was not to find efficiency and competition, but rent-seeking activities constituted the development outline of economy and industry. Implemented policies after the 1980s led to a short-term exportation increase, while no resource was reserved for long-term structural competitive power; and we were left with indirect incentives and nontariff barriers prior to customs union. However, Turkey could not use them. Nontariff customs is used to protect the domestic industry from import goods by many developed countries including EU. For many years, only large-scale investments were given incentives in Turkey. Yet, Small and Medium Sized Enterprises (SME) hold the bigger proportion. For this reason, it is crucial for small-sized enterprises who are heavily present in many sectors to have financial and consultancy support in the matters of obtaining/using new technology and transiting to new organizational structures (Kepenek and Yentürk, 2013).

Briefly, it is difficult to state that the actual growth speed which was observed in national income and industry sector in the 1980s was caused by dynamic developments in economic growth potential. We know that the productive capacity usage rates were dropped way too much under 1978–1980 crisis conditions, particularly in industry. Industrial growth which was observed in the first half of the 1980s was mainly made possible by increasing the capacity usage of the enterprises, while expansion speed of current productive capacities receded in comparison with the previous period. Industry capital under conditions of 1980 turns toward exportation by using current capacity for more production under conditions of ingravescent interest burden and shrinking domestic demand, yet creating new capacity is avoided. These assignations show that the export success of Turkey in those years was not based on technology-oriented efficiency rise, but on foreign currency policies who cause real devaluations and on abrasion of price cost (Boratav, 2003). The years of 1990s, when globalization became deeper, was a worse period in case of industry development:

> *"The ones who defend liberalization of capital movements while proceeding to 1990s expected the capital that will flow from metropolitan countries into Turkey to reduce high interest rates and to increase investment rates. Developments after 1989 did not endorse those expectations. On the contrary, the proportion of interest income in national income incrementally increased by reaching beyond 15 % between 1991 and 1995 and beyond 30 % between 1996 and 1999. Real interest rates raised rapidly in the same period. In accordance with Istanbul Chamber of Commerce data, proportion of interest expenses in total added values of 500 big industry companies raised to 45 % in 1997–2001, and ever-increasing parts of gross profits of companies were transferred to banking systems. Many of the companies started to connect their quick resources to repo, investment funds, treasury stocks instead of enterprise capital (id est production) at ever-increasing rates. In fact, in 1999–2002, interest income of 500 big private companies soared beyond their enterprise profits. Being able to shift the enterprise capital towards quick placement -in other words: rentification of industry capital with a spontaneous decision- is a privilege of big capital. Small and medium industrialist who is in debt with chronic debts is helpless against finance capital and has no other choice than to reflect the increasing interest burden onto prices." (Boratav,2003: 196–197)*

In other words, small- and medium-sized investments constituting a large proportion of Turkish industry sector were crushed under increasing real investment expenses, while big companies withdrew from production and concentrated on finance sector due to increasing interests.

4 The 2000s and Afterwards: Deindustrialization Process

The new program, created after the 2001 crisis, represented the second phase of neoliberal policies. The program not only envisaged fiscal discipline but also introduced new institutional regulations for market surveillance. The Justice and Development Party (AKP), which came to power alone in 2002, followed a more democratic stance in the early years when its objective for EU membership was not yet abandoned, and its economic policies were open to the whole private sector rather than giving concessions to specific segments (Pamuk, 2014:262). This democratic attitude was reflected positively in the Turkish economy along with the positive trend of the global conjuncture. Indeed, prior to the 2008 crisis, with its high growth rate, Turkey was praised by many international organizations, especially the World Bank and the IMF. Despite this, the fast-growing Turkish economy was unable to escape the effects of the crisis. The reality that the economy was not as strong as once thought emerged. According to Doğruel and Doğruel (2019), industrialization policies that have been implemented in recent times are the main responsibles for this.

As the chosen leading industry, the construction sector replaced the abandoned industrial policies in the 2000s. It would not be inaccurate to define the post-2000 period as a construction-based growth model or the period of deindustrialization. The construction sector, a sector which requires much less investment, can easily adapt to technology, yields immediate results, and instantly boosts growth, dazzled politicians. That way, the economy would have been revived, and growth would have been achieved in a much simpler and easier way. While the manufacturing industry demanded sophisticated labor, the construction industry was able to carry out the work with unskilled labor. This was another factor that added to the appeal of the construction sector. Over time, the leading industrialists in the country started to become constructors under the influence of all these temptations. While the state provided all the incentives to create demand for the houses being constructed, the external conjuncture too was very favorable for this demand to increase. Growing rapidly after the 2001 crisis, Turkey was able to attract foreign funds in an environment created by high real interest rates and the driving force generated by having started negotiations with the EU, and thus the Turkish lira could stay strong against foreign currency. The strength of the Turkish lira led to a decrease in inflation and interest rates, and banks increased the demand for construction by providing long-term and low-interest house loans. This was quite an ordinary situation in an environment where the global conjuncture strengthened, and liquidity was abundant and fluid. However, after the 2008 crisis, the amount of foreign currency entering the country began to decrease. The first impact of this situation was the Turkish lira losing value. This development led to an increase in import costs and hence high inflation in Turkey where imported goods costs were high due to the underdeveloped manufacturing industry. This was followed by an increase in interest rates. Banks can no longer lend loans as easily and cheap as they used to. Therefore, despite the surprising demand for housing, Turkey has now reached the end of the construction-based growth model (Eğilmez, 2015). This is indeed an expected result of giving up on a sector that makes multiple contributions to growth, i.e., the manufacturing industry, and turning to the construction sector, a one-time contributor to growth.

The most crucial of the institutional transformations that took place in the 1990s was the Customs Union Agreement signed with the EU in 1995. Turkey's trade volume with the EU did not increase immediately upon signing this agreement as the customs tariffs before the agreement were already quite low. However, following the 2001 crisis and the significant depreciation of the Turkish lira, there was a rapid increase in exports from Turkey to the EU, especially in the automotive sector as multinational companies started to use Turkey as a leading production base for exports to the EU and other countries. Exports increased first in more labor-intensive sectors such as textiles; but after the EU lifted the restrictions on China, Turkey's exports began to decline. As Turkey's prospects for EU membership weakened in the following years, due to the fact that the country was not involved in the decision-making process, Turkey was unable to influence the tariffs applied to third countries and was forced to accept the tariffs, which became a problem limiting the benefits of the Customs Union Agreement.

The overall investment weakness in the industrial sector, a problem waiting to be solved, persisted into the 2000s. Though historical averages were exceeded in the revival conjuncture of 2003 and after, it cannot be argued that the industrial sector received sufficient investment grants over the last 30 years (Türel, 2007). In the 2000s, governments attributed a central role to foreign direct investment in the competitive integration of the Turkish manufacturing industry into the global economy. Safeguards such as (i) protection against direct expropriation, (ii) ease in hiring foreign key personnel, (iii) international arbitration, (iv) real estate discount guarantee, (v) protection against losses caused by changes in legislation, and (vi) right to leave were established for foreign capital investments. In other words, Turkey put the demands of developed countries and international capital into investment incentives and coordination mechanisms in the 2000s and de facto eliminated the possibility of the fiscal policy directing investments.

Türel (2011) summarizes the fundamental changes that would affect the designing of industrial policies in international and domestic spheres in the last quarter of the century:

> *(i) The cooperation of industrial and foreign trade policies ended both in the world and in Turkey, and the institutions and rules governing foreign trade have changed. The WTO is more involved in domestic fiscal policy decisions compared to its predecessor GATT, and regional trade agreements (in the case of Turkey, the Customs Union with the EU) narrow the maneuver area of countries that are parties to them. (ii) International trade flows are increasingly controlled by multinational corporations. The relationship between large international firms and relatively small domestic firms in developing countries is an unequal and exploitative relationship. (iii) The intellectual property regime adopted by developing countries (with the expectation or blackmail that they will have access to more favorable conditions in trade and foreign capital mobility) favors not domestic entrepreneurs but international entrepreneurs and secures their intellectual property rights. With this regime, developing countries have virtually been precluded from using technology transfer methods which include copying, imitation and reverse engineering. (iv) Internal and external restrictions have emerged in the implementation of selective/reciprocal/non-operational incentives. (v) The intellectual pressure by neoliberalism discredits certain parts of fiscal policy, hence it is not preferable to use these tools even if they do not contradict international legislation. The result of all these developments is the contraction of the "fiscal policy space" of developing countries and, in this case, of Turkey.*

According to Rodrik (2004:5–6), the barrier to coherent industrial policies is not due to the impossibility of governments using them, but their reluctance to do so. Türel (2007) also shares this opinion:

> *It cannot be said that Turkey's ruling class and the top bureaucratic cadres that have been filled by the ruling class are disturbed by the process described above. On the contrary, the accepted understanding is "passive adaptation to globalization". The transivity between the reports of international finance institutions and think tanks and the reports of local public-private institutions implies that many individuals and institutions in Turkey no longer pay much attention to "which part of the table they are sitting on". If the aim is to formulate a national development and industrialization strategy, the primary priority should be to regain (albeit partially) the "policy space" which has been largely lost under the neoliberal model. The main expectation behind the support for exports and FDI in the last quarter of the century was that the effects of these activities on technology production and acquisition would solve the problem of externalities. These expectations have not been realized and it has been well understood that "foreign expansion" alone cannot be an alternative to industrial policies.*

As Rodrik (2007:13–4) points out, there is no direct correlation between a good-functioning market mechanism and institutions that operate the markets having good qualities and high industrial performance.

Another issue that should be probed with regards to the Turkish industry in the 2000s is the phenomenon of "Anatolian Tigers." Pamuk (2014:309) summarizes this phenomenon as follows:

> *Since the nineteenth century, there have been three waves of industrialization in Turkey. During the period of statism in the 1930s, government enterprises led the industrialization process. During the period of import substitution after World War II, the supervision of the industry was transferred to the private sector, especially to holding companies in the Istanbul region. The shift to new industrial centers in Anatolia despite all the limitations on the industrialization process after 1980 constitutes the third wave. This phenomenon, which emerged in certain Anatolian cities, can be construed to be the transition from agriculture and trade-focused environment to industrial capitalism. Although the industrialization process on a national scale was not very rapid, it can be said that a new bourgeoisie did emerge. The majority of industrialists who appeared on the stage in Anatolian cities supported the Justice and Development Party (AKP) after the 2000s and this support has continued to date. From the 1990s, employer institutions, like the Independent Industrialists and Businessmen's Association (MÜSİAD) and the Turkish Confederation of Industrialists and Businessmen (TÜSKON), which aimed to play the role the Turkish Industrialists' and Businessmen's Association (TÜSİAD) has been playing since the 1970s but among conservative investment groups, began to function as umbrella organizations.*

According to TurkStat data, in the post-1980 era, the efficiency of value added, it is observed that employment and labor increased faster in new industrial centers like Denizli, Konya, Kayseri, Gaziantep, Maraş, and Malatya than in old industrial centers such as İstanbul, Bursa, Kocaeli, İzmir, and Adana. Furthermore, industrialization in provinces such as Tekirdağ, Kırklareli, Sakarya, Balıkesir, Eskişehir, Manisa, and Mersin gained momentum after 1980 due to their proximity to old industrial centers. Industrial enterprises in these new centers were mostly small- and medium-sized family enterprises which used limited capital. These enterprises started production using simplistic technology in labor-intensive sectors such as textiles, clothing, food, metal processing, wooden products, and chemical industries. From the early stages, they turned to export by taking advantage of low wages in their regions. Especially in their early years, many of these firms used not banks but their own resources for their loan needs. This way, they survived through the big fluctuations of the 1990s (Filiztekin-Tunalı, 1999; Cengiz, 2013).

Businesses in the new industrial centers gave more importance to technology in subsequent years. However, Pamuk (2014) argues that when the fact that the number of new industrial centers had been limited after 30 years, total industrial production, industrial employment, and their shares in exports are taken into consideration, the industrialization process in Anatolia is not strong enough to qualify for the term "tiger." Although the term "tiger" is an exaggeration, considering its political and social implications, one must acknowledge this phenomenon as one of the most important developments of the post-80 period in terms of the expansion of industrialization and the emergence of a new bourgeoisie.

The contraction experienced in the 2000s in the textile and clothing sectors, traditionally considered to be the engines of exports and manufacturing production in Turkey, has virtually become the engine of deindustrialization. The real exchange-rate flexibility of exports from sectors where linking in to global value chains are meager and low-technology products such as textile and clothing are manufactured can be expected to be higher than in other sectors. For this reason, it can be argued that the real exchange rate increases in the 2000s determined the contraction of the textile and clothing sectors. Taymaz and Voyvoda (2017 found that a shift took place in the manufacturing industry from the textile and clothing sectors to especially engineering industries in the 2000s. In other words, there has been a shift from low-technology products to medium-high technology products, and this is a positive development. However, Turkey has recently specialized in products and stages that are more standard and have lower growth rates within medium-technology sectors such as motor land vehicles. As a result, the relative position of Turkey in the international division of labor has not changed (Taymaz et al., 2011).

Another factor contributing to deindustrialization during this period has been the increase in the level of financial openness. According to Bakır et al. (2017), the increase in the level of financial openness reduces the value-added ratio of Turkey's manufacturing industry. This finding implies that in Turkey, financial capital inflows do not turn into fixed capital investments that would increase industrial production. This gap between the financial sector and the real sector may indicate that there are several important problems in Turkey's institutional structure and macroeconomic foundations and that reforms should be made in these areas. Moreover, as barriers to capital mobility are lifted, industrial production can be adversely affected by this, leading to a significant weakening of the economy's production base and the formation of financial bubbles which would make economic stagnation more likely with foreign exchange, foreign debt, and banking crises.

5 Conclusion

One must look for the effects of the transformation that the global economy has undergone in the past 40 years in the revival of industrialization and industrial policies in recent years, both in developed countries and in developing countries (Taymaz and Voyvoda, 2017):

- Growth and development processes of a growing number of developing countries being identified by different traps (medium-income trap, low-income trap, early industrialization)
- The realization that the growth increase caused by the increase in commodity prices, especially in the 2000s, is not sustainable in the long run and
- The 2008–2009 global crisis deeply affecting the future perspective of world economies.

In the development economics literature, which developed as a subdiscipline of economics in the mid-twentieth century, the terms "developed country" and "industrialized country" are frequently used as synonyms. It is a widespread opinion among development economists that industrialization is of fundamental importance for high and permanent economic growth and development. The main reason for this is that today's developed countries have historically initiated and realized their development processes through industrialization. Many developing countries have tried to industrialize in order to catch up with developed countries in terms of their income per capita. The industry sector in general and the manufacturing industry in particular have been described as the "engine/locomotive" or the "elevator" (Rodrik, 2016) of economic growth and development.

As determined in early studies by Kaldor (1963, 1966), Kuznets (1971), and Maddison (1980), the weight of production and employment in the economic development process first shifts from agriculture to industry, and then from industry to the tertiary sector. In developed/industrialized countries, particularly the value-added share of the manufacturing industry in GDP has decreased systematically in recent years (Nickell et al. 2008). A similar trend has recently been observed in emerging market economies and developing countries apart from East Asia (Rodrik, 2016). It has been determined that the downward trend in the manufacturing industry's share, observed historically in almost all developed countries, began at a much lower per capita income level in developing countries. Hence, this phenomenon has been defined as "premature deindustrialization" (Dasgupta and Singh, 2006; Rodrik, 2016).

Compared to the industrial sector and especially the manufacturing industry, it has been argued that the tertiary sector's potential for contributing to an increase in economic growth, employment, and productivity is relatively low (Rowthorn and Ramaswamy, 1999; Rodrik 2016). Without the sufficient development of industrial production, which has been the driving force of the economy, the gradual shift in the economic structure to the tertiary sector may hinder high and permanent growth, the process of employment creation, and the increase in productivity.

In the case of Turkey, the share of the manufacturing industry steadily increased during 1960–1999, although not as much as East Asia; however, a significant decrease was observed between 2000 and 2014. While the share from 1960 to 1979 was 14 % and it increased to 23 % between the years 1990 and 1999, this percentage declined to 19 % between 2000 and 2014, meaning that the country started to experience the phenomenon called "deindustrialization."

This process, consistent with the hypotheses that the manufacturing industry is the engine of growth and that the growth of the manufacturing industry increases the demand in the tertiary sector, started to change significantly and permanently from 1999 onwards. Given the effects of the 2001 crisis, it can be assumed that the deindustrialization process started in 2002. It is known that the favorable financial conditions of 2002–2008, the period before the last crisis, supported growth in Turkey. However, despite these positive conditions for growth, deindustrialization has continued steadily. Moreover, in the recent deindustrialization process in Turkey, one cannot talk about a positive technological shift among the subsectors of the manufacturing industry from the less productive sectors to the more productive sectors. In almost all sectors, while the value-added share of the manufacturing industry and GDP has been stable, a significant contraction is observed in particularly the textile and clothing sectors. These significant decreases in the textile and clothing sectors, which have a large share both in Turkey's exports and the whole manufacturing industry and GDP, show that these two subsectors play a crucial role in Turkey's deindustrialization process.

As a result, in the case of Turkey, the process of rapid linking in to the global value chain without a matured industrialization has frayed the domestic value-added ratio in exports and production and increased the economy's dependence on imports. In other words, rapid and early participation brought along deindustrialization. At this stage, reversing this process requires well-designed industrialization, foreign trade, and financial policies that will decrease the speed of participation in a controlled manner, promoting high-tech industrial production and exports (Bakır et al., 20 17).

Excluding the first years after the founding of the Republic, industrialization in Turkey became an important policy goal since the 1930s. This process lasted until the 1980s, and in the following period, two ruptures that altered policy objectives were experienced: first in 1980 and second in the 2000s. The post-1980 and post-2000 periods had their differences. However, a common feature of both periods was that the Republic's enthusiastic and naive industrialization dream was defeated by different policy priorities in these two periods. Thus, the goal of prioritizing industrial policies that had been pursued since the founding of the Republic was abandoned. Under different policy practices, there have

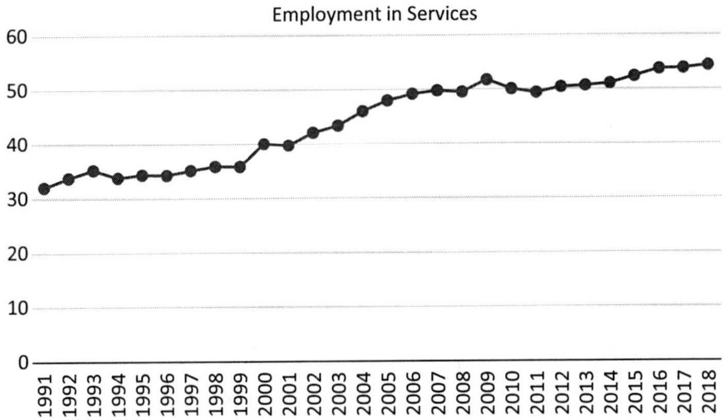

Fig. 1: Employment Rate in Services (1991–2018)

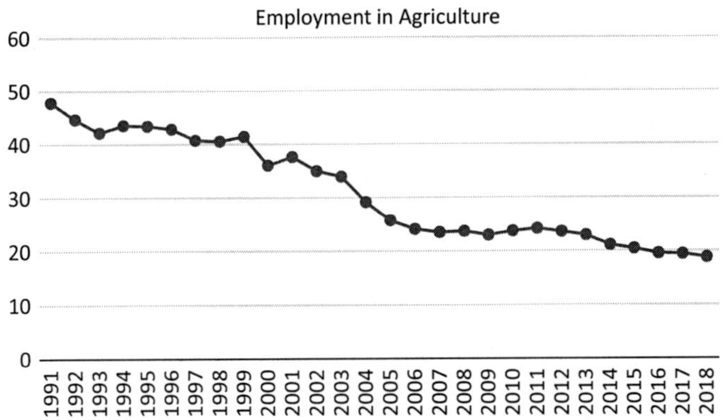

Fig. 2: Employment Rate in Agriculture (1991–2018)

been changes in the structure and development potential of the manufacturing industry in Turkey. Turkey entered the 2008 crisis with a weakening industrial structure, and this condition persisted after the crisis.

It can be said that Turkey started deindustrialization earlier than East Asian countries and later than Latin America and developing countries. As a concluding remark, the situation of developing countries can be summarized with the following sentence: "The sooner and the more unprepared you open up your economy, the sooner you become deindustrialized!"

Tables

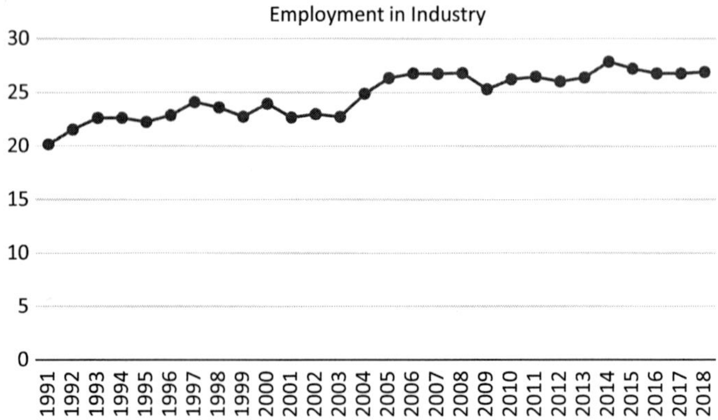

Fig. 3: Employment Rate in Industry (1991–2018)

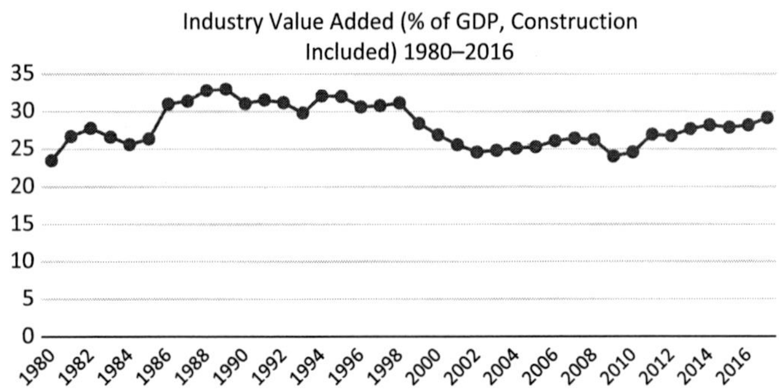

Fig. 4: Industry Value Added (Construction Included) (1980–2016)

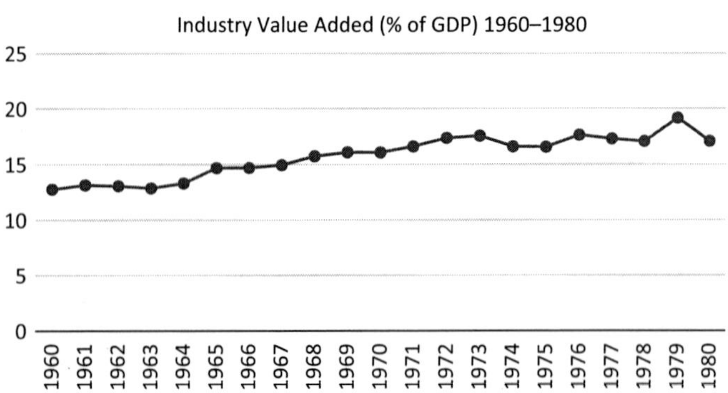

Fig. 5: Industry Value Added in the Planned Period (1960–1980)

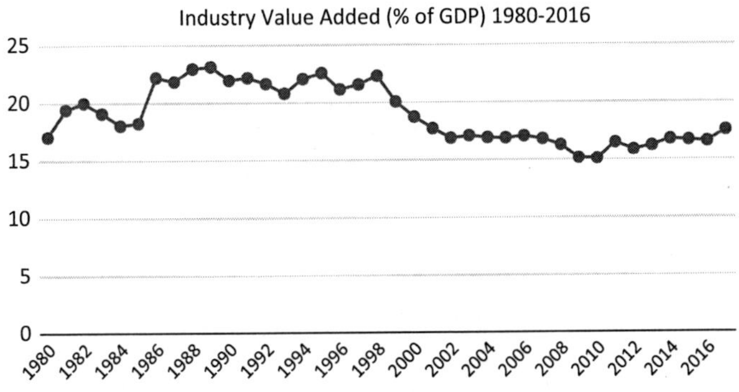

Fig. 6: Industry Value Added (1980–2016)

Bibliography

Akyüz, Y. (2007), "Global Rules and Markets: Constraints Over Policy Autonomy in Developing Countries", **İktisat, İşletme Finans**, N:257, pp. 5–43.

Bakır, E., Özçelik, E., Özmen, E. and Taşıran, A. C. (2017) "Türkiye'de Erken Sanayisizleşme", (Murat Koyuncu, Hakan Mıhçı and Erinç Yeldan, Eds.), **Geçmişten Geleceğe Türkiye Ekonomisi, Fikret Şenses'e Armağan**, İletişim Yayınları, pp. 157–192.

Barlow, R. and Şenses, F. (1995), "The Turkish Export Boom: Just Reward or Just Lucky?", **Journal of Development Economics**, Vol.48, pp. 111–133.

Barta, G., Czirfusz, M. and Kukely, G. (2008) Re-industrialization in the World and Hungary, **European Spatial Research and Policy**, Vol.15, N.2, pp. 5–27.

Bluestone, B. and Harrison, B. (1982), **The deindustrialization of America**, New York: Basic Books.

Boratav, K. (2003), **Türkiye İktisat Tarihi (1908–2002)**, İmge Kitabevi, 7. Basım.

Cengiz, K. (2013), "Yav İşte Fabrikalaşsak", **Anadolu Sermayesinin Oluşumu: Kayseri-Hacılar Örneği**, İstanbul: İletişim Yayınları.

Cheshire, P. (1991), Problems of Regional Transformation and Deindustrialization in the European Community, (L. Rodwin and H. Sazanami, Eds.), **Industrial Change and Regional Economic Transformation**, London: Harper Collins Academic.

Dasgupta, S. and Singh, A. (2006). "Manufacturing, Services and Premature Deindustrialization in Developing Countries: A Kaldorian Analysis",

WIDER Working Paper Series 049, World Institute for Development Economic Research (UNU-WIDER).

Doğruel, F. and Doğruel, S. (2019), "Küreselleşme, Unutulan Sanayi Politikaları ve Sanayisizleşme", **Çalışma ve Toplum**, Vol.2019, N.1, pp. 209–230.

Doğruel, F. and Doğruel, S. (2017), "Türkiye'de Sanayileşme ve Kriz", (Murat Koyuncu, Hakan Mıhçı and Erinç Yeldan, Eds.), **Geçmişten Geleceğe Türkiye Ekonomisi, Fikret Şenses'e Armağan,** İstanbul: İletişim Yayınları.

Eğilmez, M. (2015), **İnşaata Dayalı Büyüme Modelinin Sonu**, Retrieved from http://www.mahfiegilmez.com/2015/08/insaat-onderliginde-buyume-modelinin.html,

Eşiyok, B. A. (2018), "Kalkınmacı Devlet ve Sanayileşmeden, Neoliberal Erken Sanayisizleşmeye", **Fiscaoeconomia**, Special Issue, N.1, pp. 71–102.

Filiztekin, A. and Tunalı, İ. (1999), "Anatolian Tigers: Are They For Real?", **New Perspectives on Turkey**, N.20, pp. 77–106

Hegyi-Keri. (2016), "A Study of the Process and Types of Deindustrialization in the Visegrad Countries", **Club of Economics in Miskolc**, Vol.12, N.2, pp. 5–13

Kepenek, Y. and Yentürk, N. (2003), **Türkiye Ekonomisi**, İstanbul: Remzi Kitabevi, 13. Basım.

Kiss, E. (2010), "Territorial Restricting of the Hungarian Industry After 1989", **Dialog Campus Ciado**, Budapest: Budapest-Pecs.

Van Neuss, L. (2016), The Economic Forces behind Deindustrialization: An Empirical Investigation, HEC – University of Liège, August 2.

Nickell, S., Redding S. and Swaffield, J. (2008), "The Uneven Pace of Deindustrialization in the OECD", **The World Economy**, Vol.31, N.9, pp. 1154–1184.

Öz, S. (2018) "Dünyada ve Türkiye'de Sanayisizleşme", **Koç Üniversitesi TÜSİAD EAF Araştırma Notu.**

Pamuk, Ş. (2014), **Türkiye'nin 200 yıllık İktisadi Tarihi**, İstanbul: İş Bankası Kültür Yayınları, 4. Basım.

Paolera, Gerardo della, Xavier H. Duran Amorocho, Aldo Musacchio. **5, NBER Working Paper**. 6, January 2018.

Rodrik, D. (2004), **Industrial Policy for Twenty First Century**, Retrieved from http://www.vedegylet.hu/fejkrit/szvggyujt/rodrik_industrial_policy.pdf

Rodrik, D. (2007), A chapter in **One Economics, Many Recipes: Globalization, Institutions, and Economic Growth**, 2007 from Princeton University Press

Rodrik, D. (2013), "The Past, Present and Future of Economic Growth, Global Citizen Foundation", **Working Paper**, June 2013.

Rodrik, D. (2016), "Premature Deindustrialization", **The Journal of Economic Growth**, V.21, pp. 1–33.

Rowthorn, R. and Ramasway, R. (1997), "Deindustrialization: Causes and Implications," **Staff Studies for the World Economic Outlook,** Washington: International Monetary Fund, **December**, pp. 61–77.

Rowthorn, R. and Ramaswamy R. (1999), "Growth, Trade, and Deindustrialization", **International Monetary Fund Staff Papers**, Vol.46, N.1, pp. 18–41.

Singh (1977), "UK Industry and the World Economy: A Case of Deindustrialisation", **Cambridge Journal of Economics**, Vol.1, N.2, pp. 113–136.

Şenses, F. (1989), **Türkiye'de Sanayileşme**, Ankara: Verso Yayıncılık.

Şenses, F. and Taymaz, E. (2015), "Unutulan bir toplumsal amaç Sanayileşme: Ne oluyor? Ne olmalı?", (Ahmet Haşim Köse, Fikret Şenses and Erinç Yeldan, Eds.), **İktisat Üzerine Yazılar II, İktisadi Kalkınma, Kriz ve İstikrar, Oktar Türel'e Armağan**, İstanbul: İletişim Yayınları, pp. 429–463.

Taymaz, E. and Voyvoda, E. (2017), "Yapısal Dönüşüm, Sanayileşme ve Sanayi Politikaları: Küresel Eğilimlerden Türkiye Ekonomisine Kısa Bir Gezinti", (Murat Koyuncu, Hakan Mıhçı and Erinç Yeldan, Eds.), **Geçmişten Geleceğe Türkiye Ekonomisi, Fikret Şenses'e Armağan**, İstanbul: İletişim Yayınları.

Taymaz, E., Voyvoda, E. and Kamil, Y. (2011), **Uluslararası Üretim Zincirlerinde Dönüşüm ve Türkiye'nin Konumu**, İstanbul: Koç Üniversitesi Ekonomik Araştırmalar Forumu.

Tregenna, F. (2009). "Characterising Deindustrialisation: An Analysis of Changes in Manufacturing Employment and Output Internationally", **Cambridge Journal of Economics, Oxford University Press**, Vol. 33(3), pp. 433–466, May.

Tregenna. (2011), **Manufacturing Productivity, Deindustrialization, and Reindustrialization**, Working Paper No. 2011/57, United Nations University, World Institute for Development Economics Research (UNUWIDER), Helsinki, Retrieved from http://www.wider.unu.edu/publications/working-papers/2011/en_GB/wp2011-057/_files/86328907787665417/default/wp2011-057.pdf (01.05.2019).

Türel, O. (2011), "Dünyada Sanayileşme Deneyimi: Geçmiş Çeyrel Yüzyıl (1975–2000) ve Gelecek İçin Beklentiler", **İktisat Üzerine Yazılar I Küresel Düzen, Birikim, Devlet ve Sınıflar (Korkut Boratav'a Armağan kitabı),** İstanbul: İletişim Yayınları.

Türel, O. (2007), **Oktar Türel Sanayi Politikaları**, Retrieved from http://www.inovasyon.org/pdf/O.Turel.Sanayi.Politikalari.pdf,

Verley, P. (1997), **La révolution industrielle**, Paris: Gallimard.

Assist. Prof. Damla Özekan

Closing the Loops: Business Model Approaches for Circular Economy

Abstract: There have long been demands from industry for guidance in implementing business strategies for sustainable development. The circular economy represents the most recent attempt to conceptualize the integration of economic activity and environmental well-being in a sustainable way.The purpose of this study is to define the concept and historical perspective of the circular economy concept, to investigate the business models of the circular economy, and to examine the situation of circular economy in Turkey and the integration of circular economy business models into strategies.

Keywords: Circular Economy, Business Models, Closed Loop, Turkey

1. Introduction

Sustainability aims to address the environmental, social, and economic issues for today and future generations. The concept of the circular economy has become one of the most recent propositions to address environmental sustainability through addressing economic growth, and the lack of raw materials and energy as well as a new growing business construct (Murray, Skene and Haynes, 2015:25).

The linear economic model which consists of production, consumption, and waste (take-make-waste) is running out of road because of rising global population, increasing resource use and environmental degradation. It is apparent that business as usual is not an option for a sustainable future. There is an alternative. A circular economy would turn goods that are at the end of their service life into resources for others, closing loops in industrial ecosystems and minimizing wastes. A study of seven European nations found that a shift to a circular economy would reduce each nation's greenhouse-gas emissions by up to 70 % and grow its workforce by about 4 % – the ultimate low-carbon economy.

According to BS8001 guide report, to ensure the availability of resources in the future, current patterns and volumes of consumption and production need to change dramatically so that they are kept within planetary boundaries. To do this while continuing to thrive as a society, a complete rethink of how things are done is needed. Transitioning to a circular economy could offer a significant contribution to solving the emerging resource problems.

Ellen MacArthur Foundation indicated a number of factors that the linear model is increasingly being challenged and a profound change of the economic system is essential such as: economic losses and structural waste, price and supply risks, natural system degradation, regulatory trends that lower and price negative externalities, advanced information and industrial technologies, and urbanization and demographical growth (EMA, 2015:3).

In this part of the book, how circular business models could provide new opportunities for resilient growth despite a challenging global outlook is investigated first and the historical perspective of circular economy is explained. Business model is defined and the related literature is outlined. Then, the existing business models related to sustainability and circular economy are examined. After that, the framework for circular economy business model situation in Turkey is examined. Finally, conclusions are driven and future research paths are provided.

2. The Circular Economy

The concept of circular economy associates and builds upon several former concepts and therefore has a wide content, but does not have an articulated definition reflecting its attribute. In this section, a definition of a circular economy is given based upon several studies, and a new overview is created of all subconcepts and aspects. Practical implications of the definition and other interpretations will be treated as well, especially in relation to sustainability.

The circular economy refers to a systemic approach for redesigning the business systems, enabling sustainable economic growth by managing resources more effectively as a result of making the flow of materials more circular and reducing and ultimately eliminating waste flows. Since the first use of the concept of the circular economy, the terms "closed loops" and "circular economy" are often used in parallel.

Circular economy is not a new discussion. It blends the principles of multiple schools of thought, some of which date back to the 1960s. Kenneth Boulding predicted a "spaceman economy" that would operate by reproducing the initially limited stock of inputs and recycling waste outputs in 1966. According to Lehmann and colleagues, this concept has helped today policy-makers, academics, and the business community to recognize the need to move towards a new economic model whereby materials and energy from discarded products or by-products are reintroduced into the economic system.

Lovins and colleagues stated, in their article titled "National Capitalism," that business strategies built around the radically more productive use of natural resources will solve many environmental problems at a profit in 1999.

McDonough and Braungart in 2002 continued this discussion in their well-known book *Cradle to Cradle* by suggesting that industry should preserve and enrich ecosystems and nature's biological metabolism while also maintaining a safe, productive technical metabolism for the high-quality use and circulation of organic and technical nutrients.

Similarly, Cooper and Fava discussed that lifecycle thinking and a broad range of lifecycle assessment (LCA) methods have been utilized for assessing the environmental impacts of a product, service, business, policy, or process.

To accelerate the transition towards a circular economy, the European Union has launched an ambitious Circular Economy Package, which will contribute to "closing the loop" in product lifecycles through greater recycling and reuse, and bring benefits for both the environment and the economy (Antikainen and Valkokari, 2016:5).

Walter Stahel, in his 2016 essay, classified industrial economy as linear, circular, and performance. According to his study:

> *"A linear economy flows like a river, turning natural resources into base materials and products for sale through a series of value- adding steps. At the point of sale, ownership and liability for risks and waste pass to the buyer (who is now owner and user). The owner decides whether old tyres will be reused or recycled — as sandals, ropes or bumpers — or dumped. The linear economy is driven by 'bigger-better-faster-safer' syndrome — in other words, fashion, emotion and progress. It is efficient at overcoming scarcity, but profligate at using resources in often-saturated markets. Companies make money by selling high volumes of cheap and attractive goods.*
>
> *A circular economy is like a lake. The reprocessing of goods and materials generates jobs and saves energy while reducing resource consumption and waste. Cleaning a glass bottle and using it again is faster and cheaper than recycling the glass or making a new bottle from minerals. Vehicle owners can decide whether to have their used tyres repaired or regrooved or whether to buy new or retreaded replacements — if such services exist. Rather than being dumped, used tyres are collected by waste managers and sold to the highest bidder.*
>
> *A performance economy goes a step further by selling goods (or molecules) as services through rent, lease and share business models. The manufacturer retains ownership of the product and its embodied resources and thus carries the responsibility for the costs of risks and waste. In addition to design and reuse, the performance economy focuses on solutions instead of products, and makes its profits from sufficiency, such as waste prevention." (Stahel, 2016:435–438).*

Ellen MacArthur Foundation described circular economy as "restorative and regenerative by design and aims to keep products, components, and materials at their highest utility and value at all times, distinguishing between technical and biological cycles."

Predominantly based on the work of Ellen MacArthur Foundation and verified by the other contributors to the literature, a common basic definition can be identified as: *A circular economy is an economic system with closed material loops.*

This definition mentions that the concept of circular economy should be considered an economic concept, with "closed material loops" as an important prerequisite. "Closed material loops" implies that material is reused again, either as bulk material, as products or as components. Specific processes or economic activities such as regeneration or recycling are needed to enable this (Mentink, 2014:14–15).

One of the most important implications of closing material loops is the potential minimization of extraction of material from nature, such as resource scarcity and the emission of waste to nature such as environmental impact, can potentially be solved.

If the products, components, or materials are reused or recycled into the same or similar products, components and materials with minimum loss of quantity, quality, or function, it is called ***closed loop***. If they are reused or recycled into alternative ones, it is called ***open loop***.

Figure 1 shows how biological and technical materials and the products or components based on them cycle through the economic system, each with their own set of characteristics. Unlike biological materials, technical materials are not cascaded to other applications but the functionality, integrity, and the value of embedded energy are maintained through remarketing, reuse, disassembly, refurbishment, and remanufacture.

2.1. The Historical Perspective of Circular Economy

It is essential to understand "sustainability" concept and its roots to comprehend the logic of the circular economy. Sustainability and sustainable development issues, being the starting point and the main idea of circular economy, have been discussed since the middle of the twentieth century as the terms "sustainable" and "sustainability" appeared for the first time in the *Oxford English Dictionary*.

There had been a drastic growth in production, consumption, and wealth after the industrial revolution. Also the world's population had tripled in the period between 1800 and 1970. Mainstream economists from the neoclassical school were aware of the sustainability problems related to the huge consumption of the resources but considered that if a product or a factor input would become scarce, new technologies would be introduced to replace the scarce input.

With the effects of the worldwide recession occurring in the mid-1970s, expectations of unlimited economic growth were fractured. Also the first oil crisis

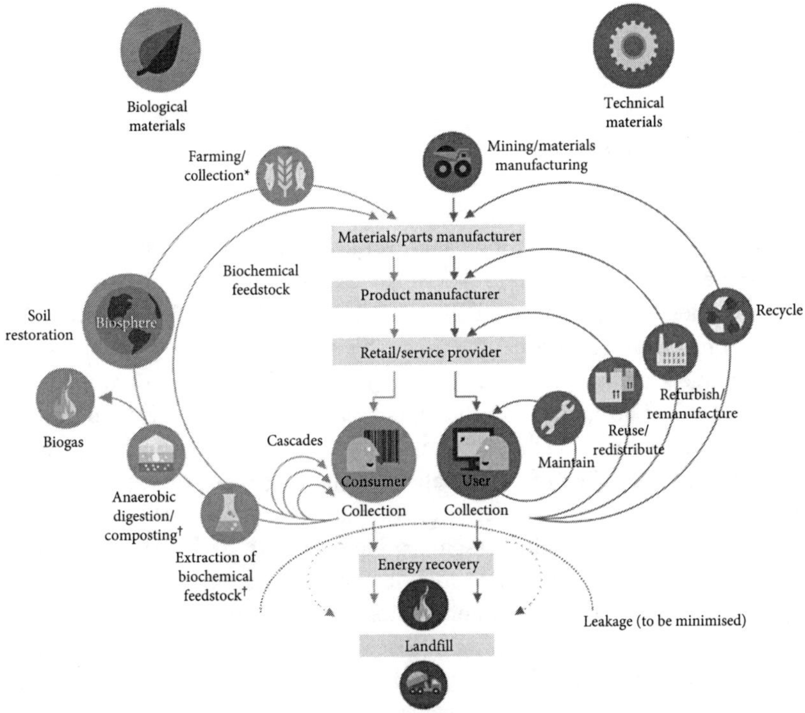

Fig. 1: Overview of Circular Economy Activities. **Source:** Ellen MacArthur Foundation, 2015:6

in 1973 had pointed the potential consequences of resource shortages. It was clear that earlier expectations of industrial development and unlimited economic growth were no longer obtainable.

In the 1980s, the new paradigm of sustainable development was popularized and became more widely used. The term was used in the International Union for the Conservation of Nature's World Conservation Strategy (1980), Lester R. Brown's Building a sustainable society (1981) and Norman Meyers's Gaia: an atlas of planet management (1984) (Pisani, 2006:92).

The World Commission on Environment and Development's report: "Our Common Future," also known as Brundtland Report, which proposed the strategy of sustainable development, was a significant attempt in 1987. The report stated the conviction that the economic growth, environmental maintenance, and social equity are possible at the same time, highlighting the three pillars of sustainable development: the environment, the economy, and the society.

The new consensus that had grown out of the adaptation of the ideas of progress, growth, and development in the light of the situation in the 1980s was that to be sustainable, development had to "improve economic efficiency, protect and restore ecological systems, and enhance the well-being of all peoples" (IISD, 2003).

The idea of circular economy dates back to 1966 while Kenneth Boulding envisioned a "spaceman economy" that would operate by reproducing the initially limited stock of inputs and recycling waste outputs. Later in 1994, Robert Ayres described industrial metabolism as "the whole integrated collection of physical processes that convert raw materials and energy, plus labor, into finished products and wastes in a (more or less) steady-state condition. The ambition level of an industrial ecology is to achieve an ideal state, one which resembles nature most. Such a system would be characterized by complete or nearly complete internal cycling of materials," and he gave an idea about a closed loop system in some sense.

The awareness of the limited resources and energy use and the importance of seeing the world as a system where pollution and waste are viewed as a defeat lay at the foundations of circular economy thinking (Ayres, 1994:28).

Although the circular economy is based on old ideas, it was first defined and conceptualized in the Ellen MacArthur Foundation's report as "an industrial system that is restorative or regenerative by intention and design" (EMA, 2015:3).

Ellen MacArthur's report in November 2015, *Towards a Circular Economy: Business Rationale for an Accelerated Transition*, claims that the circular economy rests on three principles:

- Protect and increase natural capital by controlling finite stocks and balancing renewable resource flows,
- Optimize resource efficiency by circulating products, components, and materials at the highest utility in both technical and biological cycles, and
- Encourage system effectiveness by revealing and designing out negative externalities.

2.2. The Circular Economy Schools of Thought

The circular economy concept has deep-rooted origins and cannot be attributed to one single author or date. However, its applications to modern economic systems and industrial processes have accelerated since the late 1970s as a consequence of the endeavors of a small number of academicians, businesses, and thought leaders. The general concept has been developed and refined by the following schools of thought (EMA, 2013:30).

2.2.1. Regenerative Design

In the 1970s, John T.Lyle, an American professor, challenged the graduate students with the ideas for a society in which "daily activities were based on the value of living within the limits of available renewable resources without environmental degradation." The term "regenerative design" came to be associated with this idea – that all systems, from agriculture onwards, could be orchestrated in a regenerative manner, in other words, that processes themselves renew or regenerate the sources of energy and materials that they consume.

It is not a preventative approach, reducing pollution, but also aims to **repair previous damage by designing better systems within the entity of the industry itself (Murray,** 2017:379).

2.2.2. Performance Economy

In 1976, an architect and industrial analyst, Walter Stahel outlined the vision of circular economy and its effect on economic rivalry, job creation, waste prevention, resource savings, and economic competitiveness in his report to the European Commission. Stahel asserted the idea of "functional service economy" currently widely classified into the concept of "performance economy." He also affirmed that the circular economy should be thought as a framework and a consistent model that forms a valuable part of a response to the end of "low-cost oil and materials' era."

The main idea of performance economy is selling services or the performance of the goods rather than the objects themselves. In a performance economy, many high-value items that are not currently maximized would not be sold in a one-time sale model, but rather the performance of those products would be sold to the consumer, while ownership of the item would remain with the business. Leasing machines rather than selling, being an economic advantage for both the customer and manufacturer, would be a good example of performance economy.

2.2.3. Cradle to Cradle

In the 1990s, Michael Braungart and Bill McDonough developed the Cradle to Cradle concept and certification process that considers all material used in industrial and commercial processes to be nutrients in two main categories: technical and biological. This school of thought focuses on design for effectiveness in terms of products with positive impact and reducing the negative impacts of commerce through efficiency. Braungart and McDonough have also developed a C2C certification for products.

Cradle to Cradle design identifies the safe and productive processes of nature's "biological metabolism" as a model for developing a "technical metabolism" flow of industrial materials. Product components can be designed for continuous recovery and reutilization as biological and technical nutrients within these metabolisms.

The model emphasizes the molecular composition of materials, to know what is possessed, which is the basis of every quality-based materials recycling system. The framework indicates not only materials but also energy and water inputs and builds on three key principles which are: waste equals food, use current solar income, and celebrate diversity.

"Waste equals food" principle eliminates the concept of waste by designing products and materials with life cycles that are safe for the human health and the environment and that can be reused through biological and technical metabolisms. The principle of "use current solar income" relies on the concept of maximizing the use of renewable energy. "Celebrate diversity" principle underlines respecting human and natural systems by managing water use, promoting healthy ecosystems, and guiding operations and stakeholder relationships using social responsibility.

2.2.4. Industrial Ecology

Industrial ecology is the study of material end energy flows through industrial systems focusing on connections between operators within the industrial ecosystem. This approach aims to create closed-loop processes that waste is served as an input.

It was first popularized by Robert Frosch in the late 1980s in a *Scientific American* article. Later, it has been adopted broadly with Yale University and Thomas Graedel, thought as the leaders in terms of innovative research in the area.

Industrial ecology embraces a point of view that designs production compatible with local ecological limitations also looking at their global impact from the origin, and attempting to shape them so they perform as close to living systems as possible.

This approach is also interdisciplinary being applied in the services sector also focused on social well-being.

2.2.5. *Blue Economy*

This approach initiated by Gunther Pauli, a Belgian businessman, is a movement that brings the perceptible case studies together with the "Club of Rome" cooperation. Blue Economy has twenty-one basic principles in its report that focuses on solutions being identified by their local environment characteristics with the primary source of energy. The report also provides various examples of innovation and collaborative projects.

Blue Economy is not suitable for large corporations having an established business model that will be difficult to change. It rather offers a wide platform of innovative ideas that inspires entrepreneurial minds.

2.2.6. *Biomimicry*

This approach is defined as "a new discipline that studies nature's best ideas and then imitates these designs and processes to solve human problems" by a biologist, innovation consultant, and author, Janine Benyus. It is also thought as "innovation inspired by nature." Learning from humpback whales how to create efficient wind power is an example of biomimicry.

Biomimicry stands on three principles as follows:

Nature as model: Examine nature's models and simulate these systems, forms, processes, and strategies to solve environmental problems.

Nature as mentor: Viewing and valuing the natural world based on what we can learn from it, instead of what we can extract from it and

Nature as measure: Use an ecological standard to evaluate the sustainability of the innovations.

2.2.7. *Permaculture*

Bill Mollison and David Holmgren, Australian ecologists, studied out the word "permaculture" in the late 1970s; and they defined it as "the conscious design and maintenance of agriculturally productive ecosystems, which have the diversity, stability and resilience of natural ecosystems."

Traditional sustainable agriculture and modern innovations and principles coexist in the permaculture concept. Permaculture systems have a broad range from traditional agriculture to conservation agriculture, agroforestry, organic agriculture, sustainable livestock management, and agro-ecology.

2.2.8. *Natural Capitalism*

"Natural capital" is a term used for world's stocks of natural assets such as air, water, soil, and all living things. Paul Hawkin and Amory and Hunter Lovins defined a global economy in which business and environmental interests coexist and accept the interdependencies between the production and use of human-made capital and natural capital in their book *Natural Capitalism: Creating the Next Industrial Revolution*.

There are four principles that support natural capitalism:

- Natural resources can be made to last much longer than they currently do through radical changes in production, design, and technology resulting in savings in cost, capital investment, and time.
- Natural capitalism investigates for eliminating the concept of waste by forming closed-loop production systems on nature's designs where every output is either returned harmlessly to the ecosystem as a nutrient or becomes an input for another.
- Move to a service-and-flow business model rather than the traditional sale-of-goods model arranges the interests of providers and customers in a way that rewards resource productivity.
- The need to renovate and regenerate natural resources increases as human needs and pressures on natural capital increase.

The framework synthesizes a number of longer standing schools of thought that have developed over several decades. Finally, it is obvious that each has contributed to refining and developing circular economy concept.

3. The Business Models and Innovation

A business model is a notional tool to help understand how a company does business and can be used for management, communication, analysis, performance assessment, and innovation (Bocken, Short and Evans, 2014:43).

A business model clarifies the logic and provides data and other evidence that demonstrates how a business creates and delivers value to customers. It also outlines the architecture of revenues, costs, and profits associated with the business enterprise delivering that value (Teese, 2010:173).

In another definition; the business model outlines how a company generates revenues with reference to the structure of its value chain and its interaction with the industry value system (Fisken and Rutherford, 2002:192).

A more particular definition is made by the consulting company KMLab Inc. as; "a business model is a description of how your company intends to create value in the marketplace. It includes that unique combination of products, services, image and distribution that your company carries forward. It also includes the underlying organisation of people and the operational infrastructure that they used to accomplish their work" (Chesbrough and Rosenbloom, 2002:535).

In literature, although a variety of definitions for business models can be presented, a business model is generally defined by three main elements as: the value creation, value proposition, and value capture. Value creation is the basic principle of any business model as businesses characteristically capture value by catching new business opportunities, markets, and revenue flows (Teese, 2010:183). Value proposition is interested in product and service proposition to achieve economic return. The value proposition would provide measurable ecological and social value cooperatively with economic value (Boons and Lüdeke-Freund, 2013:14). Value capture is concerned with earning the revenues from the provision of goods, services, or information to customers (Teese, 2010:178).

Zott and Amit (2010:219) describe business models as "the content, structure and governance of transactions designed so as to create value through the exploitation of business opportunities," while Teese defines that a business model articulates how the company will convert resources and capabilities into economic value. It is nothing less than the organizational and financial architecture of a business and includes implicit assumptions about customers and their needs and the behavior of revenues, costs, and competitor responses (Teese, 2010:173).

Osterwalder and Pigneur (2010:16–17) describe a business model as a series of elements such as: customer segments, customer relationships, key activities and resources, partnerships, revenue streams, cost structure, distribution, and sales channels.

Chesbrough and Rosenbloom defined the business model as a structure that intercedes between technological inputs and economic outputs while Zott and Amit took an activity-based perspective including the selection of activities "what," the activity system structure "how," and who performs the activities "who" (Zott and Amit, 2010:219).

The factors that compose business model innovation is still uncertain although there is a wide literature on business models. The literature generally enchases business model innovation in the context of changing the value proposition for the consumer. However, as business model innovation requires the way of doing business instead of what is done, it is more than just changing the product and service proposal (Amit and Zott, 2012:42).

Business models and business model innovation have received a significant attention both in literature and industry, and it is increasingly suggested that business model innovation is a key to business success (Bocken et al, 2014:43).

4. The Circular Economy Business Models

With the increasing global sustainability consciousness and enforcement, the collaboration between corporations and stakeholders is becoming more significant. The value is no longer created by companies acting autonomously while it requires serious cooperation between companies acting together. The business model can be seen as a new unit of analysis that takes into account these collaborative ties (Bocken et al, 2014:43).

The circular economy is seen as a promising approach to help reduce the pressure on global resources and climate due to human activity. It is a concept that contradicts with the traditional linear business model of "take-make-use-dispose" style production and a fossil fuel–dependent industrial system, because the aim of the business shifts from generating profits from selling artifacts to generating profits from the flow of materials and products over time (Bakker et al., 2014:308).

The whole business ecosystem is changing, and the circular economy needs systematic innovation, and therefore a multilevel analysis is required. The change towards sustainable and circular business model innovation should integrate elements from macrolevel such as: global trends and drivers; meso levels such as: ecosystem and value cocreation; and microlevels such as: company, customers, and consumers (Valkokari et al, 2014:363).

Organizations increasingly understand that meeting their sustainability aims does not only need new technologies, but also innovation on the business model level. As the new paradigm of a circular economy requires new concepts and tools to define and encourage this paradigm at the strategic level of business model innovation, more consistent terminology is needed to enable the shift of business to a circular model (Bocken et al., 2015:309). To enable the design of sustainable business models, a variety of new tools and techniques have been developed.

Business model innovations for sustainability are described as: innovations that create significant positive and/or significantly reduced negative impacts for the environment and the society through changes in the way the organization and its value-network create, deliver, and capture value or change their value propositions (Bocken et al., 2014:44).

As a business model does not only have a company focus, but it is a broader series of stakeholders requiring a wider value-network perspective for innovation (Sommer, 2012:52), likewise sustainable business models capture economic, social, and environmental value for a wide range of stakeholders (Bocken et al. 2013: 484).

Business models are viewed as an important driver for innovation, and business model choices define the structure of the business. But once established, it is generally very difficult and challenging to change business models. Shifting to a circular economy model is a radical change which will require a new path of thinking and doing business (Bocken et al, 2015:312).

There are various categories of business models in a circular economy. Lewandowski emphasized one of the examples that involves wide business actions: ReSOLVE (regenerate, share, optimize, loop, virtualize, exchange) framework in his paper in 2015. Regenerate implies the shift to renewable energy and materials and related to returning recovered biological resources to the biosphere. Share means maximizing usage of products by sharing them among users by peer-to-peer sharing of private products or public sharing of products and also reusing products as long as possible. Sharing also aims prolonging products' life by maintenance, repair, and design-enhancing durability. Optimize actions are focused on increasing the efficiency of a product and removing waste in production process and also in supply chain, leveraging big data, automation, steering, and remote sensing which does not require changing the product or the technology. Loop actions mean keeping components and materials in closed loops in which the higher importance is given to inner loops. Virtualize actions aim to deliver particular usage virtually rather than materially. Exchange actions mean replacing old materials with advanced materials and with applying new technologies also by choosing new products and services (Lewandowski, 2016:6).

Mentink used a similar approach to the business model and indicated the changes of business model elements required for developing a more circular model as: value propositions, resources, activities, processes and capabilities, revenue models, and customers or customer interfaces (2014:34).

Boons and Lüdeke-Freund identified four requirements for sustainable innovative business models such as: a value proposition reflecting the balance of economic, environmental, and social needs; a supply chain participating suppliers in sustainable supply chain management; a customer involvement motivating customers to take responsibility for their consumption; and a financial model considering a proper distribution of economic costs and benefits between the actors involved in the business model (Boons and Lüdeke-Freund, 2013:12).

Six key areas are defined by Laubscher and Marinelli for integration of the circular economy concepts with the business model as: a sales model replacing selling products with selling services, a product design and material composition changing the production process towards maximization of reuse, IT and data management to keep track of the products for resource optimization, a strategic sourcing for own operations by establishing long-term and trusted relationships with customers and suppliers, and human resource incentives for culture adaptation and development of capabilities by training programs and rewards (Laubscher and Marinelli, 2014:2–4).

5. The Circular Economy in Turkey

Turkey as a country with its fast-growing urbanization, growing energy demand per person, young population, and its economic development, has been one of the fast-growing markets of the world for the last two decades. The country has a huge dependency on expensive imported energy resources that place a big burden on the economy, and pollution is becoming a great environmental concern in the country.

Turkey has efforts in sustainability for about 20 years. The concept "sustainability" entered into the Turkish economic and environmental policy with its Sixth Five-Year Development Plan (1990–1994) when the accordance of social-economic policies with the environmental policies had been accepted as the basic principle. But over the years, except for a few multinational corporations, some large holding companies taking action, and inadequate government regulations in Turkey, it is difficult to say much could be proceeded.

Although the circular economy is a newer subject in Turkey with hardly academic research and very few applications, it is still possible to examine some good examples of large corporations and nonprofit organizations. The Business Council for Sustainable Development (BCSD) can be accepted as one of the biggest nonprofit organizations working on circular economy in Turkey. BCSD Turkey carries out activities aimed at increasing the awareness about circular economy together with the concept, and the good practices become more widespread with its projects mentioned below (BCSD, 2019):

- ***Turkey Materials Marketplace Project***: It is a digital platform which ensures that materials are exchanged between industries. The project is implemented in Turkey through the cooperation between BCSD Turkey and BCSD US and was funded for its first two years by the European Bank for Reconstruction and Development (EBRD). The EBRD included the project within the scope of "Near Zero Waste" program, which supports waste reduction projects. The project has the characteristics of a digital initiative by its structure and planned to make a significant contribution to circular economy. It creates a new business-to-business model and, thereby, aims to change traditional recycling models, waste management systems, and even the waste concept.
- ***Do (Be Sensitive) Project:*** The project was launched in 2015 and aims at promoting savings in work places by creating "Sensitive People." The savings can

cover different types of materials and energy, such as electricity, water, fuel, and paper. The project is open for members of BCSD Turkey as well as non-members. The second version of the project is more comprehensive, covering measurement, assessment, and reporting; and it was put into practice in 2017.

- ***Innovative Sustainability Solutions Contest:*** The Innovative Sustainability Solutions Contest was launched in 2013, and it is organized biennially. The contest rewards valuable sustainability solutions. This event's purpose is to emphasize the importance of innovation for industry, and to highlight good practices and make them widespread. The jury of the contest consists of stakeholders who are experts in public or private sectors, NGOs, academia, or media. As a result of the assessment made by the jury, awards are granted in "Environmental," "Social," and "Economic" Innovative Solutions branches in "Large Company" and "SME" categories.
- ***Waste to Wealth:*** Published by Accenture Strategy, *Waste to Wealth* is a book that aims at transforming circular economy into practical and implementable business models, instead of remaining as an abstract concept. The book was prepared by Accenture after analysis of more than 120 companies, and it explains five main circular economy business models, which are determined to ensure resource efficiency through innovative methods. This book was translated into Turkish by BCSD Turkey.
- ***Guide on Eco-labels for Sustainability:*** It is one of BCSD Turkey's objectives to strengthen consumer awareness in order to promote a sustainable industry. With this objective in mind, the Council analyzed various sources and prepared this guide. Eco-labeling systems developed as a result of the domestic and international circulation of products and services at an unprecedented pace. So these systems provide opportunities to all companies in Turkey, and primarily to exporting companies, in terms of risk management and new markets. Turkey's target is to become one of the top ten economies of the world, reaching an export volume of 500 billion USD. As BCSD Turkey, we believe that eco-labeling systems constitute one of the strategic phases for Turkey to create an environmentally conscious and socially sensitive industry infrastructure and sustainable products and services. In this guide, you can find information about the basic terms related with eco-labeling systems, the reasons why it is important for your entity, and different eco-labels, which prevail in 14 sectors and different export regions. It also contains short definitions of more than 300 eco-labels. This guide is an important source, prepared with purposes of raising awareness about eco-labels and enhancing knowledge accumulation.

The Environment Protection and Packing Waste Recovery and Recycling Foundation in Turkey (CEVKO) is a follower of the circular economy and "new plastics economy," initiated by Ellen MacArthur Foundation by setting up an action plan for Turkey with NGOs and the public and industrial sector.

Turkish Plastics Industry Foundation (PAGEV) is another nongovernmental organization in Turkey working on circular economy with its "Zero Plastics to Landfill by 2025" and "Plastic Carrier Bags" projects. Zero Plastics to Landfill by 2025 aims to stop the landfilling of recyclable and other recoverable post-consumer waste and support innovation in plastics recycling technologies.

D-Cube is a Scientific Research and Social Development Cooperative that aims to create awareness, solution and increase in capacity about circular economy business model for sustainable development.

Multinational corporations operating in Turkey such as Nestle, Henkel, Unilever, Hewlett Packard, and H&M also contribute to establish circular economy business models; however, government support and more consciousness is needed to increase the efforts.

6. Conclusions

All businesses, either implicitly or explicitly, operate a particular business model. A business model describes the design or architecture of the value creation, delivery, and capture mechanisms employed.

The adaptation of an operating circular economy governance requires a systemic multilevel change, including new business models, technological innovation, and stakeholder cooperation. Radical innovations and corruptive business models are needed in order to handle the current challenges and move towards the circular economy model. It is clear there is a lack of frameworks for supporting business model innovation in companies in the context of a circular economy.

Moving to a circular economic model could lead to significant benefits for the economy, environment, and business. Economic benefits can be summarized as: increased potential for economic growth, more saved resources, and employment growth; while environmental benefits can be regarded as: fewer greenhouse-gas emissions, healthy and resilient soils, and fewer negative externalities. It also has benefits on business such as new profit opportunities, volatility reduction and safeguarded supplies, the demand for new services, and getting to know the clients better.

Nevertheless, implementing a circular economic model also has important economic and institutional barriers which can be summarized as follows:

- Circular economy business models are more difficult to develop, as most investors are still working under a linear economy logic and the current economic system is geared towards the demand of the linear economy that is not yet prepared to deal with circular economy entrepreneurs,
- New business models may be challenging to implement and develop because of laws and regulations that are not prepared for this kind of innovations,
- Many companies still have goals and evaluation systems that focus on short-term value creation, whereas the circular economy model is a long-term value creation model,
- Plenty of business rely on old and/or strong alliances, making it harder to create new alliances and therefore to close loops,
- There are challenges for measuring financial benefits and the profitability of circular economy, and
- The demand for circular products and alternatives is still small.

Although Turkey has some efforts on implementing circular economy business models, the country has still a long path. As there are some nongovernmental organizations and multinational corporations working on circular economy, more endeavors in the context of national companies and government are needed.

Bibliography

Amit, R., and Zott, C. (2012), "Creating Value Through Business Model Innovation", **MIT Sloan Management Review**, Vol.53, N.3, pp. 41–49.

Antikainen, M., and Valkokari, K. (2016), "A Framework for Sustainable Circular Business Model Innovation", **Technology Innovation Management Review**, Vol. 6, No.7, pp. 5–12.

Ayres, R.U. (1994), "Industrial Metabolism: Theory and Policy", (B.R. Allenby and D.J. Richards, Eds.), **The Greening of Industrial Ecosystems**, Washington DC: National Academy Press, pp. 23–37.

Bakker, C., Den Hollander, M., van Hinte, E., and Zijlstra, Y. (2014), **Product that Last. Product Design for Circular Business Models**, Delft: TU Delft Library.

Bocken, N.M.P., Pauw, I. de, Bakker, C., and van der Grinten, B. (2015), "Product design and business model strategies for a circular economy", **Journal of Industrial and Production Engineering**, Vol.33, No.5, pp. 308–320.

BCSD. (2019), **The Business Council for Sustainable Development**, Retrieved from http://www.skdturkiye.org/en/surdurulebilir-sanayi-ve-dongusel-ekonomi, (25.03.2019).

Bocken, N.M.P., Short, S.W., Rana, P., and Evans, S. (2013), "A Value Mapping Tool for Sustainable Business Modelling", **Corporate Governance**, Vol. 13, I.5, pp. 482–497.

Bocken, N.M.P., Short, S.W., Rana, P., and Evans, S. (2014), "A Literature and Practice Review to Develop Sustainable Business Model Archetypes", **Journal of Cleaner Production**, Vol.65, pp. 42–56.

Boons, F., and Lüdeke-Freund, F. (2013), "Business Models for Sustainable Innovation: State of the Art and Steps Towards a Research Agenda", **Journal of Cleaner Production**, Vol.45, pp. 9–19.

Chesbrough, H., and Rosenbloom, R.S. (2002), "The Role of the Business Model in Capturing Value From Innovation: Evidence from Xerox Corporation's Technology Spin-Off Companies", ***Industrial and Corporate Change***, Vol.11, I.3, pp. 529–555.

Ellen MacArthur Foundation (EMA). (2013), **Towards the Circular Economy: Opportunities for the Consumer Goods Sector, Available**, Retrieved from https://www.ellenmacarthurfoundation.org/publications/towards-the-circular-economy-vol-2-opportunities-for-the-consumer-goods-sector, (12.03.2019).

Ellen MacArthur Foundation (EMA). (2015), **Towards the Circular Economy: Economic and Business Rationale for an Accelerated Transition**, Retrieved from https://www.ellenmacarthurfoundation.org/assets/downloads/TCE_Ellen-MacArthur-Foundation_9-Dec-2015.pdf), (14.03.2019).

Fisken, J., and Rutherford, J. (2002), "Business Models and Investment Trends in the Biotechnology Industry in Europe", **Journal of Commercial Biotechnology**, Vol.8, N.3, pp. 191–199.,

IISD (International Institute for Sustainable Development). (2003), **Basics and Issues**, Retrieved from http://www.iisd.org/sd/, (03.03.2019).

Laubscher, M., and Marinelli, T. (2014), "Integration of Circular Economy in Business", Proceedings of the conference: Going Green, CARE INNOVATION 2014, Vienna, Austria.

Lewandowski, M. (2016), "Designing the Business Models for Circular Economy-Towards the Conceptual Framework", **Sustainability**, Vol.8, I.1, pp. 6–28.

Mentink, B. (2014), **Circular Business Model Innovation: A Process Framework and a Tool For Business Model Innovation in a Circular Economy** (Master's Thesis), Delft University of Technology & Leiden University, Leiden, The Netherlands.

Murray, A. (2017), "The Circular Economy: An Interdisciplinary Exploration of the Concept and Its Application in a Global Context", **Journal of Business Ethics**, Vol.140, I.3, pp. 369–380.

Murray, A., Skene, K., and Haynes, K. (2015), "The Circular Economy: An Interdisciplinary Exploration of the Concept and Application in a Global Context", **Journal of Business Ethics**, pp. 1–37.

Osterwalder, A. and Pigneur, Y. (2010),**Business Model Generation: A Handbook for Visionaries, Game Changers and Challengers**, New Jersey: John Wiley and Sons Inc.

Pisani, J.A.du. (2006), "Sustainable Development – Historical Roots of the Concept", **Environmental Sciences**, Vol.3, N.2, pp. 83–96.

Sommer A. (2012), **Managing Green Business Model Transformations**, Berlin Heidelberg: Springer Verlag.

Stahel, W. (2016), "Circular Economy", **The Nature**, Special Issue, Vol.531, pp. 435–438.

Teese, D.J. (2010), "Business Models, Business Strategy and Innovation", **Long Range Planning**, Vol. 43, pp. 172–194.

Valkokari, K., Valkokari, P., Palomäki, K., Uusitalo, T., Reunanen, M., Macchi, M., Rana, P., and Liyanage, J.P. (2014), "Road-Mapping the Business Potential of Sustainability within the European Manufacturing Industry", **Foresight**, Vol.16, I. 4, pp. 360–384.

Zott, C., and Amit, R. (2010), "Business Model Design: An Activity System Perspective", **Long Range Planning**, Vol.43, pp. 216–226.

Assist. Prof. Dr. Ebru Gül Yılmaz

Foreign Trade After the 1980s and Effects of Digitalization on Foreign Trade

Abstract: In order to revive the world economy and to eliminate the protectionist and restrictive approach towards foreign trade in the aftermath of the Second World War, the General Agreement on Tariffs and Trade-GATT was signed in 1947; infrastructure to implement market economy was formed with the establishment of World Bank and International Monetary Fund (IMF) in 1944. After these dates, there has been a significant increase in foreign trade volumes worldwide. Turkey took one of the most important steps towards becoming more integrated into the global economy by applying to the European Economic Community in 1959. The country adopted an import substitution approach between the years 1960 and 1980; and in 1980, with the 24 January Decisions, an export-based industrial strategy was started to be implemented. This study aims to make an all-round analysis of the Turkish foreign trade structure from the post-1980 period in which economic integration with foreign countries started to increase to date, to identify strengths as well as issues that create improvement opportunities, and to develop suggestions for solutions to address such issues.

Keywords: Foreign Trade, 1980 Decisions, Digitalization Effects on Foreign Trade

1 History of Turkey Foreign Trade: Changes in Foreign Trade Policies After Republication Until Economic Liberalization

With the republic, many sweeping structural changes and developments began to take place in the country, and this was naturally reflected in the country's economic relations with other countries. In the literature, foreign trade in the post-Republic era is classified as 1923–1929 World Great Depression, 1930–1950 Mixed Economy, 1950–1960 Neoliberal Period, 1960–1980 Planned Period, 1980–1990 Liberalization, and 2000 Post-Crisis Period.

The basic acceptance, implementation and agreements valid in the mentioned periods are as follows:

1.1 Global Great Depression Period (1923–1929)

In the Izmir Economy Congress, which was held in February 1923 before the proclamation of the Republic, it was aimed to establish the economic foundations of the new republic. The privilege granted to foreigners in the Lausanne Peace

Treaty until 1929 was the main reason for the adoption of an outward-oriented structure in the congress. Main decisions that applied during the period may be counted as: establishment of national banks, importance attributed to industrial production, and promotion of the use of domestic goods (Özdemir et al., 2016:154).

When the impact of the decisions on foreign trade figures is measured, it is seen that the exports, which were USD 50.8 Million in 1923, increased to USD 74.8 Million USD in 1929 and the imports of USD 86.8 Million to USD 123.5 Million (Özdemir at al., 2016: 152). Although there has been a 44 % increase in the foreign trade volume, by looking at the export coverage ratio figures; which was 58.5 % in 1923 and reached only to 60.6 % in 1929 with an improvement of 2.1 %; it might be said that realizing the goal of reducing the dependency on external sources was not reached.

Another point worth mentioning regarding the foreign trade structure of the period is that the average share of agricultural products in total exports is 85 %.

In the aftermath of the global economic depression in 1929, reducing foreign dependence became the main target.

1.2 Mixed Economy Period (1930–1950)

The countries most affected by the Great Depression were those with a relatively high share in the global economy. Since Turkey just started to accelerate its foreign trade in the republican era, it was relatively less affected by the global crisis (Ozdemir et al., 2016:154).

The most important feature of the period was that the private sector which was supported by incentives until the Great Depression, yet remained below expectations, led to the adoption of a mixed economic system in the new period. Although the private sector continued to be supported throughout the period, its major investments for the development of the country was to be realized by the government (Doğan, 2013: 213).

The reflection of the mixed economic system in the banking sector was the increase in the number of public banks. Within the period, the Central Bank was established in 1931; Industrial Credit Bank was established in 1932 in order to provide loans to the industrial sector; and Sümerbank was established in 1933 in order to prepare feasibility studies of prospective state enterprises, to make investments, and to provide loans to relevant organizations (Coşkun et al., 2012:7; Özdemir et al., 2016:154).

With the success of the First Five-Year Industrial Plan, preparations for the Second Five-Year Industrial Plan for the period of 1938–1943 were initiated in

1936; however, it could not be implemented with the outbreak of World War II in 1939 (Metintaş and Kayıran, 2008:157–160).

After Celal Bayar, during the reign of Dr. Refik Saydam, a statist-populist political and economic system came to the fore once again. On January 27, 1939, The Economic Defense Plan announced by Dr. Refik Saydam was put into effect (Tokgöz, 2009:82).

Within this period, Turkey became a member of the International Monetary Fund (IMF). In evaluation of the foreign trade volumes, it is noteworthy that total foreign trade volume, which was USD 140.9 million in 1930, reached USD 549 million in 1950 with a 289 % increase and foreign trade deficit occurred only in the years 1938, 1947, 1948, 1949, and 1950 along the period. By the year 1950, 93 % of the exports were made up of agricultural products. The ratio of exports to imports decreased from 102.6 % in 1930 to 92.2 % in 1950.

1.3 The Neoliberal Period (1950–1960)

In the 1950s, policies were implemented to increase the share of the private sector in production and trade, and the state was to realize large-scale investments.

In the decade following 1950, the foreign trade volume reached USD 823.8 million. The country had a foreign trade deficit each year during the period. By the end of the period, the ratio of exports to imports decreased to 75.3 %.

1.4 Planned Period (1960–1980)

Turkey applied to the European Economic Community (EEC) membership in 1959 with the target of expanding its foreign trade volume. A partnership agreement for commercial cooperation was proposed by the EEC while Turkey was to get into the process of fulfilling the conditions membership and the said agreement, The Ankara Agreement was signed on September 12, 1963, and entered into force on December 1, 1964. The country received the first IMF loan in 1961 (Özdemir et al., 2016:159).

In the planned period, the base of economic growth was grounded on the import substitution approach. Until 1970, production for the domestic market was encouraged, and with the realization of a planned devaluation in 1970 it was aimed to increase exports. The foreign trade volume, which was USD 788.9 million in 1960, increased by 1271 % and reached 10.8 billion USD in 1980. Within the same period, the ratio of exports to imports decreased from 68.5 % to 36.8 %. The ratio of foreign trade deficit to foreign trade volume increased from 18.6 % in 1960 to 46.2 % in 1980. As of 1980, the share of agricultural products in exports declined to 56 %.

After the 1960s and during 1970s with the import-substitution strategies, Turkey's economy became highly dependent on imports and foreign borrowing. Since 1980s, open industrialization policies have been implemented and as a result, a significant acceleration in foreign trade volumes occurred. With the impact of the oil crises experienced in 1973–1974, significant deterioration occurred in terms of balance of payment, and the ratio of exports to import that was reached to the peak level (81 %) of the 1960s in 1965 decreased to 30 % in 1975.

With the applied exchange rate policies, the excessive appreciation of TL could not be prevented. In order to provide the balances, imports were suppressed with the help of necessary tools and foreign exchange controls were increased. Due to the rapid growth in imports increased over the years 1970 current account deficit, the economy, the third five-year development plan period has come to an unsustainable point along the end and Turkey's economy in 1978, it has entered into a severe economic crisis. Due to the bottlenecks in imports, the industrial sector faced serious production bottlenecks and the decline in production caused sudden and rapid increases in inflation. The economic growth has declined in the high inflation environment, where the cost of imports and the cost of the production increased with devaluations. The period of crisis between 1978 and 1980 is a turning point in terms of industrialization and economic policies.

After the republican period, Turkey has many important memberships of worldwide and regional foreign trade organizations (Tab. 1). Turkey has become a member of most of them at the establishment year or just within two–three years except Shanghai Cooperation Organization (Koçtürk & Aslıhan, 2014: 68 & Keskingöz, 2017: 21).

1.5. Foreign Trade Structure After the 1980s

By the decision of opening up Turkish economy and adopting crucial principles in order to achieve free and competitive economy, there occurred significant increase in foreign trade figures. The most important turning point in Turkish neoliberalism was the decision in August 1989 to open up the capital account completely. The decision for full openness was accepted as a premature affair due to the lack of monetary and fiscal infrastructure. Turkey has had chance to compensate the effects of this early decision after the 2001 crisis (Öniş and Şenses, 2010). The impact of the opened-up policy could have easily been monitored within just one year: exports 2.9 million USD in 1980 increased to 4.7 million USD (Fig. 1) and imports 7.9 million USD in 1980 increased to 8.9 million

Tab. 1: International Economic Organizations Registered into by Turkey. **Source:** Ministry of Social Affairs: http://www.mfa.gov.tr/sub.en.mfa?7cafe2ef-78bd-4d88-b326-3916451364f3

International Economic Organizations	Foundation Year of the Organization	Membership Date of Turkey
G-20	1999	1999
The Org. for Economic Co-operation and Devel. – OECD	1961	1961
Customs Union	1993	1995
Organization of Islamic Cooperation – OIC	1969	1969
Black Sea Economic Cooperation – BSEC	1992	1992
Economic Cooperation Organization – ECO	1985	1985
Developing 8 - D-8	1997	1997
World Trade Organization – WTO	1995	1995
International Monetary Fund – IMF	1945	1947
World Bank	1944	1947
Shanghai Cooperation Organization	1996	2012

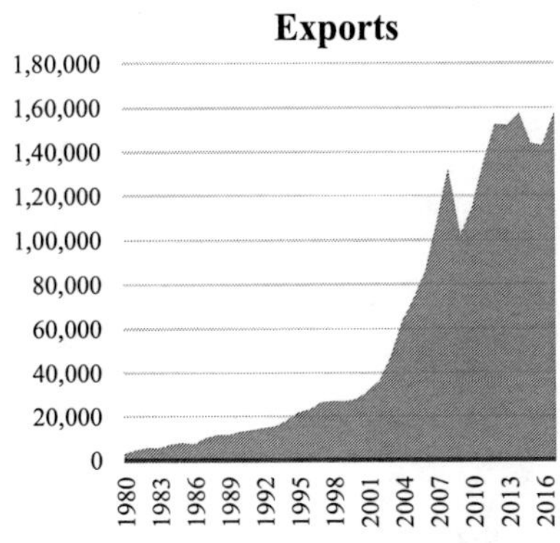

Fig. 1: Exports Trend Analysis

USD in 1981 (Fig. 2). The ratio of exports to imports increased from 36.8 % in 1980 to 52.6 % within just 2 years (Fig. 3). Before liberalization, average of exports/GDP ratio was 4.6 % for the period between 1960 and 1979. With the effects of export-led growth policy, ratio increased to 19 % for the period 1980–2017. The interperiod increase in exports was also valid for imports and the

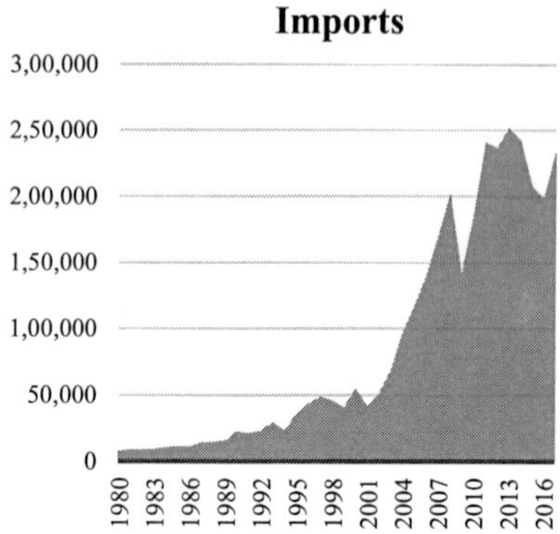

Fig. 2: Imports Trend Analysis

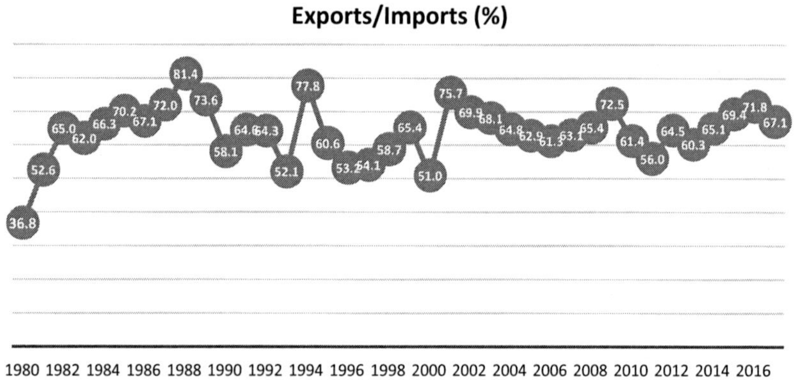

Fig. 3: Exports to Import Ratio Trend Analysis

import-to-GDP ratio of 1960–1979, which was 7.3 % on average, increased to 22.1 % in the 1980–2017 period. As it can be followed from Fig. 4, the share of imports in GDP has always been higher compared to the share of exports. The increase in the ratio of foreign trade to the gross domestic product is of course evaluated as positive.

Assessing just the change in volumes of foreign trade is not sufficient for understanding the big picture. Liberalization of economy was planned by the establishment of General Agreement on Tariffs and Trade-GATT in 1947. So, transformation in foreign trade for many countries took place. The development

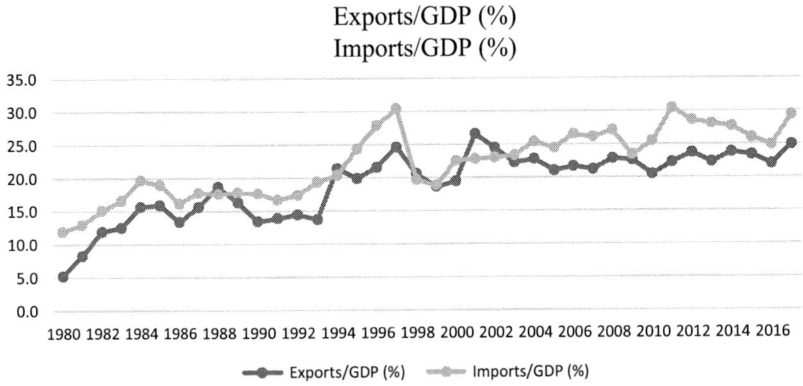

Fig. 4: Exports/GDP and Imports/GDP Ratios Trend Analysis

Fig. 5: Share of Merchandise and Service Exports in the World. **Source:** World Trade Organization (2018)

in the share of foreign trade volumes in the world is critical for seeing the full picture of Turkey's foreign trade share which was 0.1 % in 1980 and reached to 0.89 % in 2017 (Fig. 5).

The change in structure of exports and imports will be analyzed for establishing clear understanding of the full picture. Product Concentration (PCI) and Revealed Comparative Advantage (RCA) Indices of Turkey will be discussed with comparison of developing and developed countries.

1.5.1 *Foreign Trade Indices*

1.5.1.1 *Product Concentration Indices*

Importance of product concentration in foreign trade has been mentioned by the research of Hirschman at 1958. Hirchman has mentioned that diversification in exports creates new industries. Massell (1964) has investigated the relationship between export product concentration and fluctuation in export earnings and concluded that although it is tenuous, there is a relationship between product concentration of exports and instability in export earnings. Al-Marhubi (2000) has concluded that export diversification is associated with faster growth. Product concentration indices are calculated by United Nations Conference on Trade and Development (UNCTADstat) for both imports and exports on a yearly basis.

1.5.1.2 *Export Concentration Indices*

Export Concentration index is calculated for each country, and it explains the degree of concentration of goods exported. This index score shows us that if a large share of a country's good exports is distributed among a small number of commodities or if its exports are well distributed among various products (UNCTADstat, 2019). When the index score gets closer to one, this explains that exports are not well distributed among products.

The product concentration index scores for Turkey, developed, and developing countries were gained from UNCTADstat for the years between 1995 and 2017. Turkey and developed and developing countries have scores that are very close to each other; As of 2017, product production index for Turkey is 0.08, for developing countries it is 0.09, and for developed countries it is 0.07. All three are far from 1. Consequently, Turkey's exports are well distributed among products (Fig. 6).

1.5.1.3 *Imports Product Concentration Index*

This index measures, for each country, the degree of concentration of imports of goods. It tells us if a large share of country's imports relies on a small number of commodities or, conversely, if imports are well distributed among many types of products (UNCTADstat, 2019). When the index score gets closer to one, this explains that imports are not well distributed among products.

The product concentration index scores for Turkey, developed, and developing countries was gained from UNCTADstat for the years between 1995 and 2017. Turkey and developed and developing countries have scores that are very close to each other. As of 2017, product production index for Turkey is 0.10,

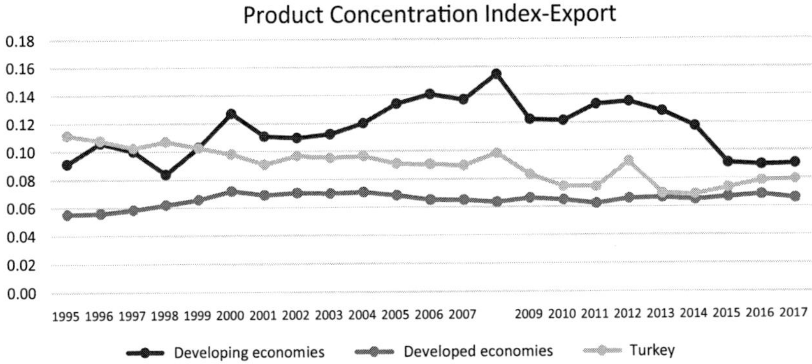

Fig. 6: Export Product Concentration Index Comparison. **Source:** https://unctadstat.unctad.org/wds/TableViewer/tableView.aspx?ReportId=120

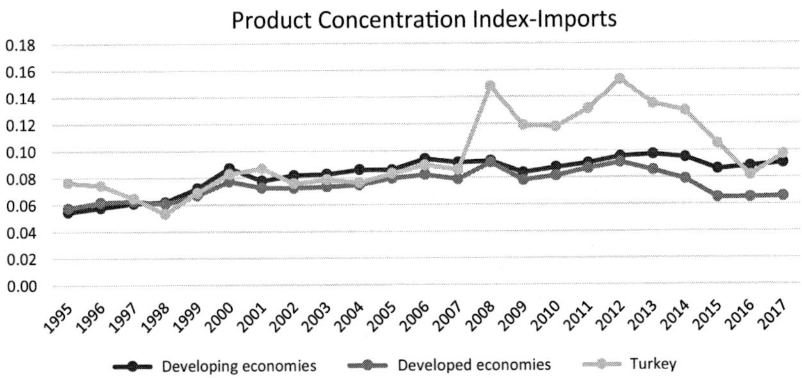

Fig. 7: Imports Product Concentration Index Comparison. **Source:** https://unctadstat.unctad.org/wds/TableViewer/tableView.aspx

for developing countries it is 0.08, and for developed countries it is 0.07. All three are far from 1. Consequently, Turkey's imports are well distributed among products, but still above developing and developed countries' averages (Fig. 7).

1.5.1.4 Revealed Comparative Advantage Index (RCA)

The idea of revealed comparative advantage was first proposed by Liesner (1958). It was later made functional by Balassa (1965) (Seymen, 2009:237). RCA is an index which is based on product groups of countries; it is calculated

Tab. 2: Top 10 Highest RCA Product Groups. **Source:** https://unctadstat.unctad.org/wds/TableViewer/tableView.aspx?ReportId=157975

TOP 10 Product Groups with Revealed Comparative Advantage	**RCA Score - 2017**
[046] Meal and flour of wheat and flour of meslin	23.1
[659] Floor coverings, etc.	14.8
[273] Stone, sand, and gravel	12.1
[025] Birds' eggs, and eggs' yolks; egg albumin	7.2
[812] Sanitary, plumbing, heating fixtures, fittings, n.e.s.	6.9
[676] Iron and steel bars, rods, angles, shapes and sections	6.9
[661] Lime, cement, fabrica. constr. mat. (excluding glass, clay)	5.8
[047] Other cereal meals and flour	5.7
[583] Monofilaments, of plastics, cross-section > 1mm	5.4
[278] Other crude minerals	5.1

by finding the ratio of that product share in total exports of the country divided by product share of exports in the world. If the value exceeds 1, it is concluded that the country has comparative advantage in the relevant product group; and if the value is less than 1, the country has a comparative disadvantage.

Formulation of RCA is as follows:

$$RCAcg = (xcg \,/\, Xct) \;/\; (xwg \,/\, Xwt)$$

xcg: Export of related product group in the related country
Xct: Total export of the related country
xwg: Export of related product group in the world
Xwt: Total export of the world

Top 10 product groups that have the highest RCA score can be followed from Tab. 2. Turkey has 95 product groups that have RCA score equal to and more than 1, 42 product groups that have a score between 0.5 and 1, and 119 product groups that have score less than 0.5.

1.5.2 Number of Products Exported and Imported

The number of products exported which was 233 at 1995 reached to 252 by 2017. It is under the level of both developed and developing countries (Fig. 8). The number of products imported which was 249 at 1995 reached to 251 by the end of 2017 (Fig. 9). Although number of products exported are very similar to developed and developing countries, the number of products imported is below

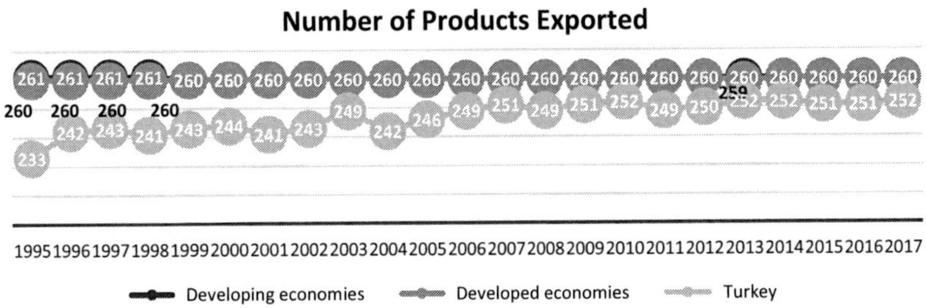

Fig. 8: Number of Products Exported Trend Analysis. **Source**: https://unctadstat.unctad.org/wds/TableViewer/tableView.aspx?ReportId=120

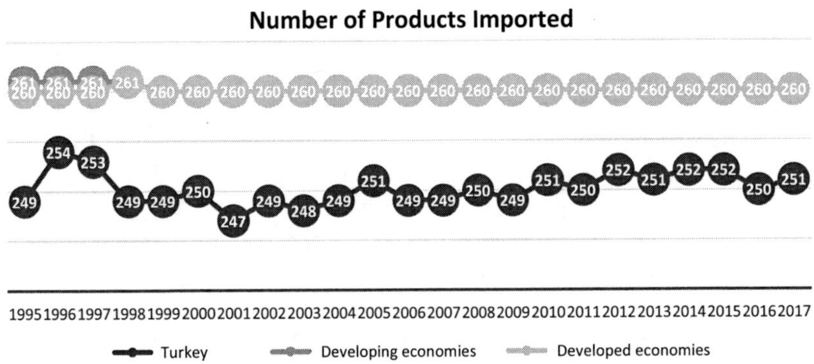

Fig. 9: Number of Products Imported Trend Analysis

the other country groups during the whole period investigated. The recent composition of the product groups will be analyzed in the next section.

2 Today's Foreign Trade of Turkey

Turkey, which was the 21st biggest economy in the world for the years between 1981 and 1985, is the 18th biggest economy in the world as of 2017. It seems that two major milestones, liberalization and the arrangements after the 2001 crisis, could not be sufficient enough for carrying the economy to upper levels in the ranking. Total volume of exports has reached to 168 billion USD, and imports have dropped down to 223 billion USD as of 2018. As a result foreign trade deficit decreased to 55 billion USD as of 2018 from 76.7 billion USD as of 2017. Imports decreased by 4.6 % and exports have increased 7.1 % compared to the previous year. Along with other aspects, one of the most important factor of this change is the devaluation of Turkish lira against USD which had an average of 4.55 in 2017 and 5.26 in 2018. The dollar exchange rate reached to its peak point: 7.2 at 12.08.2018[1].

With the intervention of Central Bank and Banking Regulation and Supervision Agency (BRSA), average of USD for the period August–December 2018 was increased to 5.69, from an average of 4.22 for the period January–July 2018.

Interventions were as follows:

- The Central Bank provided USD 6 billion and TL 10 billion to the markets.
- BRSA brought limit to foreign exchange swap transactions.
- Qatari banks and financial markets in Turkey have announced that they will invest 15 billion dollars.
- In September 2018, the Central Bank raised the policy interest rate from 17.75 % to 24.2 % by 6.25 points.

It is obvious that contraction in foreign trade deficit was not structural. The devaluation which began in August 2018 and the shrinkage in domestic demand that is highly dependent upon imports were the most important factors of this contraction. Meanwhile, talking about contraction in foreign trade deficit, it would be useful to mention about the share of imports in exports of manufacturing industry. There is a myth about this ratio which is 70 % in most of the written platforms. Akat (2019) has tested the accuracy of this myth and has tried to prove that this ratio is too high. Akat mentioned in his paper that Sönmez M. had calculated the ratio 70 % by using inward processing license permissions at 2007. Sönmez had divided the amount of imports to amount of exports recorded in the related licenses. Akat has gathered the recent data of Sönmez's method. And the result for import in export percentage is 44 % at 2018. On the other hand, Takım and Ersung mentioned in their research paper at 2010 that inward processing regime, which encourages the use of imported intermediate goods, causes great damage to domestic production. Cebeci and Yılmaz (2013) also mentioned that inward processing regime, which has a wide range of uses because of it providing opportunity to get raw materials cheaper from abroad and reducing input costs, should be reviewed for eliminating negative effects on domestic manufacturers. Definitely just imports in exports cannot be calculated just by using inward processing licenses because exports under this licenses are just approximately 45 of total exports (Tab. 3). At last, OECD's calculation for the ratio imports in exports for 2016 is 16.4 %. Under these circumstances, this topic is another research area which should be detailed later.

Total foreign trade share of Turkey is 0.89 % of the World which has become the stable ratio since 2009. The number of Turkish companies which are actively exporting has become 83.270 in 2018 from 43.456 in 2005. Although

Tab. 3: Foreign Trade Under the Inward Processing Regime. **Source**: Ministry of Commerce (2019)

	Inward Processing Reg. (IPR) - Export (Mil $) (A)	IPR Exports/ Total Exports (%)	Inward Proc. Reg. - Imports (Mil $) (B)	IPR Imports/ Total Imports	Import/Export (%) (B/A)
2010	53.7	47.2	26.0	14.0	48.5
2011	64.2	47.6	30.9	12.8	48.1
2012	65.3	42.8	31.6	13.4	48.5
2013	68.1	44.9	32.1	12.7	47.1
2014	68.6	43.5	31.6	13.0	46.0
2015	58.8	40.9	26.2	12.6	44.5
2016	58.2	40.8	24.5	12.4	42.2
2017	65.0	41.4	28.4	12.2	43.7
2018	74.9	44.6	33.0	14.8	44.0

there occurred an increase by 91.6 % since 2005, this number of companies is extremely small when it is compared with the number of SMEs: 3,470.491*.

European Union countries are the most important foreign trade partners of Turkey. 50 % of exports and 33 % of imports are realized between EU and Turkey at 2018. The fact remains that there is a concentration problem for the exporting and importing countries. By the end of 2018, 9.6 % of exports of goods were to Germany, 6.6 % to the UK, 5.7 % to Italy, 4.9 % to Iraq, and 4.9 % to USA. Exports made to five countries consist of 31.7 % of total exports. On the import side, by the end of 2018, 9.9 % of imports were from Russian federation, 9.1 % from Germany, 9.3 % from China, 5.6 % from USA, and 4.6 % from Italy; these five countries account for 38.5 % of total imports (Figs. 10, 11, 12, and 13).

Turkey's top 10 products imported are accounted for 60.9 % of the overall imports. The share of exports of agricultural products was 4 % in 2018 which was about 85 % in the 1930s. The composition of exports in terms of products has changed completely. The share of industrial product was 83 % at 2018. The top five sectors in exports are automotive industry, 31.6 billion USD; garment industry, 17.6 billion USD; chemical products industry, 17.4 billion USD; steel industry, 15.6 billion USD; and electrical and electronic industry, 11.6 billion USD (Erhan et al., 2019). Five firms have been accounted for 52 % of the whole automotive industry and these firms are Ford, Toyota, Tofaş, Oyak-Renault, and Mercedes-Benz – all of which are foreign companies (Tab. 5). Top 3 products groups are vehichles other than railway or tramway rolling-stock parts thereof,

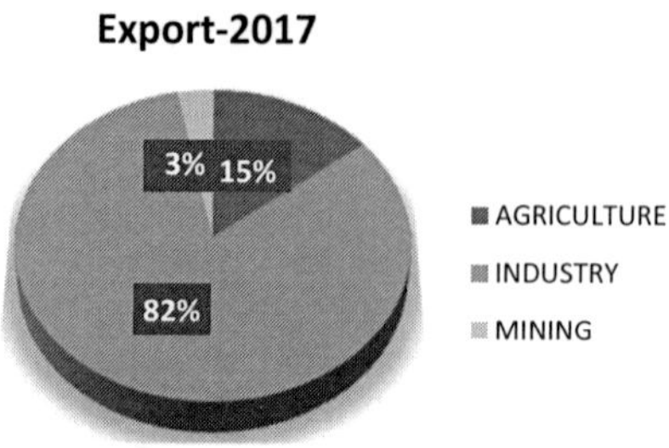

Fig. 10: Sectoral Distribution of Exports

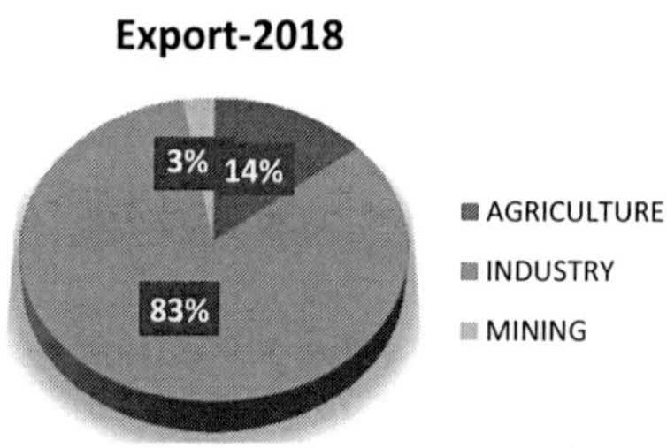

Fig. 11: Sectoral Distribution of Imports

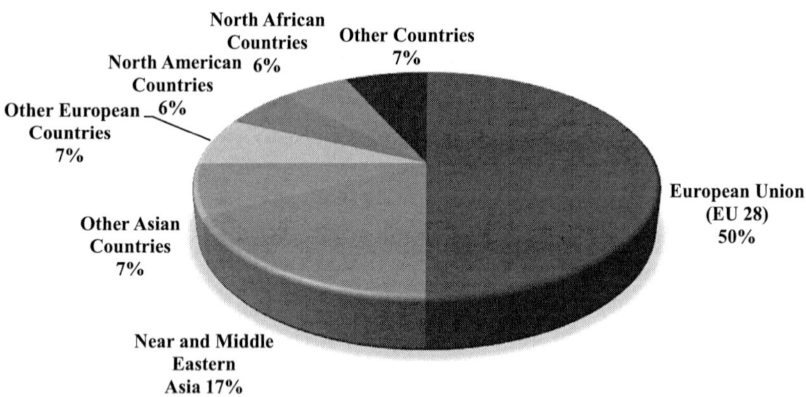

Fig. 12: Distribution of Exports Among Countries

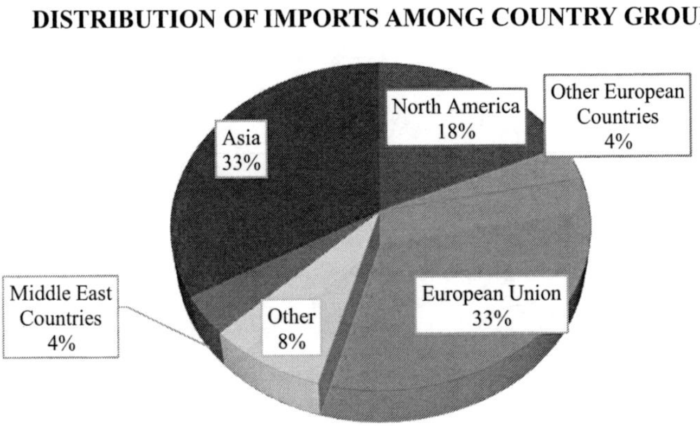

Fig. 13: Distribution of Imports Among Countries

Tab. 4: Top 10 Export Product Groups in 2018. **Source**: http://www.tuik.gov.tr/PreTablo.do?alt_id=1046

	Product Groups	**USD Million**	**Share in Total Exports (%)**
	Total	167 920	100
1	Vehicles other than railway or tramway rolling-stock, parts thereof	26 758	15.9
2	Boilers, machineries, and mechanical appliances, parts thereof	15 827	9.4
3	Iron and steel	11 546	6.9
4	Knitted and crocheted goods and articles thereof	9 042	5.4
5	Electrical machinery and equipment, parts thereof	8 723	5.2
6	Precious stones, precious metals, pearls, and articles thereof	7 172	4.3
7	Articles of iron and steel	6 534	3.9
8	Nonknitted and crocheted goods and articles thereof	6 262	3.7
9	Plastic and articles thereof	6 043	3.6
10	Mineral fuels, minerals oils, and product of their distillation	4 412	2.6

Tab. 5: Top 10 Import Product Groups in 2018

	Product	USD Million	Share in Total Imports (%)
	Total	223 047	100.0
1	Mineral fuels, minerals oils, and product of their distillation	43 005	19.3
2	Boilers, machineries, and mechanical appliances, parts thereof	25 770	11.6
3	Iron and steel	18 401	8.2
4	Electrical machinery and equipment, parts thereof	16 569	7.4
5	Vehicles other than railway or tramway rolling-stock, parts thereof	13 894	6.2
6	Plastic and articles thereof	12 937	5.8
7	Precious stones, precious metals, pearls, and articles thereof	12 556	5.6
8	Organic chemicals	5 973	2.7
9	Optical, photographic, cinematographic, measuring checking, precision	4 684	2.1
10	Pharmaceutical products	4 363	2.0

Tab. 6: Over 1 Billion USD Exporters of Turkey. **Source:** https://tim.org.tr/tr/ihracat-arastirma-raporlari-ilk-1000-ihracatci-arastirmasi.html

2018 Export ($)	Name of the Firm	Domestic	Foreign	Public	State-owned
5.682.762.433,05	FORD OTOMOTIV SAN. A.S.	%41,07	%41,04	%17,89	
4.598.412.782,39	TOYOTA OTOMOTIV SAN. TURKIYE A.S.		%100,00		
2.997.681.305,53	TOFAŞ TÜRK OTOMOBİL FAB. A.Ş.	%37,86	%37,86	%24,28	
2.719.787.015,19	KİBAR DIŞ TİC.A.Ş	%100,00			
2.591.293.127,15	TGS DIŞ TİC. A.Ş.	%55,00		%45,00	
2.466.974.750,88	TÜRKİYE PETROL RAFİNERİLERİ A. Ş.	%51,00		%49,00	
2.254.759.359,45	VESTEL TİCARET A.Ş.	%100,00			
1.936.987.240,00	ARÇELİK A.Ş.	%75,00		%25,00	
1.784.071.563,30	OYAK-RENAULT OTOMOBIL FAB.A.S.	%49,00	%51,00		
1.544.049.678,32	HABAŞ SINAİ VE TIBBİ GAZLAR İSTİHSAL ENDÜSTRİSİ A.Ş.	%100,00			
1.522.547.672,12	MERCEDES-BENZ TÜRK A.Ş.	%7,00	%85,00		%8,00
1.161.934.553,16	İÇDAŞ ÇELİK ENERJİ TERSANE VE ULASIM SANAYİ A.Ş.	%100,00			
1.013.380.682,49	BOSCH SAN.VE TİC.A.Ş		%100,00		

boilers, machineries and mechanical appliances parts thereof and iron steel, al three makes up 32,2 % of total exports (Tab. 4)

Turkey's top 10 products imported are accounted for 70.9 % of the overall imports (Tab. 6).

According to the data published in the annual Top 1000 Exporters Report 2019 by the Turkey Exporters Assembly, as of 2018, 61 % of the total exports are realized by the top 1000 exporters. Considering that the total number of exporters is 83000, it is remarkable that there is a significant concentration in the first 1000 companies. Of the top 1000 companies, 144 of them have foreign partnerships, and the share of these firms in total annual exports is 17.7 %. The number of companies exporting over USD 1 billion is 13. Six of these companies have foreign partnerships.

3. Future of the Foreign Trade of Turkey

The form of globalization and foreign trade is crucially changing depending on development of digital technologies. These changes were mentioned in mostly all parts of the World Trade 2018 Report in a very detailed way. In this section, what is changing globally and where Turkey is in this change will be discussed.

3.1 The Effects of Digital Technology on Economy and Foreign Trade

By development of smart phones and other sophisticated devices, consumers have begun to take the chance of using certain products online by accessing internet such as e-books, songs, and movies. One step later, this ability caused the birth of digital markets which can be easily reached by using sophisticated devices and internet.

Due to rapid development of Information and Communications Technology (ICT), digital markets eliminate borders between countries. Consumer from a country could easily have a chance to reach products produced in another country within just seconds.

3.1.1. Digital Marketing

Although recently it is not possible to separate domestic and foreign e-commerce volumes officially, total numbers help us for creating ideas on trends of the global commerce. Turkey's online retail sales in total retail sales is 4.1 % as of 2017. The ratio is increasing by years but it is still below the developed countries' average: 9.8 % (Fig. 14).

3.1.2. Potential Effects of Blockchain on Foreign Trade

Blockchain is a distributed data logging system that provides encrypted transaction tracking. It is not a database because saved data cannot be changed or deleted again. This is due to the fact that the data is stored by connecting the

Fig. 14: Share of Online Retail Sales in Total Retail Sales (%)

blocks to which they are accumulated, such as a chain, by linking them to each other by encryption algorithms and by distributing this chain with many people (Azevero, 2018).

Blockchain technology, called the technology of the future, has a bearing on many sectors. Digital transformation of foreign trade operations will gain a new dimension with the blockchain technologies in Turkey and globally. It is aimed that many transactions such as testing and acceptance procedures that cause products to wait at customs are no longer a problem in the period ahead. Blockchain technologies incorporate solutions that will remove many bureaucratic obstacles in international trade. Many issues such as differences in legislation between countries, nonstandardized documents, and forgery are within the solution domain of blockchain technology. Integration of blockchain technologies into public policies is also included in the second 100-day Action Plan announced by the Presidency. TIM-Turkish Exporters Assembly is to support the memorandum of understanding signed with Blockchain Turkey Platform under the leadership of the Ministry of Commerce and the work to be done in this regard and will contribute to the spreading of blockchain technology among exporters (Erhan et al., 2019:60).

3.1.3. Foreign Trade of High-Technology Products and Information Communication Technologies

Export of value-added products is one of the important building blocks of the path towards the sustainable development targets of the countries. With the

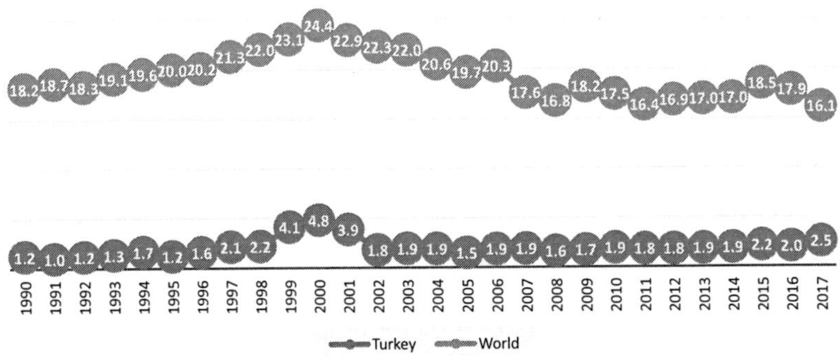

Fig. 15: High-Technology exports (%of Manufactured Exports)

acceleration of globalization, countries have started to accelerate the production and export of high-tech products in order to create added value (Güneş and Akın, 2019:1). As of 2017, the share of high-tech product exports in total manufacturing exports worldwide is 16.1 %. For Turkey, the said ratio is 2.5 %. Turkey is ranked 131 in the world with this ratio (Fig. 15).

When the share of ICT products in total exports is analyzed, it is seen that the world average is 11.3 %. Turkey lost share in this field within the periods; the figure, which was 3.7 % in 2001, decreased to 1.3 % as of 2017. ICT products' share in exports remained below the global average in all periods (Tab. 7 and Fig. 16).

Ansal and Ataman conducted an analysis on rates of owning and utilization of information in 20 countries in their study "Quest for Turkey in the Depth of Information Society" dated 2018. As a result of the study; it was determined that Finland, Iceland, Sweden, and Norway have the highest rate of information use and are at the highest level of digital division; Canada, Australia, New Zealand, the UK, and Denmark are societies about to become informatized; Austria, Belgium, the Netherlands, France, Italy, Ireland, and the Czech Republic are societies yet at the beginning of the process; Hungary and Portugal are at the bottom of the group of countries covered in the study; and Turkey has not even reached the level of Hungary and Portugal.

It does not seem possible for the digital gap to close itself automatically under free market conditions, and determination of national policies regarding education, qualification of the labor force, taking priority in industrial and commercial

Tab. 7: ICT Goods Exports (%of Total Goods Exports).
Source: World Bank

Ranking	Country Name	2016
1	Hong Kong SAR, China	50.0
2	Philippines	43.2
3	Singapore	33.6
4	Vietnam	31.2
5	Malaysia	30.5
6	China	26.5
7	Korea, Republic	22.3
8	Slovak Republic	16.6
9	Mexico	16.1
10	Thailand	15.8
	World	**11.3**
62	Turkey	1.3

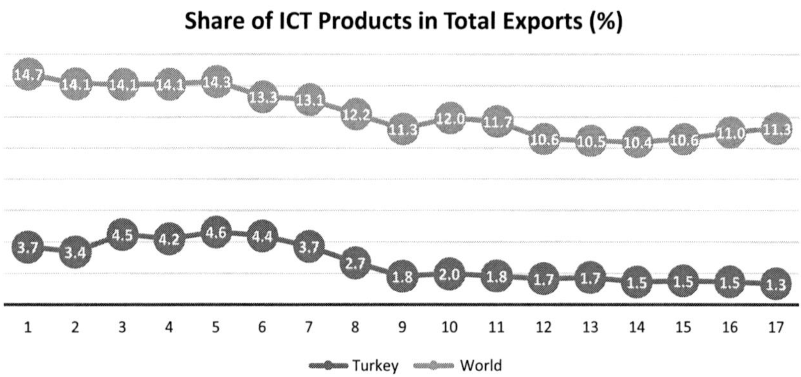

Fig. 16: Share of ICT Products in Total Exports (%)

policies, and providing the infrastructure are very important in closing the gap (Campbell, 2001).

Therefore, as a priority Turkey should establish national policies toward closing the digital gap and monitor the implementation the life of the designated policies.

4. Conclusion

Turkey is a country that has a youth population; that owns such geographic advantages as being surrounded by seas on three sides, having straits between European and Asian continents and also is a country with climatic advantages such as experiencing the four seasons in its territory. With all these features, it has a strategic significance for the world with its growth potential and in terms of providing added value to the world economy.

In order to realize the potential of the country, the economy became liberalized in the field of economy post-1980, and thus significant increases in the import and export figures have occurred and such increases have also occurred in the ratio of foreign trade to the gross national product. However, the foreign trade deficits, which have been continuing for years, failed to be covered by the cash surplus provided by net service revenues; and the country faced a chronic current account deficit problem. The periods in which the current account deficit was relatively improved were following the crisis periods such as the years of 1994, 2001, and 2008 in which the Turkish lira was devalued. The current improvement in 2018 was due to the increase in exports with the devaluation of TL as well as the contraction in demand with exchange rate increases in an import-dependent country.

One of the most important reasons for not experiencing structural improvement is that the number of exporters is limited to 82000, although there are approximately 3.5 million exporters in the country. Local producers have difficulty in locating its place in the international competition, and those who are aware of their competitive advantage are not willing to export due to lack of knowledge in entering a new market, export legislation, and operational flow.

There is a very critical finding in the "Understanding Prosperity and Poverty" chapter of Acemoğlu D. and Robinson James A.'s book *Why Nations Fail*. This finding is that in terms of economic growth, economic structures that provide equal conditions of competition and encourage investment in new technologies are far superior to those that allow the exploitation of the majority's resources by the minority, which do not provide incentives for economic activities and fail to protect property rights. Turkey; faring below its own potential and the global average in terms of digitization, as well as the share of ICT products in its exports; should, in order to address these issues, prepare technological development plans and ensure the adoption of those plans by all parties. Although the 11th Development Plan includes articles on technological development, tackling and following up this issue specially will reveal the degree of importance uttered to the subject and will provide a rapid and effective result. Another critical issue is the need for the adoption of inclusive structures and methods to address the foreign trade deficit problem, which has recently alleviated not structurally but due to the depreciation of the local currency and the decrease in consumption appetite. In order to do this, of course, it is essential that the problem be admitted honestly in the first place.

Note

1 *Resource for exhange rates*
https://.bumko.gov.tr%2FEklenti%2F10322%2Cortalama-donem-sonu-doviz-kurlarixls.xls%3F0&usg=AOvVaw1xeTYrOd8bbQmR09FlZldw

Bibliography

Acemoğlu, D. and Robinson, J.A. (2018), **Ulusların Çöküşü**, İstanbul: Doğan Egmont Yayıncılık ve Yapımcılık Tic. A.Ş.

Akat, A.S. (2019), "İhracatta İthalat", **İktisat ve Toplum**, pp. 7–13.

Al-Marhubi, F. (2000), "Export diversification and growth: an empirical investigation", **Applied Economics Letters** 7(9), pp. 559–562.

Ansal, H. and Ataman, B. (2018), "Bilgi Toplumu Derinliklerinde Türkiye'yi Arama Denemesi", (A. H. Köse, F. Şenses and E. Yeldan, Eds.), **İktisat Üzerine Yazılar II İktisadi Kalkınma, Kriz ve İstikrar**, İstanbul: İletişim, pp. 193–219.

Aykut Seymen, D. (2009), **Türkiye'nin Dış Ticaret Yapısı ve Rekabet Gücü**, İzmir: Dokuz Eylül Üniversitesi Yayınları.

Azevedo, R. (2018). "World Trade Organization Report- The future of world trade: How digital technologies are transforming global commerce", https://www.wto.org/english/res_e/publications_e/world_trade_report18_e_under_embargo.pdf

Campell, D. (2001), 'Can the Digital Divide be Contained', **International Labor Review**, 140(2), pp. 2.

Coşkun, M., Ardar, H., and Dağlaroğlu, T. (2012), **Türkiye'de Bankacılık Sektörü Piyasa Yapısı, Firma Davranışları ve Rekabet Analizi**. İstanbul: Nadir Kitap.

Doğan, M. (2013), "Türkiye Sanayileşme Sürecine Genel Bir Bakış", **Marmara Coğrafya Dergisi**, 5(3), pp. 211–231.

Erhan, Ç., Alkin, E., and Gürlesel, C.F. (2019), **Türkiye İhracatçılar Meclisi 2019 Raporu**. İstanbul: TİM.

Güneş, S. and Akın, T. (2019), "Yüksek Teknolojili Ürün İhracatı: Lider Ülkeler ve Türkiye", **Sosyoekonomi**, 27(40), pp. 11–29.

Hirschman, A.O. (1958), **The Strategy of Economic Development**, New Heaven: Yale University Press.

Kesgingöz, H. (2017), **Uluslararası Ekonomik Kuruluşların Türkiye'nin Dış Ticaretine Etkisi**, Ankara: Detay Yayıncılık.

Koçtürk, O.M. and Aslıhan, K. (2014), "Serbest Ticaret Anlaşmalarının Türk Dış Ticareti Üzerine Etkileri", **Tarım Ekonomisi Dergisi**, pp. 65–77.

Massell, B.F. (1964), "Export Concentration and Fluctuations in Export Earnings: A Cross-Section Analysis", **American Economic Review**, 54(1), pp. 47–63.

Metintaş, M. and Kayıran, M. (2008), Eskişehir Osmangazi Üniversitesi Sosyal Bilimler Dergisi, **Refik Saydam Hükümetleri Döneminde Türkiye'nin Ekonomi Politikası (1939-1942)**, 9(2), pp. 157–160.

Öniş, Z. and Şenses, F. (2010), "The New Phase of Neo-liberal Restructuring in Turkey", (Z. Öniş, F. Şenses, Eds.), **Turkey and the Global Economy- Neo-liberal Restructuring and Integration in the Post-crisis Era**, New York: Routledge Studies in Middle Eastern Economies, pp. 14–41.

Özdemir, Ü., Yiğit, G. K. and Oral, M. (2016), "Cumhuriyetten Günümüze Ekonomi Politikaları Bağlamında Türk Dış Ticaretinin Gelişimi", **Eastern Geographical Review**, 21(35), pp. 149–174.

Takım, A. and Ersungur, Ş.M. (2010), "Dahilde İşleme Rejimi: İhracat ve İthalat Üzerindeki Etkisi", **Atatürk Üniversitesi İ.İ.B.F Dergisi**, 24(2), pp. 289–305.

Tokgöz, E. (2009), **Türkiye'nin İktisadi Gelişme Tarihi**. Ankara: İmaj Yayınevi.

https://.bumko.gov.tr%2FEklenti%2F10322%2Cortalama-donem-sonu-doviz-kurlarixls.xls%3F0&usg=AOvVaw1xeTYrOd8bbQmR09FlZldw (June 2019)

https://data.worldbank.org/indicator/TM.VAL.ICTG.ZS.UN?view=chart

https://data.worldbank.org/indicator/TX.VAL.ICTG.ZS.UN

https://data.worldbank.org/indicator/NE.EXP.GNFS.ZS

https://data.worldbank.org/indicator/NE.IMP.GNFS.ZS

http://unctadstat.unctad.org/wds/TableViewer/tableView.aspx

https://unctadstat.unctad.org/wds/TableViewer/downloadPrompt.aspx

https://unctadstat.unctad.org/EN/IndicatorsExplained.html

https://unctadstat.unctad.org/wds/TableViewer/tableView.aspx?ReportId=157975

https://wits.worldbank.org/wits/wits/witshelp/Content/Utilities/e1.trade_indicators.htm

http://www.tim.org.tr/en/export-export-figures.html

http://www.tim.org.tr/files/downloads/sunumlar/Y%C3%B6nlendirme%20 Sunumlar%C4%B1/Karisik/Yeni%20Vizyon%20Yeni%20Yol%20 Haritas%C4%B1%20%C4%B0hracat%202019%20Raporu.pdf

https://tim.org.tr/tr/ihracat-arastirma-raporlari-ilk-1000-ihracatci-arastirmasi.html

http://risk.ticaret.gov.tr/data/572b3a8a1a79f50cd8a22b1a/17-gumruk%20 rejimlerine%20gore%20ihracat.pdf

http://risk.ticaret.gov.tr/data/572b3a8a1a79f50cd8a22b1a/18-gumruk%20 rejimlerine%20gore%20ithalat.pdf

http://stat.wto.org/StatisticalProgram/WSDBStatProgramHome.aspx?Language=E

Assist. Prof. Dr. Evrim İldem Develi

Innovation and Technology from Marketing Perspective (from the 1980s to 2000s) with a Case Study on Turkish Women Entrepreneurs on Agricultural Cooperatives

Abstract: In this study, the concepts; technology, innovation, and marketing; are explained through the view of integrity of ecosystem in the 1980s and 2000s. The main scope of this study is about innovation. Types of innovation and the relation between innovation and marketing strategies are discussed in the subparts of this chapter.In the 1980s, when globalization gains importance all over the world, it does also for Turkey; and economically and publicly, change begins.The study consists of the explanation on 1980 Decrees in Turkey, which mean globalization for Turkey in many areas such as foreign trade, production, marketing, and innovation.In the last part, there is a case study that is about an innovative project of a Turkish restaurant chain, which brings local products produced by rural women to the market as a social and marketing innovation.

Keywords: Technology, Innovation, Marketing, Social Innovation, 1980 Decrees, Women Entrepreneurship

1 Introduction

We experience changes in every aspect of our lives as human beings. Main reason and outcome of change is **technology**. It has a very important role in human lives; as a person, as a student, as a housewife, as a consumer, as an employer or as an employee, as a citizen, as a disabled person, etc. Technology makes us lazier, more vulnerable, more productive, more unemployed, more employed by new professions, more communicated, more intangible, closer, more separate… etc. It has number of different effects on our lives.

There is one more concept in this study: **innovation**, which has a wide range of use in human lives. For example, a chair is simple furniture that you sit on but it can be used as a bedside table, which is a good example of an innovative idea.

In the first section of the study, there is explanation on 1980 Decrees in Turkey, which mean globalization for Turkey. Literature definitions of technology, innovation – types of innovation – and marketing are the second section of the study. In the third section, the innovation in marketing mix is explained from literature and 1980s, 2000s point of view.

And the last section is about an innovative project of a Turkish restaurant chain, which brings local products produced by rural women to the market as a social and marketing innovation.

1.2 The Meaning of 1980 for Turkey

There was a major change in Turkish economical system caused by neoliberalism in 1980. In Çelik's dissertation, neoliberalism is defined as sharp separation of government affairs and economics business, where private enterprise is featured and it decreases the effect of government in social and economic affairs (Çelik, 2006:ii).

In world economic system, developing countries like Turkey is included into neoliberalism system through "structural adjustment program." In order to be a part of the system, Turkish Government made a decision named "1980 Economics Decrees" on January 24, 1980.

There was an evolution and transformation in many areas such as consumer products, import and export goods which affected thinking and buying behavior of consumers and strategies of manufacturers.

This system change was just like collapsing of invisible walls and the people, and consumers got connected with new products from global markets. Business world in Turkey became relatively alive. The manufacturers made business trips to find new markets, new business partners, and new technologies to use in production lines.

The side effect of these trips was causing manufacturers to be away from their factories, production processes, and decision-making too long. And the cost of being abroad also arose.

In 1995, when the internet started to become more popular, it is easily discovered by the people that there is a huge, global world outside without spending a lot of money for the business trips. People as students, consumers, teachers, businessmen, businesswomen, or manufacturers began to find everything online; including cooking recipes, road-trip guides, song lyrics, or new markets and consumers. Everybody began to search online for different needs and a new network was established through social media; connecting people, suppliers, consumers, and entrepreneurs. This was the time technology became a significant part of people's daily routines, and this is also innovation that played a major role in people's lives.

2 Definition of Technology, Innovation, and Marketing

In this part, the meaning of technology, innovation, and marketing are explained. The concept of marketing as a business process and its relation with innovation is also mentioned. The main scope of this study is about innovation. Types of innovation and the relation between innovation and marketing strategies are discussed in the subparts of this chapter.

2.1 Technology

Origin of the word dates back to the early 17th century's Greek word "tekhnologia" meaning "systematic treatment," which is composed of the words, "tekhnē; art, craft" and "logia; a subject of study or interest" (Mills, 2015:176). Considering the evolution of this word, it starts to become popular in the 1950s, and reaches the highest level of popularity in 2010, becoming more related with daily life because of the computers, mobile devices, and internet technologies.

According to Kline, technology mostly corresponds to human-made things, devices, and machinery (Kline, 1985:215). Technology also has a meaning of producing machines, technical equipment, and technical-based things. It has a subsidiary effect in daily life of human beings, since the utilization of technological devices like mobile phones, computers, washing machines, and printers are extensive; and even a basic object like a chair, a glass, or a window has its own technology, development, and utility.

Referencing from Li-Hua, technique covers the instruments of labor (machinery and tools), materials, and the way they are brought into function by labor in the working process. There are social effects of producing process within technology, machine, and labor (Li-Hua, 2007:193–197).

Looking from the 2000s it is observed that technology is not just a part of producing or manufacturing, it has its own versions, which today is called "industry 4.0." Industry 4.0 is the last version of technology development including robotics, machine autonomy, and artificial intelligence (Mohelska and Sokolova, 2018:2226).

2.2 Innovation

The term "innovation" originated from Latin "innovatus" which means, using new methods in societal, cultural, and managerial environment (Elçi, 2006:1).

The Organization for Economic Co-operation and Development (OECD), whose mission is to promote policies that will improve the economic and social well-being of people around the world, published "Oslo Manual" in 1991 about how to conceptualize and measure business innovation within OECD by the support of the European Union (EU). From the first Manual published in 1991 to the last Manual published in 2018, innovation surveys covering more than 80 countries have been carried out (OECD, 2019; Oslo Manual; 2018:3).

In terms of Oslo Manual, an innovation is a new or improved product or process (or combination thereof) that differs significantly from the unit's previous products or processes and that has been made available to potential users (product) or brought into use by the unit (process). This definition uses the generic term "unit" to describe the actor responsible for innovations. It refers to any institutional unit in any sector, including households and their individual members. In the Manual, innovation activities include all developmental, financial, and commercial activities undertaken by a firm, which are intended to result in an innovation for the firm. Manual describes business innovation that as a new or improved product or business process (or a combination thereof) differs significantly from the firm's previous products or business processes and that has been introduced on the market or brought into use by the firm (Oslo Manual, 2018:20).

From a literature view, firstly Schumpeter used the term "innovation" that has been associated to economic value. The definition of innovation that is given by Schumpeter and his colleagues Bessant and Tidd (2007) and Oke et al. (2007) has been used in Geldes and Felzensztein's study. According to this definition, the classification of innovation has been developing from the previously defined basic version by Schumpeter (1934) to a more comprehensive taxonomy (Rowley et al., 2011) proposed by Bessant and Tidd (2007) and Oke et al. (2007) which identifies process, products, and services innovations, as radical or incremental (Geldes and Felzensztein, 2013:110).

The scope of the term "innovation" in Turkey is put forward by Gömleksiz's study. Although there are many studies and researches about innovation all over the world for more than 50 years, discussions on this term began in the 2000s in Turkey. Meaning of the word "innovation" is "newness" and "renewal" in Turkish, but it has a wider meaning that cannot be defined by one word (Gömleksiz, 2012:3; Yılmaz and Incekaş, 2018:156). Innovation is not about discovering; it is about thinking in different ways. In the book named *Innovation, Intellectual Property, and Economic Growth* in part I – The Nature and Importance of Innovation, Greenhalgh and Rogers state innovation as the application of new ideas to the products, processes, or other aspects of the activities of a firm that lead to increased "value." They define "value" in a broad way, to include higher value added for the firm and also benefits to consumers or other firms (Greenhalgh and Rogers, 2010:4–5).

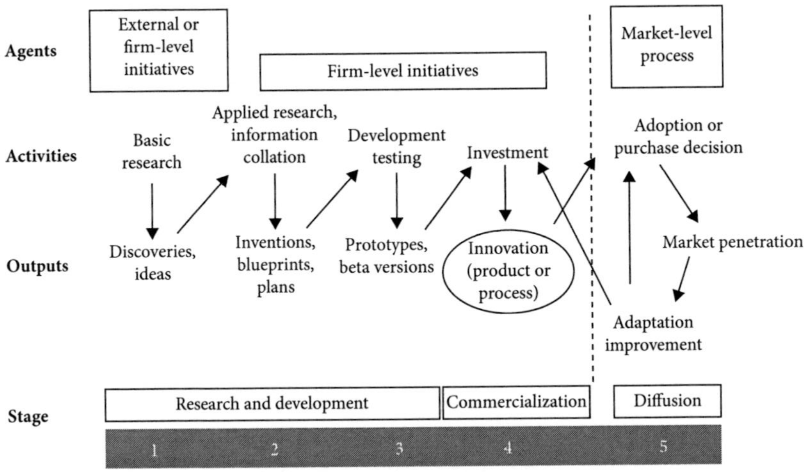

Fig. 1: The Stages of the Innovation Process. **Source:** Greenhalgh and Rogers, 2010:7

Looking from the economics and marketing aspect, it is probably best to consider "innovation" as fresh production and marketing ideas, which result in better sales and bigger market share. It is also important to recognize that the meaning of this term widely varies when it is related to computer technologies. Starting from new forms or social relations based on social networks, including mobile technologies which effects most of the daily routines like jogging, cooking, listening to music, watching movies, and reading newspapers, innovation is everywhere.

The process of innovation is shown in Fig. 1, from idea to execution and the actors taking part in the system. With this figure, the innovation system is clearly explained including stages of prototype visualization, finding investment to produce, management processing, and diffusion to market level.

According to Ogilvie's book titled *The European Guilds, An Economic Analysis*, innovation involves two main things: one is a new idea has to be thought up and the other is that it needs to be communicated so people can use it. In this study, Ogilvie states that the ideas are public goods and other institutions than markets might be better at encouraging their invention and diffusion. Nonmarket institutions might enable individuals to reap more benefits from their ideas, giving them better incentives to think them up (Ogilvie, 2019:439). The scope of the fourth section of this chapter relies on the very same idea mentioned by Ogilvie.

Lopes et al. have a study on management innovation and social innovation: convergences and divergences that involve literature review about innovation. In accordance with his study, technological innovation involves "the situationally new development and introduction of knowledge – derived tools, artifacts, and devices by which people extend and interact with their environment" (Tornatzky and Fleischer, 1990:11; Lopes et al., 2017:475). In the study, innovation is considered "technological" when it is based on or facilitated by technology.

For Ogilvie, nonmarket institutions might give inventors better incentives to diffuse their innovations to everyone who might use them (Ogilvie, 2019:439). This idea leads to two sides of innovation: business and social innovation, and these are mentioned below.

2.2.1 Business Innovation

As mentioned in Part 1 about neoliberalism, by the expanse of this system in the 1980s the countries all over the world began to integrate with each other. Companies saw different marketplaces, consumer potential, technological equipment – e.g., washing machines, colored televisions, etc., and so did the people. This view made every part of the community to compare what they have and do not with the supply. So there emerged a need to change in business, in production, and in consuming as well. Companies, which want to change and adapt to the new world system, attended to innovate through thinking, business, and production.

In Janszen's book named *The Age of Innovation*, there is the view of Schumpeter, "Innovations are the composite of two worlds, namely, the technical, and the business; so when only a change in technology is involved, this is just an invention; but as soon as the business world is involved, it becomes an innovation" (Janszen, 2000:3).

Business innovation deals with innovation in management thinking. It is motivated by changes in external and internal environmental conditions: customers, competitors, suppliers, employees, etc. (Lorente et al., 1999:3). Chew and Gottschalk's book about Business Innovation and Information Management argues that companies should have the way of thinking from innovating a single component (e.g., a product) of the business to innovating the whole business. If a firm wants to be the leader in the competitive market it should have revolutionary changes, which involves a shift on the firm's product, process, and service (Chew and Gottschalk, 2009:360).

Based on Örtlek's dissertation and Yılmaz and Incekaş' publication, principles of innovation are listed as below (Örtlek, 2015:19–20; Yılmaz and Incekaş, 2018:158):

- Innovation should have a vision.
- Innovation should be customer oriented in order to create customer value while understanding the needs of customers.
- Innovation should obey ethics.
- Innovation should be significant, clear, and intently designed.
- In order to get productivity from innovation, it should be focused on one thing simply.
- Innovation should take the risks.
- Innovation should be united with substantial interactions and varied information.

In Yılmaz and Incekaş' study, it is put forward that in economical development model there is regional development in which the whole work is done aiming to increase regional welfare and mobilizing socioeconomic potentials (Yılmaz and Incekaş, 2018:160). If there would be a factory set up, there should also be a plan for the people working in that factory, who would need houses to live, markets to shop, hospitals or medical units for their health care, etc. If there is work and production, there is also life in economics and social manner. People living in the region have a chance to integrate with each other, with the rest of the country, and globally. One factory calls another business, which increases the employment, entrepreneurship, and industrial achievement.

2.2.2 Social Innovation

Social innovation is nested with ecosystem. As a human being, also living and nonliving beings are part of the system, which is called "ecosystem." And in this environment there are business, economics, marketing, technology, public, government, rural areas, universities, and so many other actors.

According to Klein, "social innovation" entered the agendas of some research groups and governments in the 1980s, when innovation turned out to be an answer to the failures and inconsistencies of neoliberal models worldwide (Klein, 2013; Lopes et al., 2017:479), which relates with the process of 1980 Decrees in Turkey.

For Klein et al., social innovation concerns the implementation of new social and institutional arrangements, new forms of resource mobilization, new answers to problems for which available solutions have proven inadequate, or new social aspirations (e.g., autonomy and empowerment) (Klein et al., 2012:11). For Goldenberg, social innovation is used to denote the development and application of new or improved activities, initiatives, services, processes, or products designed to address social and economic challenges faced by individuals and communities (Goldenberg, 2004:1). These two statements express this chapter's main idea.

What Klein and Moulaert et al. say on innovation is that it arises from activities in collaborative networks, and these notions of social innovation are associated with civil society actions and nonprofit organizations, but they can be expanded to public and business sectors as well (Klein, 2013:9–12; Moulaert et al., 2013:13–24).

There is a view of Agnes Hubert within Ionescu's study on social innovation expressing the process of social interactions between individuals undertaken to reach certain outcomes is participative, involves a number of actors and stakeholders who have a vested interest in solving a social problem, and empowers the beneficiaries. It is an outcome as it produces social capital.

From this point of view, social innovation can be classified into three major categories. Firstly, social innovations (in general) at a local level, which respond to pressing social demands, and are not approached by the market, being aimed at the underprivileged society groups. Secondly, social innovations at a larger scale, which address society's challenges, in which the borders between "social" and "economic" are blurred; they are aimed at the whole society. Thirdly, within the changing world dynamism like climate change, technology, and needs of human being; social change plays a role in organizing what the society needs to sell their product, to be integrated with the other part of the community and other actors in the marketplace (Ionescu, 2015:57).

In the study of Sanzo-Perez et al. (2015), social innovation is explained through development and implementation of new ideas (products, services, and models) to meet social needs (Mulgan et al., 2007:9, cited by Howaldt and Schwarz, 2010:25) and simultaneously "create new social relationships or collaborations" (Murray et al., 2009:3).

For Sanzo-Perez et al., there are two basic characteristics of this concept, one is that the social mission is crucial which does not mean that social innovation initiatives cannot generate profits. The second is to entail that citizens, employees, customers, and/or nonprofit organizations play a proactive role (influencing change – Grunig, 1992:627) regarding innovation (Sanzo-Perez et al., 2015:431).

According to Dökmen, innovation – merging market intelligence and technology – becomes the driving force behind economics (Dökmen, 2009:19). Dökmen also points that, practically, electronics industry center "Silicon Valley" in South California, USA, Emilia – Romagna Region which is called "Third Italy" in Italy, and the industrial region near Cambridge in Britain are the outcomes of the relation between regional development and innovation (Dökmen, 2009:20).

As Yılmaz and Incekaş mention in their study, it is necessary to involve in the regional public to the regional development projects in case of getting integrated with the project itself and put their soul and potential on it (Yılmaz and Incekaş, 2018:162). This view is also applied in the project of Big Chefs, which is explained in fourth section of this chapter. Getting involved with public, and talking and listening to people via focus group research are the fundamentals of regional development process. As a result of this research process, the topics arose will be discussed and studied on the project that will be carried out. The innovation begins when the people feel themselves as a part of the process, and it is called social innovation.

2.3 Marketing

According to American Marketing Association (1960), marketing is the performance of business activities that direct the flow of goods and services from producer to consumer or user (Hunt, 1976:17). In Hunt's study, there is Kotler and Levy's new view to the definition of marketing in 1969 which is broadening the concept of marketing to include nonbusiness organizations. According to this article, they observed churches, police departments, and public schools that they also have products and customers and they use marketing mix as a marketing tool (Hunt, 1976:18). Hunt also gives a place to the most commonly used model even today that was popularized by McCarthy in the 1960s as 4Ps-marketing mix (Product, Price, Place, and Promotion), and expresses that the most widely used concept in scope of marketing is related with 4Ps and resulted by three concentric circles, placing the consumer to the core; and a step out of it is a second circle named marketing mix as controllable factors, and lastly in uncontrollable position macroenvironment, such as economic, technological, green, legal, cultural, political, and social resources and objectives of the company, and the existing business situation (Hunt, 1976:20).

In Achrol and Kotler's study in 1999, they begin with an assignation about marketing has made several transitions, from seller of a firm's outputs to key player in shaping a company's products, technologies, marketing policies, and strategic direction (Achrol and Kotler, 1999:146).

All business functions can be the object of innovation activity. The term "business process" includes the core business function of producing goods and services and supporting functions such as distribution and logistics, marketing, sales, and after-sales services; information and communication technology (ICT) services to the firm; administrative and management functions; engineering and related technical services to the firm; and product and business process development (Oslo Manual, 2018:72).

In Parasuraman's study published in 1981, he expresses the trends in terms of business and marketing via research and development, new products, and customer orientation of the members of the ecosystem in the 2000s today. He emphasizes the importance of the research and customer. He states that development of new technology and customer-oriented new product planning rather than just research and development is the only way leading to unique new products, (Parasuraman, 1981:38–40) which underlines the customer as the key factor effecting the production, marketing and business strategies of companies. His expression points to the importance of collaboration between customer and research and development department or any business departments producing ideas and innovation.

In Kotler and Armstrong's book *Principles of Marketing*, marketing is defined as a social and managerial process by which companies create value for customers and build strong customer relationships in order to capture value from customers in return (Kotler and Armstrong, 2008:5).

3 Innovation in Marketing Mix (4P) from the 1980s to 2000s

Rekettye's study on the regularities of innovation – a marketing perspective – tries to figure marketing tools to bring certain products or services successfully together with the target market. And this is figured as below in his study. In this figure the term "new" is used in a manner of the term "innovation." According to his hypothesis, product and marketing innovations are innovations/new when they have connection with product-related marketing innovation (Rekettye, 2003:48).

Rekettye also lists innovation in marketing linking with tangible goods-innovation process (Rekettye, 2003:54–55):

- From this view, innovation in marketing starts with an idea or invention of a new, discontinuous marketing concept. The development of this concept may go in different directions, and can appear in different forms.
- When it is getting to known with the market, one of these forms becomes dominant. Many companies start to implement the same marketing concept, involving the same marketing-mix elements and using them in a similar way, which is the learning process for companies.

- When a form of marketing idea is commonly used companies go for the other step on focusing technology and process.

In Chuwiruch et al.'s study, marketing innovation makes companies effective in competitive market (Chuwiruch et al., 2015:83). Within Axel Jones' article on Successful Marketing Innovation published in *European Journal of Innovation Management*, he connects marketing innovation with improving the mix of target markets and how chosen markets are best served (Axel, 1999:7).

The term "marketing" is firstly used in Turkey by Turkish academician Prof. Dr. Mehmet Oluç in 1957 within his academic studies. In Yükselen's study in 1994, it is mentioned that in a research reflecting the idea to 1980s in Turkey, production was seen as a problem rather than marketing. According to him making a marketing plan becomes meaningless where: the production problem situation comes out from lack of supply and import difficulties due to foreign exchange. By 1980 Decrees, deviations and instability factors changed the market opportunities and marketing strategies through economics, social-culture, technology, competitive strategies, and government regulations and executions (Yükselen, 1994:36).

With the transition to liberal economy, enterprises in Turkey needed to market their products in interaction with foreign markets as well as producing their products. Starting with the "24 January 1980 Decrees," enterprises in Turkey both in and out of the international market came to the point where they could sell their products in a whole new market. It did not take long for businesses in the domestic market to meet the concept of customer in a competitive environment. Instead of the general consumer, the concept of continuity has been focused on. In addition to importance of marketing tools being recognized by enterprises, customer requests became more important because of the competition. In this respect, the marketing mix and the 4Ps of marketing (Product, Price, Place, and Promotion) have been in transformation from the 1980s to the present. This transformation undoubtedly brought innovations and transformation in ideas parallel with the development of information technologies.

3.1 Innovation in Product

In accordance with the Oslo Manual, a product innovation is a new or improved good or service that differs significantly from the firm's previous goods or services and that has been introduced on the market (Oslo Manual, 2018:70).

In the book named *Innovation, Intellectual Property, and Economic Growth* in part I – The Nature and Importance of Innovation, Greenhalgh and Rogers state innovation as the application of new ideas to the products, processes, or other aspects of the activities of a firm that lead to increased "value." They define "value" such as, in a broad way, to include higher value added for the firm and also benefits to consumers or other firms. For Greenhalgh and Rogers, product innovation is the introduction of a new product, or a significant qualitative change in an existing product (Greenhalgh and Rogers, 2010:4). They express that product innovations may be tangible manufactured goods, intangible services, or a combination of the two. Examples of recent tangible product innovations that have a very significant impact on the way people live and work are computers, mobile phones, tablets, etc. Intangible products are the ones that complement these types of physical equipment, including the various pieces of computer software needed to control flows of information leading to the delivery of information, the supply of communication services, etc. (Greenhalgh and Rogers, 2010:4–5).

Product innovations must provide significant improvements to one or more characteristics or performance specifications. This includes the addition of new functions, or improvements to existing functions or user utility. Relevant functional characteristics include quality, technical specifications, reliability, durability, economic efficiency, affordability, convenience, usability, and user friendliness. Product innovations do not need to improve all functions or performance specifications. An improvement or addition of a new function might come with the loss of other functions or a decline in some performance specifications. **Goods** include tangible objects and some knowledge-capturing products (see below) over which ownership rights can be established and whose ownership can be transferred through market transactions.

Services are intangible activities that are produced and consumed simultaneously and that change the conditions (e.g., physical, psychological, etc.) of users. The engagement of users through their time, availability, attention, transmission of information, or effort is often a necessary condition that leads to the coproduction of services by users and the firm (Oslo Manual, 2018:71).

In Pitta's study on product innovation and management in a small enterprise, there is a reference of Cooper's study "From Experience-The Invisible Success Factors in Product Innovation" (1999) on product innovation. With this study, Cooper looks for an answer for what the critical success factors are and which of them is noticeably absent in most businesses. And in Pitta's study, he summarizes these success factors as follows (Pitta, 2008:417; Cooper, 1999:115–133):

- Solid up-front homework – to define and justify the product.
- Voice of the customer – a slave-like dedication to the market and customer inputs throughout the project.

- Product advantage – differentiated, unique benefits, superior value for the customer.
- Sharp, stable, and early product definition – before development begins.
- A well-planned, adequately resourced, and proficiently executed launch.
- Tough go/kill decision points or gates – funnels not tunnels.
- Accountable, dedicated, and supported cross-functional teams with strong leaders.

3.2 Innovation in Price

Price is the only unit of marketing mix that provides cash inflow where the other tools involve cash outflows (Kotler, 2003:470). In pricing there are actors that determine the price, such as: consumer, competitor, supplier, producer/manufacturer, logistics, government, legal decisions, and political-social and cultural environments named uncontrollable macroenvironmental tools. And there is also company's cost effect, e.g., human resource and expenditures, in producing, commercializing, or in trading product or service. These actors are related to innovative pricing as well.

For Quaye and Mensah, innovation in pricing requires key strategic marketing resources and capabilities such as employees with right knowledge, quality information, and experience. In innovative pricing, employee capabilities and all relevant primary and secondary factors are important to consider in order to set prices that are fair and acceptable to the firm, customers, market, and industry (Quaye and Mensah, 2018:1540).

In his study about innovative pricing effects, Jonason refers to Schumpeter's study (1911) that an innovation is not only the creation of something new but also involves the ability to act commercially on the opportunities that this advance in science and technology offers. From this point of view, Jonason states the pricing as an essential tool of innovation and commercial success. It may well be the case that the pricing scenario is given, while the product definition in terms of function, cost or quality is not. This idea combines pricing and product innovation with each other, and emerges a term "innovative pricing" as evolutionary price/product setting that is mentioned in Jonason's study in 1999 (2002:187). To Srinuan's, most economists consider product and service prices as supply-side variables. The issue is elasticity: if prices are lowered demand will go up (2013:63).

Within the study of Rekettye, although the price of a product can least be subject to standardization, in globalized competition a continuous convergence in the price levels is witnessed; within the same product category there is a dominant price for the identical value, and the prices of the products are dispersed around it – although to a lesser degree nowadays, due to the increasing transparency of supply in the "new economy." The price forms can also become dominant: in the information and communication industries characterized by high fixed costs, for example, price bundling, two-part tariffs, or two-block tariffs (Dolan and Simon 1996:116) tend to become dominant (Rekettye, 2003:56). From this perspective, according to Jonason, an innovative pricing can be something that is brought in from another market as long as it entails something new that other actors through inefficacy or ignorance cannot exploit (2002:188).

3.3 Innovation in Promotion

In 1960, Levitt's study on growth and profits through planned marketing innovation stated that the changes in production is not new anymore; the change has come out in departmental change like Research and Development, and Product Development Departments are replacing Advertising and Public Relations as the glamour functions of modern industry (Levitt, 1960:2). Innovation in promotion is a big developmental tool when it is looked from this century. In the 1980s as the countries being global, the media and promotion gained importance because the technology in the advertising sector was progressing.

In Turkish academician Şahinde Yavuz's study on advertisement and advertisement sector in the 1980s in Turkey, it is stated that the 1980s are the era of new market for advertisement sector in Turkey because of the globalization and neoliberalist system. In this system, consuming becomes the new lifestyle that affected the number of advertisements in an increasing manner, where the advertisement is seen as the proof of product reliability. After 1980, as the multinational companies got in the Turkish market, multinational advertising agencies also came to the market to learn about the Turkish market, consumer behavior and work with the local advertising agencies. As the local advertising sector stays in touch with multinational advertising companies, it broadens the vision of local companies. This vision also changed the thinking of companies taking the advertisement as a tool of cost (Yavuz, 2006:157).

When the internet gets in the market and people's lives in every manner, people and the companies' curiosity began to affect the market. "Which company has a web site, what the companies produce, what the profit of the company is" are the questions that easily could find an answer via the internet-information world. This means that consumers also affect each other by word of mouth (WOM). WOM is the new era of promotion, which is free of charge to share the information about the product or service if there is a satisfied, happy customer. If the customer is not satisfied or happy with the product or service, WOM makes the promotion harder and more expensive.

While the satisfied customer recommends the product or service to others and this results in repeated buying behavior, the unsatisfied customer discredits the product or service by affecting especially the loyal customers who have emotional or habitual relationship with the product/service/company, through not to buy that product or service again.

Technology and internet changed the perspective of media from mass to target oriented. As a result of this change, social media has become more preferred for selling, especially utilizing promotion to the targeted customer by means of filtering.

3.4 Innovation in Place (Distribution Channels-Supply Chain Management)

To Kotler, a marketing channel manages the work of moving goods from producers/manufacturers in a small/medium/large scale to consumers. Members of marketing channel have key functions. Such as (Kotler and Armstrong, 2008:506):

- Gathering information from the field about potential and current customers, competitors, and other actors,
- Developing and using persuasive communication methods for purchasing,
- Making long-term agreements within the actors in distribution channel, which is named today value chain-supply chain management.

For Chopra and Meindl, supply chain management is a system to have efficient management of supply chain assets, products, information, and cash flows in order to maximize the excess that results from the difference of the price paid by a consumer and all the operational costs that comes out from the supply chain (e.g., 2007:16). Supply chain innovation involves the flow of information, changing the structure like way of thinking, management, and enhancing collaborations with partners to give flexibility, speed, and effectiveness to market (Chew and Gottschalk, 2009:364).

As proposed by Bello et al. (2004), supply chain innovations are new logistic, production, or marketing processes – or the combination of innovations in information and communication technologies with new logistic, production, and marketing procedures – to improve operational efficiency and enhance service effectiveness. Technological innovations improve the efficiency of information and material exchange in the supply chain. For instance, tracking and tracing systems enable manufacturing and logistics companies to follow objects – such as components, semifinished, and final products – during production and along transportation routes. For instance, Radio Frequency Identification (RFID) and barcodes capture data in real time and support operations in reducing inventory levels and costs (Li et al., 2010; Abdelkafi et al., 2018:590–591).

E-commerce and electronic/mobile communications are the new generation channels to commercialize, sell product or services to customers and also to industries like alibaba.com and aliexpress.com. All these connect all supply chain members with real-time information exchange (Cagliano et al., 2015; 930).

In Rekettye's study on the regularities of innovation – a marketing perspective published by Akadémiai Kiadó – Acta Oeconomica, distribution channel is defined through reflective view of supply chain management that manufacturers in a strong position make efforts to keep their distribution channels under their control and sell their products through a network that they have and the control over. Some other selling channels like franchising are acceptable too, whereas controllable by them (Rekettye, 2003:57).

Actually, this statement is relatively hard for the small- or microscale manufacturer who has no power and no network ability to sell his/her product which becomes more weak and inactive. In the 1980s economy and marketing system, there was the control and management of government as a business partner due to closed economy. But after 1980 Decrees on economics, the system became more open to abroad, and business market started to have an interaction with the countries around. However, big manufacturers who have money have the chance to interact. So there became the unbalanced market through strong and weak ones. The small manufacturers gained their own capability to survive, to produce, and to find customers.

By the time the technology changed, the public experienced internet and also mobile technology and social media. This was the new market that opens the door to the world.

With the internet, the unknown people, small manufacturer, entrepreneur, shopkeeper, producer, or farmer has the chance to be seen by the world, which makes the business global. The internet is a big innovation in distribution channel. It has a power to interact with people, producers, consumers, and business world. And this feature makes the life of human being innovating.

From gathering the whole point of view, there emerges a chance for producer who has no network connection, or who wants to change the job performed before and to be an entrepreneur. In section four there are 14 women stories about producing their own product as supplier and selling it to market.

4 Case Study – Turkish Women Entrepreneurs on Agricultural Cooperative

The cooperative movement is an important role in the development of agriculture and agro-business. From marketing to credit, cooperatives have been at the center of many of the most successful developments, and they have succeeded in bringing together sound management and fiscal discipline with broader social perspectives. In many developing countries, NGOs (nongovernmental organizations), which are effectively cooperatives, are playing an increasingly important role (Stiglitz, 2004:2), which is the same case in Turkey in Anatolian Sisters' project, supported by Ankara Developing Agency, fiscally and in marketing and selling.

In Geldes and Felzensztein's study, there is a view of Edwards and Shultz on agribusiness that it is a dynamic and systemic endeavor that serves consumers globally and locally through innovations and management of multiple value chains that deliver valued goods and services derived from the sustainable orchestration of foods, fiber and natural resources, which refers to supply chain (Edwards and Shultz, 2005:66; Geldes and Felzensztein, 2013:112).

In Ionescu's study about the conceptualization of social innovation, there is a clear view that social innovation has greatly increased society's willingness to cooperate and innovate. Governments, communities, and people are concerned about the future and are trying to find viable solutions to adapt to an ever-changing world, with the purpose and need to overcome poverty and solve serious issues that humanity is dealing with. Therefore, one of the resources, and solution, is social innovation (Ionescu, 2015:55).

In some cases like people find their own solutions to publicly common issues. In this study, the solutions are coming from the women cooperatives.

According to Zusman's study in 1982, the existing theories of cooperative enterprise commonly portray it as a goal-directed entity that is highly objective.

In the 2000s with the technological, social-cultural, and economical changes around the world as globalization, life in rural area becomes more precious rather than living in big, noisy cities. Urban life slightly goes to rural, and the knowledge that the urban people have also shifts to rural. This knowledge is very important and productive where used effectively.

The case study, which is based on Turkish Women Entrepreneurs on Agricultural Cooperative, is focused on productive, knowledgeable rural women.

The new way of entrepreneurship in the case study is the reflection of innovation through new marketing tools, new selling channels, and logistics. Rural women reaching out to marketplace through agricultural cooperatives is an example of social innovation resulting to the commercialization of the their products.

For an activity to be considered as a social development it needs to have some specific features as listed below (Gibson, 2005:3):

- Entrepreneurship must come from the bottom,
- To be based on volunteerism,
- Must be based on the principle of democratic management,
- To strengthen community ownership,
- To construct human resources (leadership development, cultural development, provision of employment environment, etc.),
- To increase local capacity,
- To combine economic and social goals,
- To encourage the community to go beyond its patterns,
- To have financial management,
- Both educational and organizational enterprises, and
- Development of the activity within the strategic plan and analysis.

Social innovation leads to rural areas through social entrepreneurship. This entrepreneurship includes mentoring people about how to find a market to sell their product and have network with the marketplace and also with life outside of rural areas.

Big Chefs' project named Women of The Soil, which is about working with local women producers and cooperatives is aiming to support local development through social innovation activities as a result of the marketing approach where emerges a contribution to economy, employment, income and life standards.

4.1 The Development of Women Entrepreneurs Cooperative

The contract was signed for the "Anadolu Bacıları (Anatolian Sisters) Are Strengthening" project between Ankara Development Agency and Anadolu Bacıları Women's Entrepreneurs Cooperative in accordance with "Local Product Commercialization Financial Support Program of Ankara Development Agency." With the project, women entrepreneurs from Polatlı/Ankara will commercialize their local products and present them to the world.

The project, which will last for 18 months and cost 523.000 Turkish lira (TL), aims to contribute to the development of the region and close the social-economic gap with the surrounding regions by means of strengthening the production and marketing processes by supporting women entrepreneurship and increasing the added value of local products. In this context, beet molasses will be produced and commercialized, as a local product with brand value in Polatlı, and a market network will be developed to bring the product to the international market. The project also aims to develop income-generating activities in the agricultural industry and to increase women's employment in Polatlı (Mynet, 2019).

Anatolian Sisters (Anadolu Bacıları) Cooperative has been producing many local products such as orange-carrot jam, Polatlı noodle, melon jam, watermelon jam, and beet molasses from the day it has been established, selling their products online, and sending 300–400 kg of their products to Big Chefs Restaurants, which is more than their yearly selling amount (Milliyet, 2019).

Big Chefs is a well-known, highly profiled segment restaurant in Turkey. It opened first in Ankara in 2007. Now, it is in 11 cities – Istanbul, Ankara, Izmir, Antalya, Adana, Bodrum, Bursa, Denizli, Iskenderun, Gaziantep, Mersin – and four foreign countries including United Arab Emirates, Kuwait, Saudi Arabia, and Iran, with more than 50 branches (Bigchefs, 2019).

There is a following social responsibility project "From Women of The Soil, To The Tables" initiated by Big Chefs Restaurants' Chief Executive Officer (CEO) Gamze Cizreli. Within the scope of this project, there are 14 entrepreneur women living in Manisa, Gaziantep, Ankara, Amasya, Antakya, Kastamonu, Bursa, Balıkesir, Canakkale, Bolu, Mugla, Düzce, and Izmir, who are making a living from agriculture. There are cherry, pepper, peanut, artichoke, crushed green olives, black bulgur, and tomato producers among these women. The amount of supply from these producers is 10–12 million TL annually. Currently, there are 10000 products registered with geographical indications in the world. Although there are 2500 candidate products in Turkey, only 337 of them are registered with geographical indication and application for 422 products has been completed and is awaiting registration.

With the "From Women of The Soil, To The Tables" project, Big Chefs Restaurants are aiming to increase the number of women entrepreneurs they work with to 50, and will be supplying half of its product supply from local women producers in 2021 (Raillife, 2019).

From this information given about the production, supply system, and collaboration of Anatolian Sisters, Big Chefs, and other women cooperatives, there is a scheme created and recommended for this network as shown in Fig. 2.

In Fig. 2, producers are women from various cooperatives, who produce locally for Big Chefs restaurant. With the figure it aims to recommend software for supply chain optimization. The information flow between supplier, seller and market needs to be supported by an optimization software.

With this flow, the partners of the supply chain will gain time in every step of the process, such as ordering, producing, etc. The most important point of this flow is to increase productivity with time and material flow efficiency. The items

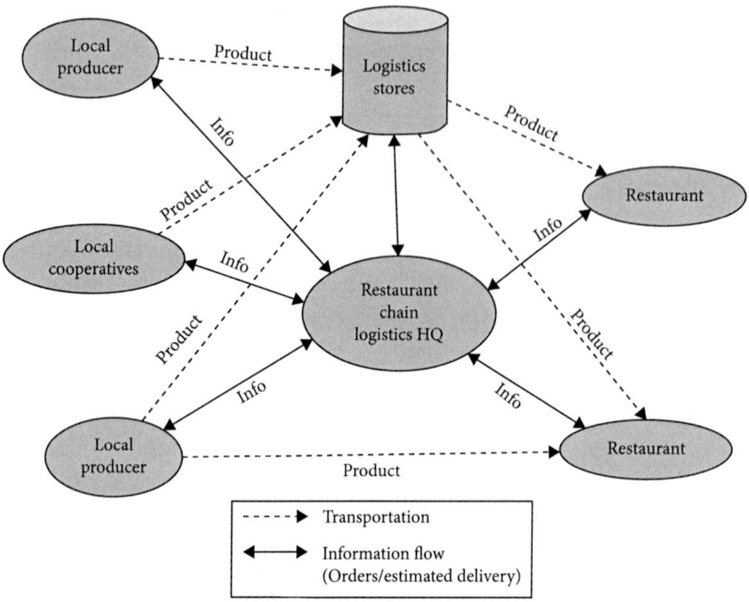

Fig. 2: The Production, Supply System, and Collaboration of Anatolian Sisters, Big Chefs, and Other Women Cooperatives Through Applied Network System

that are mentioned below show the information, which should be in the Applied Network System in order to increase efficiency within the network system.

- Information of the producers with their resumes,
- Product description (name and features like product type, kg, lt., price, etc.),
- Quantity of order,
- Time for harvest and planting,
- Weather conditions,
- Marketers' info with their objective and needs, and
- Estimated time for logistics from the producer to the delivery location.

4.1.2 Stories of 14 Entrepreneur Women

Of the 14 women producers in which Big Chefs cooperates,

- Rabia Yılmaz produces both cherry pepper and cotton in the Saruhanlı district of Manisa. Yılmaz has been farming since she was 10 years old and is 68 years old now.

- Gülter Açıkgöz, a peanut producer from the Ticar Village of Gaziantep, is 43 years old.
- "Anatolian Sisters Cooperative" member Nilüfer Kart and İklime Yaşar are producing the first orange-carrot jam of Turkey in Ankara Polatlı.
- Medina Alkoç from "Amasya Bee Women Cooperative" prepares delicious noodles in the village of Amasya Yolüstü.
- Hülya Altınöz, who lives in Hatay, stands out as a producer of crushed green olives.
- Iksir Aydın, the founder of Iksirli Ciftlik, and his daughter Ece Aydin both produce black bulgur and employ women in the region with their farms and accommodation facilities.
- Eda Çelebi, 37, who grows artichokes in the Mustafa Kemalpaşa district of Bursa, is aiming to cultivate mushroom as well as lettuce and pumpkin production.
- Gülsüm and Hasibe Akın, the founders of "What's on My Table" brand, produce goat cheese in Balıkesir Kaz Mountains.
- Ezel Temiz and Ayşe Kocagöz from Karaağaç Village of Bolu produce delicious village breads with sourdough. The biggest dream of the duo is to carry the village bread, which they produce with 100 years of sour yeast, to the world table.
- Suzan Mantar and Sezin Çetin sisters from "Biga Women's Cooperative and Women's Labor Valuation Foundation" produce tarhana (soup with dried yoghurt) in Çanakkale's Biga district. The duo also makes Turkish ravioli, sweet, and pies.
- The 43-year-old Hatice Havle Alptekin, who lives in the town of Fethiye in Muğla, stands out as the fresh and dried tomato producer.
- Aliye Akbulut, 45, living in Menemen District of Izmir, produces vegetables such as arugula, parsley, purslane, and dill.
- A graduate of the Middle East Technical University Department of Business Administration, 38-year-old Aslı Aksoy is the producer of fresh asparagus for Big Chefs. Her biggest goal is to see Turkey among asparagus exporter countries.
- The last one of these 14 women producers is Filiz Aynacı, a 63-year-old hazelnut producer living in Soğuk Su Village in Düzce (Raillife, 2019).

5 Conclusion

Globalization and neoliberalism movement spreading over the world in 1980s started to affect Turkey with the "The 1980 Economics Decrees." This situation caused Turkey to open to the outside world along with the neoliberals economy, abandoning the policy of import substitution and transition to a free market economy.

During the structural adjustment process carried out under the supervision of the International Monetary Fund and the World Bank, problems requiring the immediate intervention to national economies such as high inflation, the melting of foreign exchange reserves, capital escape from the country, and the growth of deficits in the balance of current payments were solved by the stability packages (Tellan, 2008:5).

This evolution process started with 1980 Decrees was not only economical but also was social-cultural, technological, and about visionary diversity.

When these changes are examined as a whole, it is easily understood that the people's lives are changed both at micro and macrolevels.

The consumer's choices, that were making purchases within the limited product range, increased with the transition to the new economic model; and accordingly, the consumption habits began to change. This change extending from production to consumption patterns caused a new era to begin where innovation word started to be used frequently both in the world and in Turkey.

As technology becomes more important and indispensable in the daily life of people, innovation becomes critical in every aspect. Starting from creating fresh ideas about daily life, innovation takes part in every scale of industry and marketing.

While social innovation reaches out to people and improves their life standards, just like we observe with the "Women of the soil" and "Anatolian Sisters" projects, it also creates new marketing ideas.

As a result of production and marketing's becoming global, with the endless possibilities of lightning-fast information flow over the internet, innovation ideas are exchanged easily all over the world.

Thanks to the demanding nature of human beings, innovation ideas exchanged globally lead industry and producers to come up with better and cheaper products widely available for everyone.

Innovation whether it is social, industrial, or technological should be based on communication with people and supported by information technologies, mainly internet and mobile technologies.

As long as businesses take peoples' ideas into consideration seriously, there is a wide range of selections easily accessible utilizing web pages, mobile applications, and growing possibilities of communication.

Coming back to social innovation, "Anatolian Sisters" and "Women of The Soil" projects discussed earlier in the case study in section four are real-life examples but seem to be lacking a little more technological support. There is certainly a gap in this area to be filled with information technologies. Considering every actor in the supply chain has a mobile device and internet connection, there is a good chance of optimization of logistics and adding more local producers to the supply chain network.

Bibliography

Abdelkafi, N. and P., Margherita (2018), "Supply Chain Innovation-Driven Business Models: Exploratory Analysis and Implications for Management", **Business Process Management Journal**, Vol.24, N.2, pp. 589–608.

Achrol, R. S. and Kotler, P. (1999), "Marketing in the Network Economy", **Journal of Marketing**, V.63, pp. 146–163.

Bello, D. C., Lohtia, R. and Sangtani, V. (2004), "An Institutional Analysis of Supply Chain Innovations in Global Marketing Channels", **Industrial Marketing Management**, Vol.33, N.1, pp. 57–64.

Bessant, J. and Tidd, J. (2007), **Innovation & Entrepreneurship**, Chichester: John Wiley and Sons, pp. 6–58.

Bigchefs. (2019), **Bigchefs**, Retrieved from http://www.bigchefs.com.tr/en, 30.03.2019.

Cagliano, A. C., De Marco, A., Rafele, C., Bragagnini, A. and Gobbato, L. (2015), "Analyzing the Diffusion of a Mobile Service Supporting the E-Grocery Supply Chain", **Business Process Management Journal**, Vol.21, N.4, pp. 928–963.

Chew, E. and Gottschalk, P. (2009), "Business Innovation and Information Management", **Information Technology Strategy and Management: Best Practices**, New York: IGI Global, pp. 392–427.

Chopra, S. S. and Meindl, P. (2007), **Supply Chain Management: Strategy, Planning, and Operations**, 3rd ed., New Jersey: Prentice-Hall, pp. 13–30.

Chuwiruch, N., Jhundra-Indra, P. and Boonlua, S. (2015), "Marketing Innovation Strategy and Marketing Performance: A Conceptual Framework", **Allied Academies International Conference. Academy of Marketing Studies. Proceedings**, Vol.19, N.2, pp. 82–93.

Cooper, R. (1999), "From Experience – The Invisible Success Factors in Product Innovation", **Journal of Product Innovation Management**, Vol.16, N.2, pp. 115–133.

Çelik, H., (2006), **1980–2000 Yılları Arasında Türkiye'de Uygulanan Neo LiBeral Politikaların İşçi Sınıfına Etkileri** (Yüksek Lisans Tezi), Pamukkale Üniversitesi, Denizli, pp. ii–56.

Dolan, R. J. and Simon, H. (1996), **Power Pricing: How Managing Price Transforms the Bottom Line**, New York: Free Press, pp. 110–126.

Dökmen, G. (2009), **Bölgesel Kalkınmada Yenilik Sistemleri ve Devletin Rolü: Türkiye**

Örneği (Doktora Tezi), Dokuz Eylül Üniversitesi, İzmir, pp. 19–20.

Edwards, M. and Shultz, C. (2005), "Reframing Agribusiness: Moving from Farm to Market Centric", **Journal of Agribusiness**, Vol.23, N.1, pp. 57–73.

Elçi, Ş. (2006), **İnovasyon: Kalkınmanın ve Rekabetin Anahtarı**, Ankara: Feryal Matbaacılık, pp. 1–10.

Geldes, C. and Felzensztein, C. (2013), "Marketing Innovations in the Agribusiness Sector", **Academia Revista Latinoamericana de Administracion**, Vol.26, N.1, pp. 108–138.

Gibson, R. (2005), **The Role of Co-operatives in Community Economic Development**, RDI Working Paper, pp. 3–6.

Goldenberg, M. (2004), **Social Innovation in Canada: How the Nonprofit Sector Serves Canadians and How It Can Serve Them Better**, Research Report No. W/25, Canadian Policy Research Networks, Ontario, pp. 1–4.

Gömleksiz, M. (2012), **Bölgesel İnovasyon Sistemleri ve Türkiye: İstatistiki Bölge Birimleri Sınıflandırması Düzey 2 Bölgeleri İnovasyon İndeksi** (Yüksek Lisans Tezi), Selçuk Üniversitesi, Konya, pp. 3–50.

Geldes, C. and Felzensztein, C. (2013), "Marketing Innovations in the Agribusiness Sector", **Academia Revista Latinoamericana de Administracion**, Vol. 26, N.1, pp. 108–138.

Greenhalgh, C. and Rogers, M. (2010), "The Nature and Importance of Innovation", **Innovation, Intellectual Property, and Economic Growth**, New Jersey: Princeton University Press, pp. 4–20.

Grunig, J. E. (Ed.) (1992), **Excellence in Public Relations and Communication Management**, Routhledge: Taylor and Francis Group, 1st Edition, https://doi.org/10.4324/9780203812303, pp. 627–635.

Howaldt, J. and Schwarz, M. (2010), **Social Innovation: Concepts, Research Fields and International Trends**, Dortmund: International Monitoring, pp. 25–33.

Hunt, S. D. (1976), "The Nature and Scope of Marketing", **Journal of Marketing**, Vol.40, N. 3, pp. 17–28.

Ionescu, C. (2015), "About the Conceptualization of Social Innovation", **Theoretical and Applied Economics**, Vol.22, N.3(604), pp. 53–62.

Janszen, F. (2000), "The Shape of Innovation", **The Age of Innovation**, USA: Pearson Education, pp. 3–24.

Jones, A. (1999), "Successful Marketing Innovation", **European Journal of Innovation Management**, Vol.2, N.1, pp. 6–11.

Jonason, A. (2002), "Innovative Pricing Effects: Theory and Practice in Mobile Internet Networks", **European Journal of Innovation Management**, Vol.5, N:4, pp. 185–193.

Klein, J.-L. (2013), "Introduction: Social Innovation at the Crossroads Between Science, Economy and Society", (Moulaert, F., Maccallum, D., Mehmood, A. and Hamdouch, A., Eds.), **International Handbook On Social Innovation**, Cheltenham: Edward Elgar, pp. 9–12.

Klein, J.-L., Fontan, J.-M., Harrisson, D. and Levesque, B. (2012), "The Quebec System of Social Innovation: A Focused Analysis on the Local Development Field", **Finisterra**, Vol.47, N.94, pp. 9–28.

Klein, S. J. (1985), "What Is Technology", **Bulletin of Science, Technology & Society**, N.1, pp. 215–218.

Kotler, P. and Armstrong, G. et al. (2008), **Principles of Marketing**, 12th Edition, Prentice Hall: Pearson, pp. 4,5,506 .

Kotler, P. (2003), **Marketing Management**, 11th Edition, Prentice Hall: Pearson, pp. 470.

Levitt, T. (1960), "Growth and Profits Through Planned Marketing Innovation", **Journal of Marketing**, Vol.24, N.4, pp. 1–8.

Li-Hua, R. (2007), "What Is Technology?", **Journal of Technology Management in China**, Vol.2, N.3, pp. 193–197.

Lopes, D. P. T., Vieira, N. S., Barbosa, A. C. Q. and Parente, C. (2017), "Management Innovation and Social Innovation: Convergences and Divergences", **Academia Revista Latinoamericana de Administración**, Vol.30, N.4, pp. 474–489.

Lorente, A. R. M., Dewhurst, F. and Dale, B. G., (1999), "TQM and Business Innovation", **European Journal of Innovation Management**, Vol.2, No.I, pp. 12–19.

Milliyet. (2019), **Kadın Kooperatiflerine Bir Destek Daha**, Retrieved from http://www.milliyet.com.tr/kadin-kooperatifine-bir-destek-daha-ankara-yerelhaber-2959711/, 30.03.2019.

Mills, M. (2015), **Technology**, (Adams, R., Reiss, B. and Serlin, D., Eds.), New York: NYU Press, pp. 176.

Mohelska, H. and Sokolova, M. (2018), "Management Approaches for Industry 4.0 – the Organizational Culture Perspective", **Technological and Economic Development of Economy**, Vol.24, N. 6, pp. 2225–2240.

Moulaert, F., MacCallum, D. and Hillier, J. (2013), "Social innovation: intuition, precept, concept, theory and practice", (Moulaert, F., MacCallum, D.,

Mehmood, A. and Hamdouch, A., Eds.), **International Handbook on Social Innovation**, Cheltenham: Edward Elgar, p. 13–24.

Mulgan, G., Ali, R., Halkett, R. and Sanders, B. (2007), **In and Out of Sync. The Challenge of Growing Social Innovations**, London: NESTA, pp. 9–27.

Murray, R., Caulier-Grice, J. and Mulgan, G. (2009), **Social Venturing: The Social Innovator Series**, London: NESTA, pp. 3–8.

Mynet. (2019), **Anadolu Bacıları Ajans Desteğiyle Güçleniyor**, Retrieved from https://www.mynet.com/anadolu-bacilari-ajans-destegiyle-gucleniyor-180104083999 (30.03.2019).

Tornatzky, L. G. and Fleischer, M. (1990), The Processes of Technological Innovation, Lexington: Lexington Books, pp. 11–15.

OECD. (2019), **Who We Are?**, retrieved from http://www.oecd.org/about (27.03.2019).

Ogilvie, S. (2019), **The European Guilds: An Economic Analysis, Innovation**, USA: Princeton University Press, pp. 438–510, https://www.jstor.org/stable/j.ctv3s8sm9.14.

Oke, A., Burke, G. and Myers, A. (2007), "Innovation Types and Performance in Growing UK SMEs", **International Journal of Operations and Production Management**, Vol.27, N.7, pp. 735–753.

Oslo Manual. (2018), "The Measurement of Scientific, Technological and Innovation Activities, Guidelines for Collecting, Reporting and Using Data on Innovation," **OECD, European Union**, 4th Edition, pp. 19–172

Örtlek, Z. (2015), **İnovasyon ve Bölgesel Kalkınma Perspektifinden Türkiye** (Yüksek Lisans Tezi), Aksaray Üniversitesi, Aksaray.

Parasuraman, A. (1981), "Hang on the Marketing Concept", **Business Horizons**, Vol.24, N.5, pp. 38–40.

Pitta, D. (2008), "Product Innovation and Management in a Small Enterprise", **Journal of Product & Brand Management**, Vol.17, N.6, pp. 416–419.

Quaye, D. and Mensah, I. (2018), "Marketing Innovation and Sustainable Competitive Advantage of Manufacturing SMEs in Ghana", **Management Decision, Management Decision**, Vol.57, No.7, pp. 1535–1553.

Raillife. (2019), **Toprağın Dilinden Anlayan Kadınlar**, Retrieved from http://www.raillife.com.tr/topragin-dilinden-anlayan-kadinlar, 30.03.2019.

Rekettye, G. (2003), "The Regularities of Innovation – A Marketing Perspective", **Acta Oeconomica**, Vol.53, N. 1, pp. 45–59.

Rowley, J., Baregheh, A. and Sambrook, S. (2011), "Towards an Innovation-Type Mapping Tool", **Management Decision**, Vol.49, N.1, pp. 73–86.

Sanzo-Perez, M., Álvarez-González, L. I. and Rey-García, M. (2015), "How to Encourage Social Innovations: A Resource-Based Approach", **The Service Industries Journal**, Vol.35, N.7–8, pp. 430–437.

Schumpeter, J. (1934), **The Theory of Economic Development: An Inquiry into Profits, Capital, Credit, Interest and Business Cycle,** Vol. 46, Cambridge, Harvard University Press, pp. 71–242.

Srinuan, C., Srinuan, P. and Bohlin, E. (2013), "Pricing Strategies and Innovations in the Thai Mobile Communications Market", **Info** Vol.15, N.1, pp. 61–77.

Stiglitz, J. (2004), "The Role of Cooperatives in Globalization" Conference The Culture of Development, Globalisation and Cooperative Enterprise Working Paper, 9, Genoa, Italy.

Tellan, D. (2008), "Tüketimin Karşı Devrimi: Türkiye'de 1980 Sonrası Uygulanan İktisat Politikalarının Toplumsal Sonuçlarına Eleştirel Bir Bakışı", **Ekonomik Yaklaşım**, Vol.19, N.67, pp. 1–19.

Yavuz, S. (2006), "Reklamlar ve Reklamcılık Sektörü Açısından 1980'lerde Türkiye Panaroması", **Galatasaray Üniversitesi İşletme Dergisi**, Vol.5, pp. 157–182.

Yılmaz, Z. and Incekaş, E. (2018), "Türkiye'de İnovasyon ve Bölgesel Kalkınma", **Kırklareli Üniversitesi Sosyal Bilimler Dergisi**, Vol.2, N.1, pp. 154–169.

Yükselen, C. (1994), **Temel Pazarlama Bilgileri**, Ankara: Adım Yayıncılık, pp. 36–89.

Assist. Prof. Dr. Furkan Evranos

Turkey's Asset Management Companies and Projections for the Sector

Abstract: In the financial crisis of 2001 in Turkey, many banks with a high level of non-performing loans (so-called Nonperforming Loans, "NPLs") found their sources of capital dissolved, which occurred because of lack of risk focused management. Huge amounts of NPLs imply both a lack of management methods and lack of capital. Because huge NPL volume has affected banks' operations and credit capacity. The purpose of this study is to present one of the NPL management and resolution methods called Asset Management Companies (AMCs) that already exists in the application. These firms provide agility, liquidity, tax advantage, and robustness to the banking sector. These organizations, which are increasingly professional in their fields, operate in financial markets.The study ends with the projections regarding receivable and asset management sector and AMCs.

Keywords: Asset management company, asset management, receivable management, financial restructuring, financial improvement

1 Introduction

First of all, it is appropriate to define loans which are called nonperforming. Nonperforming loans are characterized as specific loans which are past due over 90 days. To be more specific, if a borrower has a loan and he has not fulfilled his loan obligations to the bank for more than 90 days, then his loan is considered as nonperforming (BDDK, 2016:2).

That is a matter of essential importance for regulatory authorities, banks, and governments concerned on financial stability. NPLs can arise in a bank's balance sheet because of poor credit risk management.

Banks desire to have the lowest possible level of NPLs in their balance sheets. If a bank has low levels of NPLs, this directly implies that it will have low levels of risk. Moreover, banks build their foundations on consumers' confidence. In the case that a bank appears to be "weak" or "fragile" then costumers might choose to withdraw their deposits and put them elsewhere. This unpleasant event may be happened when high (Anastasiou, 2016:2).

Internal and external factors are important in the banking system to make loans problematic. Internal factors are problems and inadequacies arising from the parties involved in lending and reimbursement. External factors refer to the reasons that occur outside the will of the credit parties (Sipahi, 2003:5).

The research results and past episodes of financial crises strongly suggest that rising NPLs must be addressed rapidly and effectively due to an immediate feedback impact on economic and financial variables. NPLs reduce banks' lending abilities and drag on banks' profitability (that is, they increase the opportunity cost of capital, since they yield no returns and require capital provisioning, management, and financial resources). Excessive and rapid buildup of NPLs can also cause a credit crunch, leading to a banking crisis, and financing for small- and medium-sized enterprises, trade, infrastructure, and households may take a serious hit. Banking instability strongly affects other capital market segments (bonds, equities, and commodities).

Accordingly, the early cleanup of NPLs from bank balance sheets can help restore private sector lending to the real economy and facilitate recovery from a crisis. Effective and preemptive handling of the deterioration of banks' asset quality can also help inclusive growth, by mitigating the negative impact of NPLs on unemployment and the poor. In addition, the finding that rising unemployment plays a key role in the buildup of NPLs also suggests that, during a crisis, policy measures to mitigate unemployment could be considered part of a comprehensive crisis response package, and decrease the negative impact on financial instability. As such, dealing with a rapid rise of NPLs can be seen as part of either microprudential or macroprudential policies depending on the underlying cause of the vulnerability and country-specific circumstances (Lee and Rosenkranz, 2019:25).

2 The Scope and Functions of AMCs

AMCs are defined as the institutions whose functions have been taken under the law for the purpose of purchasing, collecting, restructuring, and selling the assets and other assets of banks and other financial institutions within the financial system. These companies try to collect these problem loans using their financial, legal, and technical infrastructure (BDDK, 2006:4).

After the global economical crisis, many countries began to apply various approaches to take measures because of the corruption in the financial structures of the firms (especially of Small- and Medium-Sized Enterprises) that occupy an important place in their own economical arrangements. The process that began with London Approach continued with Istanbul Approach and Anadolu Approach. It is necessary to provide the small medium sized enterprises which are really important in the progress and macroeconomical structures of the countries, a scope to rejoin the system by refining their states. In this study it is determined comparatively if Istanbul Approach and Anadolu Approach, which were put into practice in Turkey, reached their goals. General public opinion is that both of the approaches did not work well in the rearrangement of the firms. When compared with each other, it is seen that the Istanbul Approach is more successful than Anadolu Approach (Koç, 2010:35).

AMCs undertake an important mission and provide significant support to banks in order to eliminate toxic assets and bank balance sheets that will affect equity and liability structure. By transferring the troubled assets to the AMCs, the banks have the opportunity to improve their balance sheets and write down the profits they have set aside. Although the liquidation of nonperforming loans by AMCs has been a method applied by many countries in recent years, practice characteristics have changed from country to country.

AMCs buy NPL from banks and other financial institutions with submission of a proposal for substantial discount and then they try to collect as much as they can via contacting customers to convince them to pay back loans and negotiate with them by pressuring them with laws to be enforced that AMCs are one of the structural methods that banks use in restructuring their financials by solving their NPL.

Debt buyers and the collection industry play an integral and necessary role within the complex credit-based economy. The ability of debt buyers to purchase distressed accounts from originating creditors provides benefits not only to the originating creditors but to all consumers and businesses that rely on the availability of credit at reasonable rates for their purchasing needs.

Debt buyers are companies that purchase contractual-based accounts receivables (hereinafter referred to as "accounts") from originating creditors on the secondary market. The types of accounts can differ dramatically based on the asset class that was the foundation of the contractual agreement, not to mention other factors such as whether the accounts:

- Are associated with "consumer" or "corporate" obligations,
- Are "performing" or "nonperforming,"
- Have "guarantees" made by third parties, or
- Have "collateral" for payment.

A debt buyer analyzes all of these factors as well as numerous others when valuing accounts prior to purchase. For example, whether an account is characterized as "performing" or "nonperforming" will significantly impact what the originating creditor can expect to receive for the sale of the account on the secondary market. Performing accounts are frequently valued at or near face value whereas nonperforming accounts are usually valued at a discount due to the challenges associated with rehabilitating contractual performance.

When a debt buying company purchases an account from a creditor, it essentially purchases the contract and all rights, benefits, and liabilities that were held by the creditor that are associated with the contract – which includes receiving payments on performing accounts and the right to collect on all nonperforming accounts (Reid, 2015a:4).

Debt buyers may be companies that purchase consumer debt from originating creditors or from other debt buyers. The types of consumer debt that are purchased can differ dramatically, based upon the contractual agreement revolving credit card debt, auto debt, medical debt, etc., not to mention other factors, such as whether the debt is performing or nonperforming; whether payment guarantees have been made by third parties; or whether collateral has been provided (Reid, 2015b:5).

AMC model, like "RTC" and "FDIC" in USA since the 1980s, "FOBAPROA" in Mexico, "KAMCO" in South Korea, "CHAMC" in China, "IBRA" in Indonesia, "FRA" in Thailand, "DANAHART" in Malaysia, "APT" in Philippines and "NPART" in Ghana and is part of a system proposed by the IMF to Turkey. Due to the financial crisis in 2001, banks were unable to overcome the crisis. As a result of this phenomenon, many firms in the real sector have come to the brink of bankruptcy.

The transferring of nonperforming loans to AMCs is welcomed by both banks and regulatory authorities. The sale of nonperforming loans is favorable in terms of providing revenue from an asset that does not have any value, improving financial ratio and cleaning the balance sheet. Regulatory authorities, on the other hand, have a positive approach to the transfer of nonperforming loans due to the recovery of the balance sheets of the banking sector after the transfer of nonperforming loans and become more readable (Selimler, 2015:274).

Empirical analysis has shown that probability distribution of expected inflows from nonretail NPLs considerably deviates from symmetric distribution and is asymmetric to the right. Accuracy of derived model depends upon available data in banks about NPLs by corporate sectors and recovery rates by time intervals (Devjak, 2018:3).

The bank-specific variables used are the ratio of return on assets (ROA) and return on equity (ROE) as proxies for management quality, the ratio of loans to deposits (LTD), and bank size (SIZE). ROA reveals the managerial efficiency of a bank to convert its assets into net profits, while ROE reveals mostly how efficiently a bank has used its equity. "Quality of management" indicators (high levels of ROA-ROE) will be related to low NPLs, that is, a negative sign is expected (Anastasiou, Louri and Tsionas, 2016:11).

3 Development of AMCs and NPL Management Sector in Turkey

Loans are the most important source of income of banks, and the amount of loan is defined as risk. The credit risk in the banking system is the most significant percentage compared to other risks in the sector. This situation has increased the importance of credit risk management in the banking sector.

Banks implement various policies in credit risk management and try to control the credit risk. Some of these policies are proactive policies for the prevention of risk before loss, and others are passive policies aimed at meeting the effects of the loss after the risk has occurred. By using passive policies, banks try to cover the effects of the risk by taking advantage of internal and external sources by assuming that the risk cannot be fully eliminated. They do this by holding sufficient equity capital, creating additional capital to cover the loss or providing nonbank guarantees. Proactive policies are intended to prevent banks from exposure to credit risk; they are the primary ones for risk management. These policies include risk exposure, risk mitigation, risk allocation, hedging, and risk differentiation. Reflection of the risk is applied to the bank as collateral in case the principal of the loan is not repaid or interest repayments are realized. If the bank encounters a negative development, it can cover the loss completely or partially.

The "Transition to Strong Economy" Program was put into practice by the government in order to eliminate the instability that occurred after the November 2000 and February 2001 crises and to establish the infrastructure for the restructuring of the economy. One of the main elements of this program is the restructuring of the banking sector (TCMB, 2001:1).

The Reel Sector and Finance Advisory Board, which was formed by the representatives of the real sector and finance sector, who decided to overcome the economic crises of 2000 and 2001 before the structural change of the Turkish banking sector, came together and threatened the banking sector's ability to pay and the reduction of the troubled assets that caused the reduction, so that due to the debts to the financial sector restricted the activity of the real sector companies in order to relieve the proposed İstanbul Approach which had been inspired by the London Approach.

The experience of the Istanbul Approach has given opportunity to develop the skills of the banks to solve their problems without public authority. The rate of application to the approach and the conversion to contract reached a satisfactory figure.

Turkey had been experienced financial crises in November 2000 and structural reforms implemented after the February 2001 crisis, there has been a reduction in the number of banks. However, the fact that this decrease was realized in the banking sector in which banks with international capital adequacy ratio remained within the system allowed the sector to be reconstructed on a solid basis.

Within the scope of aforementioned approach, a distinction has been made between the firms that can live and the companies that cannot live, and they have been put into practice for the companies that can experience the plan. Companies that have difficulty in payment are not forced into bankruptcy by the banks where they are indebted, but rather they are supported and their operations are maintained and their debts are structured.

According to Article no.143 of the Banking Law no. 5411; for the purpose of purchasing, collecting, restructuring, and selling the receivables and other assets of banks and other financial institutions including the fund, AMCs may also be established. To provide additional financing to borrowers or to participate in their capital in order to collect and finance their real estates or other goods, rights and assets acquired for the purpose of collecting receivables under the scope of collection and collection of receivables and/or other assets within the scope of the restructuring of receivables and/or other assets. AMCs are authorized to perform all kinds of activities (BDDK, 2005:76).

AMCs take over the overdue loans of bank, leasing, factoring and other financial institutions; transferring both cash resources to banks and preventing them from performing unproductive activities in a nonspecialized area. These companies try to make a profit by meeting with creditors and by proceeding with the legal processes initiated by banks, thus making their investments in purchasing credit portfolios, the expenses incurred in the collection process, and interest expenses (Güvenal, 2015:1).

The main purpose of the AMCs, which are established by private or public, is defined as the companies that take over the troubled assets that cause problems on financial institutions and facilitate the financial restructuring and maximize the recovery value of the troubled assets. Another method that banks will use to liquidate their problem loans is to transfer such loans to AMCs.

Why AMCs? To minimize the fiscal and/or private cost associated with the restructuring of distressed financial institutions, financial restructuring program should be aimed at maximizing the value of restructured financial institutions and that of the assets of closed financial institutions over time. To achieve these objectives, it has been sometimes suggested that good assets of distressed financial institutions should be separated from their bad assets and that AMCs should be set up as receptacle vehicles to take over the latter.

The typical arguments in favor of separating nonperforming from performing assets of distressed financial institutions are listed below (Woo, 2000:9, 10):

- Division labor,
- Facilitation of valuation,
- Strengthening of credit discipline,
- Economy of scale, and
- Enhanced bargaining power.

AMCs can assist to close the NPL pricing gap by allowing banks to invest in AMCs and retain some of the upside returns from restructuring in a way that does not conflict with accounting rules. By purchasing foreclosed collateral and converted equity from banks (after debt-equity swaps), AMCs can also reduce the market risk that banks face from NPL restructuring (Jassaud and Krang, 2015:16).

3.1 Effects and Importance of AMCs

AMCs provide numerous advantages to the financial system. It can be argued that they help restructuring of the financial system in a way that when financial institutions sell out their bad debts, they obtain robustness, liquidity, and trust.

Moreover, written losses may bring credit discipline for further deals. Banks transfer risks to AMCs. These firms also provide rapid solutions to liquidation sales, they provide high returns in liquidation process of bad debts, and they also help asset prices to normalize; book value of debts and market value of them differs significantly which may mislead investors, creditors, and stakeholders.

Economies of scale and economies of scope may be achieved when deals are pooled and sold to an entity. Increase in financial leverage and improved management conditions do also favor these sales.

3.2 NPL Management and AMCs' Approach of Turkey

In the world, carrying the distinction of being the only sector regulated and supervised under the authority of the BRSA (BDDK), the purpose of establishment of the Asset Management sector of Turkey is: to provide the individuals and companies with the opportunity to pay their debts to the economy; to provide liquidity to the financial system; and to contribute to the improvement of banks' balance sheets and to save them from the operational burden. The law on the establishment of AMCs, which is one of the structural reform targets planned for the restructuring of the banking system according to international standards, entered into force in 2003 (VŞYD, 2019).

Since the enactment of the communique governing the foundation and operations of NPL servicing platforms in Turkey in November 2006, financial institutions, despite being volatile, have consistently sold NPL.

The NPL purchasing market has experienced considerable growth over the years with the increase in number of banks selling portfolios, entrance of new AMCs to the market, as well as banks selling larger portfolios. In 2017, private banks, factoring, leasing, and other financial institutions sold a total of TRY 8.6 billion NPLs, in terms of UPB (unpaid principal balance), to AMCs, the highest number since the inception year of 2008.

The major driving factors behind this growth were:

- Banks and other financial institutions realizing the benefits of selling NPLs (e.g., avoiding operational costs, reducing NPL ratios, and ability to focus more on core business) and
- Increasing maturity and sophistication of AMCs in the market (PWC Reports, 2018:4).

Further growth is expected to be seen in the next few years driven by several factors:

- Total volume growth regarding growing loan and NPL balances,
- Expectation of state banks to start to enhance volume of selling NPLs, and
- Expectation of companies of technology, energy, and telecommunication to start selling of NPLs.

3.2.1 Purpose of Receiving Receivables by AMCs from Banks and Other Financial Institutions

The purpose of AMCs is to buy and/or liquidate these assets with the highest possible value by purchasing the receivables/other assets of banks and other financial institutions with the most reasonable prices. For this purpose, AMCs have taken the problematic presence; in order to take into account the cost of transactions to be carried out behind it (the improvement, restructuring, and sale of the problematic asset and the loss of the asset) and the profit to be obtained, it is necessary to make the pricing of the problematic asset right and dispose of this asset as soon as possible (Oy, 2009:83).

AMCs are interested in: Credit Card Receivables, Corporate Loan Receivables, Commercial Loan Receivables, SME Loan Receivables, Personal

Loan Receivables, Housing Loan Receivables, Vehicle Loan Receivables, and all other assets and receivables.

In addition, AMCs should select the assets they can manage and/or liquidate their receivables/other assets in the most efficient manner. These are especially large assets, fixed assets, and loans to be liquidated. Loans to be restructured and loans to debtors aiming to establish a long-term relationship with the bank should be left in banks.

3.2.2 Process of Selling Receivables by Financial Institutions to AMC

In our country, the purchase/sale process of the receivables and the existence of AMC with sufficient capital, experience, and knowledge to be able to contribute to the financial sector in Turkey and the purchase/sale transactions should be made in accordance with the benefits through mutual agreements and right pricing.

The procedures followed in the receivables and asset purchase/sale transactions performed in our country are as follows:

- Determination of the receivable portfolio to be sold by banks or other financial institutions which will be sold,
- Determination of the amount of the receivable portfolio to be sold by banks or other financial institutions which will be sold at the minimum price of the tender,
- Preparation of receivable files related to receivable portfolios to be sold by banks or other financial institutions that will be sold,
- Preparation of the presentation document for the receivables portfolio to be sold,
- Preparation of specifications for the tender,
- Preparation of asset documents and receivable files between the banks or other financial institutions that will sell and AMCs preparing to receive,
- Preparation of confidentiality agreement before the examination,
- Review of the receivable files,
- Purchasing of receivable portfolio after review of AMC,
- Determination of the amount and the nature of the tender specification together with the bid,
- Informing AMCs,
- Contracting between the banks and other financial institutions and AMC,
- AMC purchased receivables portfolio, and
- Transferring of the credit file by banks and other institutions to AMC.

3.2.3 Analyzing of Assets and Receivables Portfolios by AMC

AMCs are obliged to do the necessary work before purchasing the receivables/other assets. They cannot evaluate every bid or every tender they are in front of; own internal procedures, he/she will have sufficient experience and experience related to the problem/asset, financial structures, the nature of the receivable/other asset (collateral, guarantor, foreclosure-pledged-precautionary-annotated, etc.). They are examined according to different criteria:

- Determination of the value of collaterals/other assets in the form of real estate/securities pledges, commercial enterprise pledges, bails, receivables assignment, and the value expressed by the guarantees,
- Determination of the amount of all the foreclosures and the value of the property subject to the foreclosure,
- Detailed examination of legal compliance, validity, and availability of all collaterals,
- The legal proceedings initiated and executed by the borrower; and administrative interviews are also made:
    - To learn the importance and operability of this agreement if an agreement is made with the borrower on the payment of debt,
    - To learn the accuracy and adequacy of the scope of the legal proceedings and to have other legal follow-up opportunities.
- Determination of the debtor and his/her guarantors' legal status, such as bankruptcy, concordat, or counterclaim against goods, restructuring bankruptcy or reconstruction through reconciliation,
- Determination of the mortgages and pledges, their appraisal values and their sales capabilities,
- Determining whether there is a possibility of a new receivable and a new receivable if there is a credit transfer, and whether there is another previously transferred receivable,
- Determination of the amount of the previous pledges with more than one hostage,
- Determination of the type of transactions and the current status of these transactions, rather than the pledge amounts, rather than the amount of the pledges and other guarantees, and the status of the follow-up procedures, if any, related to the follow-up of their receivables/other assets,
- Determination of the debts and debts of the debtor to the markets and banks and the business condition and assets of themselves and their vouchers,
- Investigating all of the legal proceedings initiated by the creditors/other assets of the borrower, for their receivables/other assets, and determining their results,

- Determination of the period in which the receivable/other asset can be collected and the collateral to be received within this period can meet the debt,
- Whether the debtor and/or the collaterals, if any, of the asset/other asset is not the collateral, whether or not the agreement basis for the collection of debt attention should be paid to such details and carefully studied on these issues (Oy, 2009:87–89).

3.2.4 Determining the Price of Assets and Receivables Portfolios by AMCs

All businesses can take place in the market or in the sector within the scope of their achievements. For AMCs, this success means that the receivables/other assets they will undertake are correct. Pricing is important for the real value of the receivable/other asset. It is undesirable for pricing to be made above or below the value of the receivable/other asset; in case of high cost, publicly financed AMCs are subject to the public, while in case of low pricing, there is a transfer of funds from banks to these AMCs in terms of private sector-based AMCs. This is a negative effect of public banks traded on the BIST in banks for investors.

The solvency and capacity or performance of the borrower, the ability to direct this capacity or performance to debt repayment and the preparation of a realistic collection schedule, the legal suitability of the receivable, the other debts, priorities and guarantees of the borrower, the debts of the debtor to the state and the priority of these debts, arising from tax/picture, etc., calculating the costs, determining the cost of the asset/other asset considering the criteria such as calculating the cost of the AMCs from the external factors such as exchange rate or interest rate risk, and calculating the cost of the receivable according to the type of financing to be used in the purchase process.

In addition, another issue to be considered in terms of the pricing of the receivable/other asset is the determination of the net price by subtracting the nominal values of the banks' provisions for receivables/other assets. Otherwise, these receivables/other assets will be transferred from banks to AMCs over their net values, and banks will make a profit in excess of net value.

In order to estimate the growth in the coming years, three scenarios are developed in this study based on different macroeconomic assumptions (i.e., expected baseline economic growth, prospering economy with higher growth, and conservative economic growth). GDP is one of the key drivers of credit and NPL balance growth in the financial sector, and thus our scenarios primarily differ by the expected GDP in the forecast period.

3.2.5 Litigation of Asset and Receivables Portfolios by AMCs

In order for AMCs to operate effectively, both the existing legal structure in the country should be conducive to this and the borrowers must acknowledge AMCs have a say in their debts. If we look at the road map of AMCs in conducting their collections, in the first instance, the principal and interest receivables from the borrower companies and the collateral status of these receivables should be examined carefully (Oy, 2009:90,91).

To do this:

- Real estate or securities pledges and their ratings, the value of the properties of the pledged goods, the pledge and the actual amounts of the pledges of the previous pledges, if any, whether the previous and/or subsequent pledge holders are subject to the enforcement proceedings of the pledges, and the status of the proceedings of the pledges covered by the receivable file should be determined,
- Borrowers are taken into account in the context of the file taken over the real estate or securities and whether they are foreclosed by other creditors, if they have been applied, the level of these foreclosures and/or foreclosures, the values of the goods subject to foreclosure, foreclosures of the previous foreclosures and the actual amounts of real receivables, to determine the status of the follow-up of the holders of the right to be subject to the enforcement proceedings of the subject of the foreclosure, and if so, the follow-up of the follow-up and the foreclosures in the scope of the receivable,
- In addition to the real estate and/or movable goods, the amount of the transferred receivable, the institution to which the right to receivable will be borne, and the status of the business relationship between this institution and the debtor and whether there is any right to have previously transferred receivable,
- Whether there is a result of the receivables from third parties related to the acquired receivables/other assets, if there is, the amount of foreclosures related to this receivable, the institution to which the right to claim will be borne and the status of the business relationship between this institution and the debtor, and the other ones made by other creditors. It should be determined whether there are foreclosures,
- If the borrower has not been transferred to legal proceedings, the AMCs will take action to determine which follow-up routes to apply and a business plan for that follow-up.

3.3 Analysis and Projections for NPL Market and AMCs' Sector

According to PWC's base scenario, gross NPL outstanding balance is to reach TRY 117.9 billion by 2020 with an NPL sales volume of TRY 9.2–13.7 billion by private banks between 2018 and 2020. In addition to this, for state banks, we envisaged NPL sales of 1.0 billion each in 2019 and 2020. Note that the resulting NPL ratio after sales, out of gross loan volume, would range between 3.1 % and 3.4 % from 2018 to 2020. This study does not incorporate any NPLs to be disposed by nonfinancial institutions, such as telecoms and utilities. Attractive opportunities for AMCs in the Turkish NPL purchasing market are foreseen.

Turkey's lending market is still in a growth phase. It had a loan/GDP ratio of 75 % in 2017, below established markets and select developing markets (Germany, the UK, Spain, Italy, South Africa, Chile), but a few percentage points above the average of developing economies (67 %) within the select group.

Following the banking crisis in 2001, the lending market loan size grew at a fast pace of 26 % per annum on a TRY basis until 2017, to reach a size of TRY 2.292 billion (USD 629 billion). The main drivers of this growth have been macroeconomic growth, stabilizing inflation, portfolio inflows, and government initiatives (e.g., the Credit Guarantee Fund), especially in 2017 (PWC Reports, 2018:5).

Within the overall market, banking industry loans make up majority of the gross loans, representing a share of 94 % in 2017, and have demonstrated a YOY growth of 26 % between 2002 and 2017. Factoring, leasing, and other financing companies' share of loans have remained below 10 % in Turkey since 2005. Most of the leading factoring and leasing companies are affiliates of banks.

The percentage of retail loans increased from 2002 to 2011. However, after 2011, this percentage decreased, partially due to regulations to control consumer spending (e.g., the introduction of limits on credit cards and consumer loans, higher risk weights on credit cards, and limitations on usage of instalments for certain product groups) and more recently the government's Credit Guarantee Fund, which provides collateral for loans, specifically to SMEs (totaling up to TRY 250 billion in guarantees in 2017). As of 2017, the majority of loans (77 %) were disbursed to corporate, commercial, and SME segment customers.

3.3.1 Evolution of Nonperforming Loan Balance

Turkey's growing lending market's NPL volume reached TRY 69.5 billion in 2017 (and stood at TRY 63.6 billion in 2016). The NPL ratio is within the lower group of select developed and developing economies. This is due to several factors: strong monitoring of banks by the BRSA following the 2001 crisis, the relatively low impact of the 2008–2009 global crisis on the Turkish banking sector, and the introduction of regulations supporting bank restructuring and recovery practices. Turkey's gross NPL balance has grown at 13 % per annum since 2002, which is lower than gross loan volume growth (26 %). The NPL balance YOY growth would have been 16 % if there had not been any NPL sales, which is still lower than loan volume growth.

3.3.2 NPL Balance Breakdown by Origination Channel

Similar to loans, the primary contributor to NPL volume is Turkey's banking sector, at 92 %, specifically the country's private banks (accounting for 70 % of total bank NPL volume in 2017). Furthermore, except in 2002, the gross bank NPL to loan volume ratio remained relatively stable within the 2.5–5 % band.

3.3.3 NPL Balance Breakdown by Asset Type

Looking at the NPL balance by asset type, the retail NPL share grew to over 30 % in 2011, driven by an increase in retail loan volume as well as flexible limits on credit card spending and the number of instalments. However, the retail NPL share decreased to 26 %, mainly due to stricter credit card regulations (e.g., limits on the number of instalments, limits on total spend), and more NPL sales for retail than corporate and SME.

3.3.4 Evolution of Nonperforming Loan Sales

NPL sale to AMCs began with the Savings Deposit Insurance Fund's transactions in 2004 and 2005, the purpose of which was to dispose of large sums of problematic loans which originated as a result of the 2001 banking crisis.

Following the introduction of the communique specific to AMCs in Turkey in November 2006, Turkish private banks and other financial institutions (e.g., leasing, factoring, and financing companies) started selling NPLs to AMCs in 2008.

Total NPL sales totaled approximately TRY 38 billion, with YOY growth of 20 % per annum between 2008 and 2017. NPL sales were above TRY 6 billion in 2014, when 22 private banks (including Tier 1 and 2 banks: Yapı ve Kredi, Akbank, İş Bankası, Garanti, TEB, Denizbank, and Finansbank) initiated auctions in that year. In the last 4 years (2014–2017), banks started selling their NPLs on a regular basis (except for 2015), contributing to the increasing NPL sales volume. The decrease in sales volumes in 2015 was mostly due to prices offered by AMCs not meeting the expectations of banks. Recovery expectations for AMCs were lower than usual, primarily due to preelection campaign pledges from political parties promising to erase or defer consumer credit debts. The largest NPL sales volume in terms of unpaid principal balance was in 2017. It totaled TRY 8.6 billion.

3.3.5 NPL Sales Breakdown by Asset Type

Historically, retail NPL sales have made up the majority (58 %) of total sales. This has been mostly due to:

- Lower average ticket size requiring a systematic approach to collection for financial institutions,
- The higher share of unsecured loans, hence lower recovery expectations of financial institutions, and
- The moral hazard problem for financial institutions (i.e., granting favorable terms to some borrowers may lead to a moral hazard among performing borrowers).

3.3.6 NPL Sales Prices Evolution

After trending upward from 2009 to 2013 (but not in the first year of sales in 2008) due to the introduction of new players and increased participation by AMCs in auctions, sales price ratios have declined from 15 % to 6.5 % (excluding transactions with publicly undisclosed UPBs and prices).

This decline is because of:

- Less intense competition due to exits and mergers of AMCs,
- Lower quality NPL portfolios sold by banks, and
- Increased funding costs of AMCs.

Examining the historic sales price trend in the market in detail highlights a number of facts: 2008 had a high sales price ratio because the NPL portfolio sold that year had a higher percentage of secured loans.

After 2013, the maturing NPL purchasing market experienced exits, mergers, and acquisitions within the competitive landscape, resulting in fewer players. In addition to these market developments, the decreasing quality of bank portfolios also contributed to the decline in sales prices.

The nonperforming loan outstanding balance is influenced by four drivers:

- NPL inflows: loans that attained NPL status during the period,
- NPL collection: banks and nonbank financial institutions collecting or seizing assets from NPL customers during the period,

- NPL write-off: banks and nonbank financial institutions writing-off uncollectible NPLs in line with the local regulations during the period, and
- NPL sales: bank and nonbank financial institutions selling part of their NPLs to AMCs during the period.

3.3.7 Projections for Sales of NPL Portfolios

For private bank and nonbank financial institution sales:

- In the macrobase scenario, we believe the aggregated volume of NPL sales will be similar to the average sales ratio of the past 4 years, 2014 to 2017 (2014 was the year when all the top nine private banks, in terms of cumulative sales volume, sold NPLs).
- In the macro-good scenario, where higher economic growth is assumed compared to the base scenario, we envisage financial institutions will sell at a lower volume due to lower NPL outstanding balances as well as lower NPL growth expectations. Hence, we base our sales forecasts on the average sales ratio of the past 3 years (2015 had a lower sales volume compared to the 2012–2014 interval).
- In the macro-conservative scenario, we envisage financial institutions will sell higher volumes compared to the base scenario due to higher overall NPL outstanding balances and higher NPL growth expectations. In this scenario, we assumed that sales will be similar to the average of the most recent 2 years, 2016 and 2017, when sales ratios were relatively high as the top nine private banks, in terms of cumulative sales volume, sold NPLs regularly.

For state-owned bank sales: There is still an uncertainty as to potential disposal of NPLs from state banks, since no sales were realized from these banks since the inception year of 2008.

On the other hand, with the assurance of legislation passed in 2017, envisaged state banks will commence sales in 2019 at the average historic sales ratio of private banks and nonbank finance firms. It is likely that they will prioritize retail NPL sales in the first few years for similar reasons to those of private banks which prefer selling retail NPLs over SME and corporate:

- Lower average ticket size requiring a systematic approach to collection,
- Higher share of unsecured loans, hence lower recovery expectations, and
- The moral hazard problem.

Since 2008, an NPL portfolio with a cumulative total of TRY 37.5 billion, in terms of UPB, has been sold.

We foresee that the upward trend in NPL sales, which occurred in the last 2 years, will continue in each of our three scenarios. The total NPL sales volume is expected to reach TRY 11.7–14.9 billion by 2020, growing at 11–20 % p.a. This estimate includes potential NPL sales of state banks in 2019 and 2020 (TRY 1.0 billion sales in both years).

Similar to total sales volumes, retail NPL sales are expected to continue increasing and reach TRY 6.2–8.5 billion by 2020, which represents 5–17 % p.a. growth (without state bank sales, retail NPL sales are expected to reach TRY 5.2–7.5 billion). SME and Corporate NPL sales are expected to reach TRY 5.5–6.5 billion by 2020, growing at 19–25 % p.a., primarily driven by increase of the SME and corporate NPL balance share within the gross NPL outstanding balance from 2017 to 2020.

4 Conclusion

With the effect of globalization, the needs of individuals and the search for finance have increased. In parallel with the developments in the world, consumption expenditures were easily funded when global and interdependent economies, financial markets, and financial expectations were good. However, when we look at the times, we have seen some disruptions in the return of banks' previously provided financing, which has left banks in a very difficult position in many respects. For example, while loans are a large asset item in a bank balance sheet, nonperforming loans within this asset item are higher than the acceptable amount, which adversely affects the bank's balance sheet and its position in the sector.

Another example is the provisions that should be legally reserved for nonperforming loans, which results in lower profitability and some of the shareholders' equity, as they are separated from profits and shareholders' equity. Banks cannot use the funds they allocate to finance new and high-return investments; they cannot transfer the resources they allocate to other areas.

In addition, the time it takes to keep track of these loans and the workforce to spend will be another difficult situation that will bring the workload to the bank outside of its own area of expertise.

The financial crises, political-economic uncertainty and instability and the increase in some undesirable situations like these, and the banks that continue their activities by dealing with the various risks that may pose a problem sufficiently meet these problems and the institutions and organizations concerned with the banking sector it was entered. First, measures were taken to tighten credit processes and policies within banks, to introduce risk management bodies and activities, to make national regulations such as these, and to take into account international regulations.

However, in the following periods, when the legal follow-up of the troubled loans could not be carried out effectively, and therefore the late collection or nonpayment of the loans and the effects of the nonperforming loans on the banks were taken into consideration, the need for the existence of specialized institutions was mentioned; and the AMC proposal emerged. When the AMCs started to deal with nonperforming loans, the banks that sell their problem loans to these institutions escalated the costs of these loans as well as strengthened their balance sheets by improving their asset quality, and provided the opportunity to invest in other areas where the loans they derive from the sale of nonperforming loans have been extended to loans or to be brought. This situation led to the removal of nonperforming loans from banks' balance sheets and increase of the amount of good assets and loans and assets of the sector.

AMCs provided the banking sector and markets with speed, fluidity, and durability and making banks to focus on their own activities by rescuing them from the follow-up costs for their troubled loans. In the case of restructuring of debts to customers with problematic loans, they provided the opportunity to pay a portion of their debts, not all of them.

In addition, AMCs have the practice of discounting the customer's debt in case they declare that they will pay the full amount of debt, and they can offer the loan customers the loans they have purchased with a certain discount at the flexibility they cannot offer.

AMCs, the legal basis of the AMCs operating in our country, the tax advantages, working methods and company structures of the sector's regulatory and supervisory authorities within the current economic situation and needs of both the AMCs and the borrowers of these organizations by taking into consideration the expectations of the credit customers. In the event that the borrowers use the opportunities and rights offered by the AMCs in accordance with the mutually agreed agreements, mutual trust, loyalty, and the loyalty of the corporations will be facilitated and they will be able to benefit effectively. It is thought that a functioning order will be provided. Thus, the trust in AMCs and the functioning of the sector will increase and AMCs will be able to work more easily and comfortably.

As a result, AMCs can recover their credit customers from their debts and their negative image in their financial identities by introducing the problematic loans and nonperforming credit customers that cannot find their place in economies, and they can collect the problem loans again.

Bibliography

Anastasiou, Dimitrious. (2016), Management and Resolution Methods of Non-performing Loans: A Review of the Literature, MPRA Paper Series, No. 77581.

Anastasiou, Dimitrious, Louri, Helen and Tsionas, Mike G. (2016), Non-performing Loans in the Euro Aera: Are Core Periphery Banking Markets Fragmented?, Bank of Greece Working Papers, December 2016.

BDDK. (2005), 5411 sayılı Bankacılık Kanunu, Retrieved from http://www.mevzuat.gov.tr/MevzuatMetin/1.5.5411.pdf, (12.03.2019).

BDDK. (2006), Varlık Yönetim Şirketlerinin Kuruluş ve Faaliyet Esasları Hakkındaki Yönetmelik, Retrieved from http://www.mevzuat.gov.tr/Metin.Aspx?MevzuatKod=7.5.10744&sourceXmlSearch=&MevzuatIliski=0, (14.03.2019).

BDDK. (2016), Kredilerin Sınıflandırılması ve Bunlar İçin Ayrılacak Karşılıklara İlişkin Usul ve Esaslar Hakkında Yönetmelik, Retrieved from http://www.mevzuat.gov.tr/Metin.Aspx?MevzuatKod=7.5.22599&MevzuatIliski=0&sourceXmlSearch=kredilerin%20sınıflandırılması, (20.03.2019).

Devjak, Srecko. (2018), "Modeling of Cash Flows from NonPerforming Loans in a Commercial Bank", Nase Gospodarstvo/Our Economy, Vol.64, N.4, pp. 3–9.

Güvenal, Hilmi. (2015), Varlık Yönetim Şirketlerinin Kredi Sistemindeki Yeri ve Tahsili Gecikmiş Alacakların Yönetimine Dair Düzenlemelerin Kredi Sistemine Etkisi, Retrieved from https://www.hayatvarlik.com/file/e50bec4e-cb48-4515-96c2-31793b95e618/pdf (14.06.2018).

Jassaud, Nadege and Kang, Kenneth H. (2015) "A strategy for developing a market for nonperforming loans in Italy", IMF Working Paper, WP /15/24.

Koç, Selahattin. (2010), "Finansal Yeniden Yapılandırma: İstanbul ve Anadolu Yaklaşımları, Sonuçları", Cumhuriyet Üniversitesi İktisadi ve İdari Bilimler Dergisi, Vol.11, N.1, pp. 35–55.

Lee, Junkyu and Rosenkranz, Peter. (2019), "Non-performing Loans in Asia: Determinants and Macrofinancial Linkages", Asian Development Bank Economics Working Paper Series, No. 574, March 2019.

Oy, Osman. (2009), Varlık Yönetim Şirketleri, İstanbul:Beta Basım Yayın.

PWC Reports. (2018), Turkish Purchasing Market, Overview and the Way Forward, Retrieved from https://www.pwc.com.tr/tr/sektorler/yatirim-yonetimi/turkiye-tahsilli-gecikmis-alacaklar-satis-piyasasi-raporu-final.pdf (01.05.2019).

Reid, David E. (2015a), "The Debt Buying Industry", Receivables Management Association International White Paper.

Reid, David E. (2015b), "Out of Statue Debt: What Is a Smart Balanced, and Responsible Approach?", Receivable Management Association International White Paper.

Selimler, Hüseyin. (2015), "Sorunlu Kredilerin Analizi, Banka Finansal Tablo ve Oranlarına Etkisinin Değerlendirilmesi", Finansal Araştırmalar ve Çalışmalar Dergisi, Vol.7, N.12, pp. 131–172.

Sipahi, Nihal. (2003) Problemli Kredilerin Yeniden Yapılandırılması Uluslararası Uygulamalar ve Türkiye Örneği (Uzmanlık Tezi), TCMB Bankacılık ve Finansal Kuruluşlar Genel Müdürlüğü, Ankara.

TCMB. (2001), Türkiye'nin Güçlü Ekonomiye Geçiş Programı, Retrieved from https://www.tcmb.gov.tr/wps/wcm/connect/26640b7b-9641-4c35-99ec-cd10a9d4e51b/program.pdf?MOD=AJPERES&CACHEID=ROOTWORKSPACE-26640b7b-9641-4c35-99ec-cd10a9d4e51b-m3fB7oF

VYŞD. (2019), Varlık Yönetim Şirketleri Derneği, Retrieved from http://www.varlikyonetim.org.tr, (10.02.2019).

Woo, David. (2000), "Two Approaches to Resolving Nonperforming Assets During Financial Crises", International Monetary Fund (IMF) Working Paper, WP/00/33.

Assist. Prof. Dr. Hakan Özcan

Turkish Insurance Market

Abstract: Insurance companies are now an economic unit helping people to cope with the damages that may be caused by risk factors and directing that help systematically in line with the laws, and the customs of the industry depending on the structural features of societies. The liberalization trend observed in the economy after 1980 took its hold on the insurance industry as well. The industry witnessed some arrangements directed at liberalization beginning from the late 1980s.When we look at the development of the insurance industry, which is the most important corporate investment organ of financial markets in Turkey, we see that our private insurance industry was stuck in a stable structure for long years and unable to create a significant source for financial markets (particularly capital markets). In other words, the funds created by private insurance industry remains in very small quantities at the global scale. Turkey has indeed always ranked at the bottom in global terms in comparison to other countries both in terms of the premium production and per capita premium and premium/GNP ratio.

Keywords: Turkey, Insurance, Liberalisation

1 Introduction

Insurance is a system not based on production of any goods, covering economic activities and transactions and aiming at making good any possible losses by joining forces against the dangers that people may encounter. For the insurance industry, 1980s come to the fore as the years when the relative control of the State on the industry decreased and the liberalization movements started in the industry. Turkish Insurance industry was also influenced by these developments and achieved a growth. However, it is well known that this development remained at a lower level compared to the other financial sectors. One of the most significant indicators of this development is the share of the production of insurance premium in GNP and the production of per capita insurance premium. The production of premium which was $1 billion in the 1980s increased to 12 billion dollars in 2018. Again in the same period, per capita production of insurance premium reached from $10 to $149. The share of the production of insurance premium in GNP increased from 0.5 % to 1.5 %. Increases were also observed in the employment figures and number of insurance agents. The number of people employed in the insurance companies increased from 9,000 to 15,000 and the number of agents from 10,000 to 20,000. New business partners joined the industry as a result of the regulations introduced particularly after 2017.

2 Insurance and the Concept of Risk

The phenomenon of insurance first came into being with the idea that people must unite against the risks that they encounter and may encounter and consequently distribute the losses, which they would otherwise have to endure on their own, among themselves. It has later passed through significant stages within the course of time. Developments in the insurance industry have brought about the function of saving or investable funds and increasingly gained prominence. Uncertainty means the inability to anticipate the outcome of an incident or not knowing the general impact of the factors which have an impact on the outcome of the incident on the outcome. Risk may be defined as the probability of occurrence of loss or occurrence of an undesired incident. If the probability of the occurrence of an incident is 10 % and its probability of nonoccurrence is 90 %, we may say that the ratio of a certainty in this case is not very high. Uncertainty is at the highest level when the two possibilities are equal (Blanchard, 1965:1).

Insurance companies are now an economic unit helping people to cope with the damages that may be caused by risk factors and directing that help systematically in line with the laws, and the customs of the industry depending on the structural features of societies. In other words, insurance companies do not eliminate the risks but try to eliminate negative impacts of risk on the policy holder with the contribution of other policy holders. As the insurance companies provide service in return for premium, it is possible to consider benefiting from insurance services as a behavior of individuals to preclude the potential losses that they may incur in the future which are difficult to endure, with the help of affordable costs (Erdoğan, 1993:5).

2.2 Functions of Insurance

We see that insurance has numerous social and economic functions.

2.2.1 Insurance Provides Security in Economic and Social Life both for Individuals and Institutions

Insurance provides the opportunity to live, work, and the ability to start new businesses without fear of the potential risks that the future may bring along. Individuals and institutions feel themselves secure in economic and social life in this way.

2.2.2 Bolsters Financial Stability and Effectiveness of the Financial System

Insurance provides assurance for the lives, health, properties, and financial assets of individuals and institutions and thus helps creation of a financially stable environment. Furthermore, it also contributes to reducing transaction costs, provision of liquidity, and creation of a scale economy. Companies do not have to allocate large-scale funds for the risks they incur thanks to insurance and consequently can transfer their resources to production and investment more easily.

2.2.3 Develops Savings, Creates Funds and Contributes to Formation of Capital

Life insurances and similar insurances contribute to the development of savings because they are long-term insurances. Furthermore, premiums collected by the insurance companies generate big funds, which are in turn used for investments.

2.2.4 Supports Entrepreneurs and Trade and Maintains Business Continuity

Insurance contributes to the development of trade and industry, creation of new business opportunities and employment. Production of many products and services depends on the assurance provided by insurance.

2.2.5 Helps Extending Loan

Neither industry nor trade may be considered without loans. Rights of the creditors are better secured, and it becomes easier to obtain a loan if the assets to be pledged for a loan are insured. Furthermore, it is also important for the banks that the borrowers take out a life insurance policy.

2.2.6 Alleviates the Pressure on the Social Security Programs

Life insurances and private pension system in particular fulfills a complementary role for the social security programs of the State which require large amount of expenditures. For example, the private pension system contributes to the social security system by means of additional payments for retirement, and consequently the State budget is relieved of the pressure.

2.2.7 Maintains Peace and Confidence in the Society

Insurance maintains peace and confidence in the society by forestalling social and economic problems and losses that may arise out of occurrence of the risks like death, fire, natural disasters, disability, etc.

2.2.8 Develops International Relationships

Success of insurance depends on its ability to spread as extensive as possible. Insurance companies may ensure participation of a wider community in the risk by opening branches in foreign countries or entering into reinsurance contracts with the companies in foreign countries.

2.2.9 Ensures More Efficient Management of Risks

Risks are more easily measured, managed, and transferred thanks to insurance. Insurers predict potential damage levels against the probability of occurrence of the risk and determine the premiums accordingly. Likewise, insurers take the necessary measures in order to pay less premiums and incur the minimum amount of damage when the risk occurs (SEGEM, 2015).

3 Turkish Society and Insurance

The concept of insurance means that individuals secure themselves in advance against the prospective losses and damages that they deem possible. The possibility that the individuals do not get in trouble during the insurance period and consequently the money they have paid for insurance shall be retained by the insurance company induce them to obtain unfair advantages from the insurance companies. This phenomenon of deriving unfair benefit becomes even more important in the societies where insurance is not accepted as a need and the insurance companies run after clients. The possibility that they will never recover the premiums they paid induces some policy holders to commit frauds.

People from all income levels of the society consider favorably claiming more than justifiable indemnities from the insurance companies or claiming the existence of damages not actually existing. One of the foremost reasons for this attitude is the difficulty to prove insurance frauds.

Furthermore, in cases where the dispute is referred to the court, decisions are given generally in favor of the policyholder due to the difficulty to disprove his/her claims. On the other hand, examination of fraud incidents by governmental bodies consists of a totally legal transaction. It is possible to carry out the transactions by taking many documents just based on the statement of the policyholder. The fact that the individuals who commit insurance fraud do not lose their social prestige and the absence of any legal sanction may even induce decent people into negative behavior.

The view of Turkish society on insurance may be summarized under the following headings:

1. Traditional fatalism
2. Insurance is expensive
3. Insurers do not pay
4. High level of feeling of confidence
5. Negligence (Özcan, 2018b).

4 Historical Development of Insurance Industry in Turkey

Significant developments took place especially in the commercial life of the Ottoman Empire in the 19th century. This development triggered change in the lifestyle in all areas from architecture to consumption habits. Many goods from Europe were sold especially in the capital Istanbul. The need for insurance was not a current issue in Istanbul until the big fire broke out in Istanbul Pera in 1870. However, Istanbul Pera was the center of commercial life during that period, and the world of finance in particular was controlled by foreigners. The financial market was frightened by this big fire and consequently an insurance system became a current issue to provide security against risks. Three English companies, namely Sun, Northern, and North British, launched operations in the insurance industry in 1872 for the first time in our country. Eleven insurance companies were operating as agents in our country as of 1899. These companies were operating within the boundaries of the Ottoman Empire, especially in Istanbul based on the instructions they receive from their head offices, and issuing their policies in English and French. They were appointing the courts of London or the courts of the place of their head offices as the competent courts with sole jurisdiction in case of dispute, canceling policies and divesting the insurance contacts whenever they wanted. Many insurance companies made money hand over fist, and insurance ethics corrupted with the impact of capitulations (Erdoğan, 1993). The first insurance company founded in the Ottoman State was Osmanlı Umum Sigorta Şirketi founded with the partnership of Ottoman Bank, a foreign capital bank and Tobacco Administration. Insurance agent business of the company was carried out by the branches of the Ottoman Bank and Tobacco Administration.

Significant initiatives were taken to develop the national insurance business both at the legal and institutional levels during the years following the proclamation of the Republic. Türkiye İş Bankası had started to be interested in insurance business along with the banking operations. The bank expanded its operations which had begun as a bank agency and later founded Anadolu Sigorta, which was the first national insurance company of that period. Almost all the Turkish insurance companies founded during that period had foreign partners. In 1929, the company Milli Reasürans was founded as a partnership of Türkiye İş Bankası, Milli Sigorta, and Company Suisse de Reasassurance. Milli Reasürans was founded for the purpose of setting the grounds and paving the way for nationalization of insurance business, making savings in foreign currency in order to retain the insurance premiums in the country and for bringing in revenue to the Treasury. Furthermore, another goal pursued by founding insurance companies was to create monopolies in order to bring in revenues for the State, reduce the domination of foreign companies in the insurance industry, and for being used as means of social and economic policies of the government. Inclusion of motor vehicles into the scope of Compulsory Accident Insurance beginning from 1953 played an important role in the development of insurance.

One of the foremost developments achieved in the 1950s in terms of the insurance industry was the law on the supervision of insurance companies numbered 7397 passed in 1959. This law prescribed the supervision of all kinds of operations of the insurance companies and production instruments by a board formed by insurance specialists and further prohibited price reductions for the purpose of precluding competition, which is not in harmony with the insurance technique and content, puts the rights and interests of the policyholder into risk, and weakens the financial structures of insurance companies. The general conditions of insurance and price tariff were regulated by the Ministry of Trade for the purpose of standardization of the general insurance conditions in order to ensure application of the same general conditions for all companies instead of different conditions changing from one company to another based on the price tariff. This law aimed at ensuring and sustaining the trustworthy features of insurance companies and the adequacy of their financial and technical structures, and organizing the operations of insurance agents and specialists on a professional level (Temur, 2007:6).

A glance at the period of planned economic development shows that there has been an increase in the premium production in the insurance industry. We see that there was a tendency towards increase in the premium production of in real terms, albeit in a small amount. However, the share of the premiums produced in GNP vary between 5 % and 6 %. The number of the insurance companies was about 38 along with the implementation of the decision of the development plan directed at keeping the number of insurance companies constant during that period. This situation affected competition negatively and was reflected in the insurance industry as low development rate in the annual growth speed of premium production. The average annual growth rate of the insurance industry in real terms during 1963–1983 planned period was 6.6 %. We see that the growth rate remained low in comparison to especially the growth figures achieved in the post-1980 period. Average annual growth rate of the industry approached 15 % in real terms in the period 1980–1991 and a growth rate of approximately 10 % was achieved in the period 1991–1996 despite the economic crisis of 1994.

5 Industry in the Post-1980 Period

For the insurance industry, 1980s come to the fore as the years when the relative control of the State on the industry decreased and the liberalization movements started in the industry. The liberalization trend observed in the economy after 1980 took its hold on the insurance industry as well. The industry witnessed some arrangements directed at liberalization beginning from the late 1980s. Some problems inherent in the Social Security System also provided various opportunities to the private insurance business. These problems covering a wide range of issues from collection of social security premiums to the regulations on retirement age have expanded the area of the private insurance business.

The regulations directed at liberalization during the process of ensuring harmonization with the EU at the industry level and intensified in the late 1980s include: setting free the foundation of new insurance companies, regulations directed at foreign companies, regulations directed at updating the capital of companies, transition to the free tariff system, separation between life and nonlife branches, and new regulations concerning the Agents.

Entry of new companies into the insurance industry was prohibited due to the principle decision taken during the planned economy period between 1968 and 1984, and only the foundation of a few numbers of new insurance companies was allowed during those 16 years. The interest of the domestic and foreign capital in the insurance industry tended to increase, and the number of insurance companies increased two to three fold along with the permission of foundation of new companies by the Treasury beginning from the mid-1980s.

5.1 Transition to Free Tariff in 1990

The Turkish insurance industry adopted the free tariff system in May 1990. This system granted the insurance companies the right to apply free premium, excluding life insurances and compulsory insurances. Some arrangements regarding relationships of the insurance companies with their agents were also introduced in order to allow the insurance companies to collect premiums in due time. Various arrangements have been made for this purpose. This regulation aimed at transferring premiums to the companies at the intended time, and important sanctions were imposed on the agent-policy holder-company chain by making amendments on the article 1297 of the Turkish Commercial Law in 1.1.1995.

5.2 Increase of Premium Production in the Industry

Significant increases were achieved in premium productions in real terms during the post-1980 period, which was reflected in the average annual growth rates. For example, the sector premium production showed an increase of 21.5 %, 37.1 %, 32.3 %, and 25.7 % in 1982, 1985, 1990, and 1993, respectively. The average annual growth rate of the sector premium production was 14.7 % during the period 1981 to 1990, quite exceeding the average annual growth rate of the service sector for the same period (5.7 %). Growth rate of the premium production dropped to 8.7 % along with the crisis of 1994. Under the impact of this outcome, the average annual growth rate of the real sector became 9–8 % during the period 1991 to 1996. Notwithstanding the negative developments, it is obvious that the industry achieved an increase in the real sector premium production by years. However, when we have a look at the shares of the premiums produced in the service sector in GNP, we see that it only reached 1 % after the 1990s, which is indicating that the industry still failed producing sufficient amount of premium (Kazgan, 2008).

6 Insurance Law

6.1 An Overview of the Insurance Law

The Turkish Insurance industry is regulated by the insurance law no. 5684 passed in 2007. Insurance Law no. 5684 repealed the Insurance Supervision Law no. 7397. One of the foremost developments giving rise to the drafting of the Insurance Law no. 5684 was the developments in the Turkish economy and the process of integration with the global economy. The importance of the insurance industry and of the insurance companies in the financial sector has increased even more during the course of time, but the Law no. 7397 became incapable of meeting the needs of the industry and could not adapt itself to the developing structure of the industry. Furthermore, emergence of the need to harmonize the Turkish insurance legislation with the norms and insurance directives of the European Union in the process of harmonization with the European Union has also been a factor accelerating adoption of a new law. The objectives of the law no. 5684 may be listed as follows:

- Ensure development of insurance activities in our country,
- Protection of the rights and interests of individuals who are a party to insurance contracts, and
- Introduce arrangements concerning real and legal entities subject to the law in order to ensure safe and stable operation of the industry.

6.2 Structure of the Law

The law is a framework law. First, the main principles were determined and the details were left to the secondary legislation. It was aimed to ensure adaptation of legal regulations to the dynamic structure of the industry without delay. As a matter of the structure of the Turkish legal system, the regulations made in the laws like the Turkish Commercial Law, Law of Obligations and Enforcement and Bankruptcy Law were transferred to the insurance law.

6.3 The Scope of the Law

The operations of the insurance companies, reinsurance companies, Insurance Association of Turkey, intermediaries (agents and brokers), insurance experts, and actuaries operating in Turkey is regulated by the Law numbered 5684.

Social security institutions, Export Credit Bank of Turkey, and other establishments engaged in the insurance business according to special laws are not under the scope of the Law numbered 5684 (excluding the provisions on supervision).

6.4 Novelties Introduced by the Law for the Insurance and Reinsurance Companies

- Implementation of capital adequacy and minimum guarantee funds were introduced.
- Technical provisions were rearranged and additional technical provisions were introduced.
- The situations accepted as the weakness of financial structures were explained in more detail. Coverage system has been rearranged. Price tariffs were set free in principle.
- Establishment of an internal audit system is compulsory for the companies.

6.5 Other Novelties Introduced by the Law

- An arbitration system was introduced for the purpose of facilitating settlement of the disputes between the policyholder and the insurance company more easily.
- Insurance Training Center (SEGEM) was established for the purpose of regulating the insurance-related exams and meeting the training needs in this area.
- Council of Ministers was allowed to make the insurances other than liability insurances also compulsory.

- A separation was made between the administrative fine and judicial fine, and the new Turkish Penal Code and Misdemeanor Law were taken into consideration in the new regulations.
- Amendments were made on the organization of the Association of Insurance, Reinsurance and Pension Companies (Insurance Association of Turkey) and procedures for membership to the Association.
- The nonlife insurance companies were required to employ an actuary (SEGEM, 2015).

7 Changes in the Industry After 1980

We observe that the developments of the industry had a more stable structure between 1980 and 2000. The main change and movement started beginning from the year 2000 and accelerated after the insurance law was passed in 2007.

In 2000, 68 insurance companies were operating in the industry and 15 of them were foreign-capital companies. There were 13,567 insurance agents working with the insurance companies and 9,715 employees working in these companies. The amount of premium production was $5 billion and the share of the foreign-capital companies in production was 17 %. The amount of per capita premium production was $25 (ISB, 2000).

In 2005, 52 insurance companies were operating in the industry and 20 of them were foreign-capital companies. There were 14,453 insurance agents working with the insurance companies and 12,837 employees working in these companies. The amount of premium production was $6.9 billion, and the share of the foreign-capital companies in production was 30 %. The amount of per capita premium production was $77 (ISB, 2005).

In 2010, 58 insurance companies were operating in the industry and 43 of them were foreign-capital companies. There were 16,029 insurance agents working with the insurance companies and 16,205 employees in these companies. The amount of premium production was $9.2 billion and the share of the foreign-capital companies in production was 58 %. The amount of per capita premium production was $125 (ISB, 2010).

In 2015, 60 insurance companies were operating in the industry and 43 of them were foreign-capital companies. There were 19,311 insurance agents working with the insurance companies and 15,195 employees in these companies. The amount of premium production was $11.1 billion, and the share of the foreign-capital companies in production was 65 %. The amount of per capita premium production was $141 (ISB, 2015).

In 2017, 62 insurance companies were operating in the industry and 44 of them were foreign-capital companies. There were 19,883 insurance agents working with the insurance companies and 15,832 employees in these companies. The amount of premium production was $12.1 billion, and the share of the foreign-capital companies in production was 60 %. The amount of per capita premium production was $149 (ISB, 2017).

8 Foreign Capital Inflow

Insurance activities occupy an important place in the financial sector. One of the most important functions of the insurance business is to distribute and reduce risk by transferring it. Transactions made in relation to economic issues involve risk factor most of the time. For that reason, one of the main economic functions of insurance companies is to take over the risk for a price determined based on a risk analysis. Another important function of insurance is the generation of funds. Insurance industry introduces the collected premiums to the economy through various investment instruments. These funds generated by the insurance industry are directed to investments in rational areas. The share and role of the insurance industry in the financial sector in Turkey is rapidly increasing in parallel to the number of insurance companies.

While the ratio of the total amount of premiums produced in the Turkish insurance industry to GNP varies between 1 % and 1.5 %, it is between 5 % and 10 % in the EU countries and many other developed countries. In other words, the insurance industry in Turkey is a significant market with growth potential and attracts attention of foreign capital as such. The Turkish insurance industry has a significant growth potential for the future despite it still being under the expected level in terms of size of balance sheet. Turkey puts forth its growth potential in the process of harmonization with the EU insurance industry with its young population structure, increase in the per capita income, increasing interest of foreign capital in its globalized financial sector, and the low level of use of policy in the Turkish insurance industry and the newly offered insurance products. Furthermore, financial structures of the companies have strengthened, disputes have been resolved more rapidly, and consequently flexibility and security have been achieved in respect of the expansion of the industry along with the new insurance law passed in June 2007. It may be said that the increase in the share of foreign capital in the industry will increase the productivity and contribute to the corporate development and competition of companies and to more rapid growth of the industry along with the increase of their financial instruments. Potential effects of the foreign capital tending towards the Turkish insurance industry may be evaluated with respect to their positive and negative aspects based on theoretical infrastructures. When we first have a look at the positive aspects of the foreign capital in the Turkish insurance industry, we may say that its ability to provide additional financial means as a solution for the problem of scarcity of sources suffered by the industry is important. The investments in the industry may increase along with the increased savings. These investments may either be in the form of increase in product diversity and service quality or increase in the quality of the actives of the insurance companies. The need for labor force increasing along with the growth of the industry contributes positively to the recruitment of labor force in the industry and creates new jobs. Furthermore, qualified and specialized labor force coming in along with the foreign capital may contribute to increasing the technological and management knowledge in the industry by transferring accumulation of knowledge to those working in the industry. In this context, technological novelties may be introduced to the insurance industry by the companies with a high market share by realizing technology transfers through license agreements, technical publications, trainings, and various communication channels. The incoming foreign capital may have an increasing effect on the foreign trade volume by facilitating the foreign trade thanks to the high credit rating and ability to provide high level of security for the insurance companies. This may also be expected to have a positive impact on the balance of payments. The foreign capital directed towards the insurance industry may also increase the tax revenues in the country thanks to its efficient and effective operations. The interest towards the Turkish insurance industry is increasing every day (Tanınmış et al., 2011). However, the number of foreign capital entering the industry through mergers and acquisitions and reorganization has begun to slow down starting from 2017. The share of foreign companies in the total premium production dropped to 60 % in 2017 from 65 % in 2016.

9 Conclusion

Insurance is an economic service covering economic activities and transactions, not based on production of any goods, but based on the principle of joining forces and sharing the losses that may arise from the dangers that people may encounter or have already encountered. And the entities operating for the purpose of providing such an important service by covering the losses and damages that may be caused by the risks that may occur are called insurance companies. Insurance companies regulate and ensure management of various relationships within the society. Besides their services aiming at recovering the economic losses, they direct the funds created by the premiums that they collect to various investments in order to contribute to the economy and development of the country. They also contribute to the development of the capital markets by investing those funds in investment instruments like stocks, bills and bonds, etc. On the other hand, participation of insurance companies in the capital markets primarily depends on the ability of the insurance industry to create funds that may be transferred to those markets. In the developed economies in particular, the insurance industry has been the driving force behind the economy of the country with the funds and investments they create. The funds accumulated in the insurance companies reach big figures to the extent they shape the national economy in the developed countries in particular. Consequently, the insurance companies become able to finance limited number of investments with a considerable size all over the world, and they even have a capacity to provide long-term credit facilities to the developing countries. Furthermore, the confidence factor provided by the basic function of insurance (providing assurance) in these developed countries to the country and national economy is more conspicuous, and the insurance enhances the general welfare level of people.

When we look at the development of the insurance industry, which is the most important corporate investment organ of the financial markets in Turkey, we see that our private insurance industry was stuck in a stable structure for long years and unable to create a significant source for financial markets (particularly capital markets). In other words, the funds created by private insurance industry remains in very small quantities at the global scale. Turkey has indeed always ranked at the bottom in global terms in comparison to other countries both in terms of the premium production and per capita premium and premium/GNP ratio. As a result, we see that the insurance companies acting as an intermediary institution regarding the realization of the savings forming the basis of accumulation of capital and transformation thereof (funds) to investments through the capital markets have been unable to fulfill this function in Turkey effectively. It comes out that the Turkish private insurance industry is not very effective in the capital markets even if the whole amount of funds (direct premium production) created in the insurance industry was transferable to the capital market. Consequently, the possibility for the insurance sector to take its place in the capital markets in the Western sense primarily depends on increasing the direct premium production which serves as a basis for creating sources for funds. In other words, the share of direct premium production in GNP must be raised to the level of 5 % to 6 % from its current level of around 1.5 %, if not to the levels in the developed countries.

For that purpose, it is of great importance for our country to take necessary measures and introduce incentives aiming at creating an effective insurance industry so that the private insurance industry is able to:

- Create funds for the economy,
- Bring in foreign currency,
- Be encouraging, and
- Ensure security and stability.

The insurance industry is a part of the financial sector which achieved a significant development particularly as a result of the liberal economic policies implemented after the 1980s in our country. Indeed, the insurance industry has a very small share in GNP, but it becomes an important industry, a candidate to make a breakthrough comparable to the one realized by the banking sector in the past. The insurance industry has been affected the most by the recent acceleration in privatization and company sales in Turkey. The Turkish insurance companies were generally founded as affiliates of banks or big companies, and the size of a considerable part of them has remained in small scales due to undercapitalization compared to their precedents in the world. Consequently, the Turkish insurance companies have attracted the highest level of interest from foreign investors with their suitable prices during the process of foreign expansion in the economy. The Turkish insurance industry has a small share as 1.70 in GNP, and its annual per capita premium production is around $145. This share in GNP reaches approximately 8 % in many Western countries, and the annual per capita premium production exceeds $1,000 in some Western countries. The Turkish economy aims at attaining the European Union norms and has a continuously growing dynamic structure. That is why the Turkish economy and the Turkish insurance industry attract the interests of foreign insurance companies. It was believed that the productions and profits of insurance companies would increase in a short time along with the development of the insurance industry which is expected to grow without much additional effort due to the need for insurance estimated to emerge parallel to the economic growth. Foreign companies coming to Turkey through acquisitions or mergers based on their confidence in the economic stability in the country have acquired 2/3 of the capital of Turkish companies operating in the Turkish insurance industry as of 2017. The distance taken by the insurance industry with an ever-increasing importance as explained above has increased, and the structure of employment in the companies operating in the industry has expanded parallel to that development. The insurance industry has become a business field that concerns minimum 100,000 employees, including the agent network, insurance experts, and the employees working in the enterprises providing service to the industry.

Bibliography

Blanchard, Ralph H. (1965), **Risk and Insurance**, Lincoln: University of Nebraska Press.

Erdoğan, İ. (1993), **Attitude against Voluntary Insurance Service**, İstanbul: Beta Publications.

ISB. (2000), **Insurance Supervisory Board, Official Statistics, Report for 2000**, Ankara.

ISB. (2005), **Insurance Supervisory Board, Official Statistics, Report for 2005**, Ankara.

ISB. (2010), **Insurance Supervisory Board, Official Statistics, Report for 2010**, Ankara.

ISB. (2015), **Insurance Supervisory Board, Official Statistics, Report for 2015**, Ankara.

ISB. (2017), **Insurance Supervisory Board, Official Statistics, Report for 2017**, Ankara.

Kazgan, H. (2008), **Koç Allianz: 75 Years Old Insurer of Our Republic**. İstanbul: Koç Allianz Publications.

Özcan, H. (2018a), **Damage Management**, İstanbul: AUZEF Istanbul University Publications.

Özcan, H. (2018b), **Insurance Frauds and Abuses**, İstanbul: Kriter Publications.

Özcan, H. (2018c), **Agent-Company Relationships in the Insurance Sector**, İstanbul: Kriter Publications.

SEGEM (Insurance Training Center). (2015), **Agent Technical Personnel Lecture Notes,** İstanbul: Insurance Training Center Publications.

Tanınmış, B., Akpınar, Ö., and Okay, G. (2011), **Potential Impacts of the Share of Foreign Capital on Turkish Insurance Industry: An Assessment from EU Perspective**, Marmara University European Community Institute, Vol.19, No.1, pp. 53–75.

Temur, A. (2007), **Employment in Insurance Industry** (PhD Thesis), Istanbul University, Istanbul

Assist. Prof. Dr. Hazar Dördüncü

Crisis and Development of Financial Markets in Turkey After 1980

Abstract: Since the 1980s, Turkey entered a period of economic stability policies, on the one hand, and an exit from an inward-looking economic structure of the import substitution type, on the other. The liberalization process led to serious transformation in many areas in the early periods. In this process, which started in the 1980s, the aim was to open the economy to foreign competition, to liberalize the determination of exchange rates and interest rates, to liberalize capital movements, and to implement many structural reforms, in particular privatization, to make the economy more productive according to the optimization principles. Although the policies followed in the period between 1980 and 1990 were essentially stable, there were some ups and downs from time to time. In the 1990s, the country's economy was affected by high chronic inflation and unbalanced growth. Inflation reduced the purchasing power of money and caused uncertainties in economic and social life. Due to the financing of high budget deficits, real interest rates increased and the domestic debt burden has become unsustainable as a result of frequent domestic borrowing. After the bumpy 1980s and 1990s, in the 2000s, an export-oriented, technology-intensive, and high-value-added production structure that complies with international standards and mobilizes local resources has gained importance.

Keywords: Financial Market, Capital Market, Turkish Economy

1 Financial Market

The market is where buyers and sellers interact and exchange goods, services, and money. Stock exchanges, which are the places where investors traded in physical or electronic environment and traded in the framework of certain rules, in which the supply and demand are met by processing, are the most suitable examples for the financial market concept.

Markets are divided into two as real markets and financial markets. Real markets are the markets where goods and services are faced by supply and demand. While financial markets are the markets in which the documents which are qualified as financial assets are bought and sold. The concept of financial market includes the fund suppliers, fund seekers, institutions that regulate fund flows, instruments, and equipment that provide the flow and the legal and administrative rules that regulate them. If there is a need to open up more, the transfer of funds through intermediary institutions is realized between those who have excess savings and those who are in need of debt. Each country has an organization that controls and regulates the financial market system. In Turkey, this organization is Capital Markets Board (CMB). It is possible to divide these markets into two where small and large investors benefit, while at the same time, the companies that want to develop are able to meet the resources they need for return and fixed assets investments; money market and capital market (Sermaye Piyasası Kurulu Uzmanları et al., 2017).

1.1 Money Market

Money markets, which can be considered as the sub-markets of the financial market, can be defined as markets where short-term funding supply and demand are met. The highlight of such markets is that they consist of short-term funds, which generally do not exceed one year. Funds provided through money markets, which bring short-term liquidity surpluses and liquidity deficits, are evaluated in order to finance the current assets of the enterprises.

In Turkey, there are three forms of work and money market trading volumes ranging from:

- Central Bank Market,
- Interbank Market, and
- Takasbank Market.

We can list the instruments subject to money markets as follows:

- Treasury Bond
- Bank Bonds
- Repo/Reverse Repo
- Financing Bonds
- Bank Guaranteed Bills

1.2 Capital Market

In the capital markets, financial assets with a maturity of more than one year are traded. The loans obtained from these markets are mostly used to finance the major fixed assets of the enterprises such as buildings, machinery, and equipment. As in the money market, resources in these markets are savings. In the capital market, fund owners may purchase the documents from the first issuance or second hand. This gives rise to two basic groups: the Primary Market and the Secondary Market:

Primary Market: Securities that are circulated in the market for the first time are traded in these markets. In primary markets, they can come together directly or through a brokerage firm with securities issuers.

Secondary Market: The secondary market is the market in which the securities which are not new, bought and sold before, are processed. The secondary market, which increases the liquidity of securities, thus creates demand for the primary market and contributes to its development.

Capital market instruments can be listed as follows:

- Share certificates
- Government securities
- Investment fund participation shares
- Private sector bonds
- The usufruct of participation
- Income partnership
- Act profit–loss partnership documents
- Real estate certificate
- Asset-backed securities
- Eurobonds (Matriksdata, 2014; Morgül, 2013; Keser, 2015)

2 Financial Markets in Turkey (Before 1980)

Turkey had a closed and tightly regulated economy model before 1980. It had an import substitution industrialization policy (Karabıçak, 2000). Before 1980, the economy had three basic problems. These were:

- Inflation caused by high demand,
- Reduced international competitiveness due to high cost, and
- Noninvestment due to low savings.

3 January 24, 1980, Decisions and Financial Liberalization Process

When we look at the economic stabilization program implemented in Turkey's economy, it is observed that firstly the short-term goal is taken into account; and it can be considered that there were no liberal policies then. However, when looking at the decisions of January 24, short-term goals have been set, but especially towards long-term goals. Especially the measures that were put into effect between 1980 and 1983 and determined within the framework of the stand-by agreement signed with the IMF were as follows:

- Reduction of money supply and free interest,
- The high devaluation of the Turkish lira,
- Reducing the public expenditures, reducing the budget deficit,
- Giving the authority to raise the state economic enterprises to close their deficits,
- Minimization of subsidies and reduction of price controls,
- Flexible exchange rate, daily exchange rate application,
- Taking measures to accelerate the entry of foreign capital,
- Continuous support for exports (tax, cheap credit, and foreign exchange facilities) while encouraging export-based industrialization.

These measures, which encourage anti-inflationary and outward opening, have started to give positive results since the beginning of 1981. Also in 1981, the private sector had two new applications. The Central Bank announced the daily exchange rate since April 30. On July 30, the Capital Market Law entered into force. As targeted in the January 24th stabilization program, the rate of increase in money supply was reduced in the first 3 years. The use of the Central Bank loans in comparison to previous years was effective. With the start of the creation of resources through the banks system, the public sector started to leave its place to the private sector. As a result of the implementation of the decisions, we see a relative decline in inflation. The inflation rate, which was 107.2 % in 1980, decreased to 36 % in 1981 and to 25.2 % in 1982. It can be said that the decisions were effective on the inflation rate for the first 2 years. Turkey carried out simultaneous stabilization and financial liberalization policies in the years 1980–1983.

Interest rates were released, so they were determined by several large banks. Tight monetary policies and competition from bankers led to small banks entering the race of interest. The real interest rates that were negative due to the ceilings applied until the 1980s turned positive and significantly increased as shown in Tab. 1. But soon after this arrangement, large banks came together to decide on a common interest rate to prevent interest rates from rising above a certain level. Another liberalization in line with financial liberalization was that banks and some holdings established intermediary institutions and sold their deposit certificates by discounting them. This decision, which contributed to the formation of the brokerage institution, provided the basis for the emergence of an unhealthy financial structure and brought bankruptcies (Oktayer, 2009).

Finally, in 1982, Turkey experienced its first financial crisis of the liberalization; most bankers and a few small banks went bankrupt. Following the crisis, a fluctuating course on the determination of interest rates occurred between banks and Central Bank.

Tab. 1: Interest Rates (%) Between 1980 and 1989 (*Turkish State Planning Institute, 2001*)

	Saving Deposit Interest Rates	Interest Rates on Central Bank Discount	Interbank Overnight Interest Rates
1980	33.0	26.0	*
1981	35.0	31.50	*
1982	50.0	31.50	*
1983	45.0	48.5	*
1984	45.0	52.0	*
1985	55.0	52.0	*
1986	48.0	48.0	39.09
1987	58.0	45.0	42.36
1988	89.9	54.0	46.77
1989	58.8	54.0	26.87

In 1982, opening a foreign exchange bank account was allowed. In 1983/1984 foreign trade was largely liberalized. In 1984, foreign exchange transactions were partially liberalized.

In 1985, the Central Bank launched public paper auctions. In 1986, the Central Bank opened the Interbank money market. The target was to meet the short-term liquidity requirement of the banking system and to reduce the demand for Central Bank resources. The stock market was opened in 1986. In 1987, the Central Bank started the open market operations and opened the foreign exchange market.

Between 1981 and 1988, Turkey was at the first stage of the liberalization program. The second phase started with the liberalization of foreign capital inflows in 1989. In 1989 the Decree No. 32 led the foreign exchange regime to be fully liberalized. In 1989, capital movements were liberalized. The Turks began to buy foreign papers, and foreigners were able to buy local papers.

In this first period, export incentive policies are in the forefront. These policies used both foreign exchange and direct export subsidies.

3.1 Regulations Regarding Exchange Rate

In the financial liberalization process, the second step regarding the emphasis on market-based policies was taken with the regulations made in the foreign exchange regime.

The fixed exchange rate regime was implemented in the pre-1980 period, and the value of the Turkish Lira was adjusted by the government to the changing economic conditions. However, the delays in the adjustments to be made resulted in a significant and excessive appreciation of the Turkish lira in some periods. A more realistic and flexible exchange rate policy was introduced with the stabilization program that went into effect in 1980, and the value of the Turkish Lira against foreign currencies was reduced. In 1982, commercial banks were allowed to hold foreign exchange positions. The aim of this regulation is to increase foreign exchange transfers from abroad and parallel markets to the banking system and to prevent capital escape. With the Decree No. 30 dated July 7, 1984, the most important step was taken in the liberalization of the foreign exchange regime. This decision allowed commercial banks to engage in foreign exchange operations and transactions with a ratio of foreign exchange liabilities.

Another step of the ongoing liberalization movement in the foreign exchange regime was taken with the establishment of the Interbank Foreign Exchange and Effective Market under the auspices of the Central Bank on September 21, 1988, to help the exchange rate to be determined according to the market conditions.

The date August 1989 represents an important turning point for the Turkish economy. At that date, with the Decree No. 32, regarding the Protection of the Value of Turkish Currency, an amendment was enacted. With this decision, the first steps of transition of Turkish Currency to full convertibility were taken, and the liberalization in the foreign exchange system was increased (Oktayer, 2009).

3.2 Establishment of Interbank Money Market

The Interbank Money Market was established on April 2, 1986, to meet the short-term liquidity needs, to support interbank reserve movements, to regulate liquidity in the system, and to help the distribution among banks in a balanced manner, and to ensure the use of resources more effectively. With the establishment of the interbank money market, it is aimed to expand the banks' borrowing opportunities during the day and thus contribute to the growth and deepening of the market (Oktayer, 2009).

3.3 Establishment of Securities Market

Reform efforts related to the securities markets in Turkey began with the removal of the Capital Market Law. Then, in accordance with the Law, to regulate, develop, and audit capital markets, in 1982, the CMB was established. Following the amendments made in the Capital Markets Law, in 1985, the Istanbul Stock Exchange was reopened with its current identity and started its operations. The establishment of the Istanbul Stock Exchange is one of the milestones that make a significant contribution to the development of Turkish financial markets. Important tax incentives have been introduced to stock market gains to ensure the development of the market in question (Oktayer, 2009).

3.4 Establishment of Gold Market

Gold trade liberalization was one of the other step in the process of financial liberalization which began with the January 24 Decision. With the regulations made in 1983 and 1984, the trade and importation of gold within the country was released, and its exports were subject to specific permits. Again, within the framework of these regulations, the Central Bank was authorized to determine the value of gold and exchange rates against Turkish lira.

This authority given to the Central Bank formed the basis for the formation of an official gold market in Turkey.

Within the framework of this authorization, the Central Bank established the Gold Market in TL equivalent in 1984 and began to import gold, and sold these gold to the individuals and institutions for TL, and the market price of gold was determined on the basis of TL (Oktayer, 2009).

4 Economic Liberalization Period (1980–1989)

Civilian government in Turkey ended on September 12, 1980, with a military coup. With the military administration, 24 January Decisions became more easily applicable. With the implementation of these heavy measures and decisions, the economy breathed for a while and the country's economy began to recover. In 1984 Turkey left the fixed exchange rate policy and took the first steps to a variable rate policy. In this new system the exchange rate was allowed to be determined by the market.

Outward or Export Oriented Growth Perspective policy as is named, not only in Turkey also in the US and the stabilization policy in the UK have created the main axis. With this new policy by reducing the role of the state in the economy, the market economy is tried to be implemented. With an open restructuring, new policy has focused on bringing stability to the economy and ensuring economic growth. One of the key elements of the 24 January Decisions was the control of money supply and public spending, and the reduction of high demand that had caused high inflation (Şahin and Karanfil, 2015).

With these decisions, it was planned to reduce priority to the public sector and to give the same instead to the private sector. Thus, public intervention would be reduced and the market economy would become operational. It has not been possible to reduce public spending alone. Some of these expenditures were public expenditure and have not been reduced since they were services such as general public services, education, justice, security, and health. Budget expenditures have not fallen below 22 % in the 1980–1989 period. However, there was a complete contradiction in public revenues. In order for the market economy to settle, the tax burden must decrease; on the other hand, public revenues should be increased in order to reduce budget deficits.

Together with these, Turkey has abandoned its protectionist import substitution industrialization policy and has shifted to an industrialization model within the framework of export-oriented, open-to-open and market economy. A large part of Turkey's export portfolio was comprised by the agricultural products then. In this context, Turkey planned to increase the exports of industrial products. As a result of this transition, exports of $ 2.9 billion in 1980 increased to $ 12.9 billion in 1990. In addition, the amount of imports was $ 7.9 billion in 1980 and reached $ 22.3 billion in 1990. During this period, Turkey began to experience integration into global markets and economies. In the same period, the IMF and the World Bank have become decisive for Turkey's economic policies. Turkey provided an economic growth of over 5 % annually in this period, and it has achieved a growth of over 8 % in industrial production. However, inflation has increased continuously in this period (Fırat, 2009; Arabacı and Çavdar, 2015; Eğilmez, 2018a).

5 Transition to Market Economy (1990–2001)

Upon Turkey's economy entered a gradual liberalization effort since 1980, first in foreign trade, followed by the process of completing a transaction with financial liberalization and deregulation that took place in 1990 for the domestic financial market.

Although Turkey began to be a part of the world economy, it had not made a significant change in economic policy tools.

So, on the one hand, Turkey's economy felt the negative effects of fluctuations in the global economy; on the other hand, it had not made the necessary institutional arrangements. Besides, the economy remained dependent on hot money. With the reliance on an unstable economic resource such as hot money, the balance of resource use in the country began to deteriorate. Thus, inflation has been high and volatile since the beginning of the 1990s, growth has been unstable, and high growth years have been replaced by contraction years.

Although it was envisaged to reduce the role of the Central Bank in the financial system by the resolutions of January 24, 1980, the rapid growth policy introduced after 1980 prevented the Central Bank's role in the financial system from diminishing.

In the monetary program of 1990, the Central Bank's balance sheet was targeted to be reduced and transparent. In this context, the Central Bank aimed to achieve price stability and to increase foreign exchange assets in the medium term. In an environment where capital movements are released, interest and exchange rate policies are linked. Thus, the Central Bank is able to use only one of these tools (Alpay and Alkin, 2017).

In 1990, the Turkish economy gained a structure open to the international capital movement. However, following the stabilization program announced in 1980, the Central Bank tried to meet the increasing domestic and foreign debts. Especially in 1990, public sector deficits increased rapidly, tax revenues were insufficient even for domestic debt service, and this situation negatively affected the budget balance and exchange rates.

In 1993, the newly elected government increased the borrowing from abroad due to the high interest rate of the Turkish lira. At the same time, the new government tried to increase the money supply and pay the domestic debt through this money. Also, they tried to reduce the domestic borrowing interest rate. Nonetheless, to reach the goal government lowered interest rates on treasury papers. Together with the high current account deficit, low interest rates, and the expectation of devaluation; people turned their savings to foreign exchange. While there was such a foreign exchange demand in the domestic market, there was a currency shortage within the country. The ratio of foreign exchange deposits to Turkish lira deposits increased from 35 to 73 %, and the Turkish lira became unable to realize some of its features. On March 11, 1994, the interest rate per night increased to 700 %, but the foreign exchange demand of the markets could not be reduced. ISE could not withdraw speculative capital, and demand for foreign exchange did not stop. Under these conditions, the exchange rate of 1 dollar, which corresponds to 19 Turkish liras in January 1994, increased to 38 Turkish Liras in April 1994. The foreign exchange reserves of the Central Bank, which was $ 7 billion in January 1994, declined to $ 3 billion in April 1994.

Following the elections held in 1994 under these economic indicators, the government responded to the economic crisis by launching an IMF-backed economic stabilization program on April 5, 1994. With this program, the government aimed at decreasing the high inflation rate, stabilizing the Turkish lira, and reinforcing the economic structure for future economic growth. In other words, the government aimed to create economic stability in the short-term and implement structural reforms to maintain economic stability in the long-term. The main measures of the April 5 stabilization program were:

1. Devaluation of the Turkish lira by 39 %. The exchange rate of the United States Dollar increased from TL 23 to TL 32 on April 5th.
2. Abolition of the 5 % tax on the revenues earned in the government securities market.
3. A one-time tax surcharge on private enterprises.
4. Liberalization of the exchange rate determination. With the new system, the exchange rates would be determined according to the data provided by 10 major commercial banks along with the Central Bank.
5. An increase in the amount of the government's insurance coverage on bank deposits. The insurance limit increased from TL 50 million to full coverage.
6. Increases in public sector prices. Before the economic crisis, the government artificially kept the prices of public goods low by subsidizing them. Following the announcement of the stabilization program, public sector prices increased sharply: the government increased the prices of sugar by 50–62 %, tobacco and liquor by 70–100 %, tea by 64–72 %, and fuel by 46–90 %.
7. Reduction in public expenditures. With this measure, the government would cut its current nondefense expenditures by 30 %.
8. Increases in interest rates to curb the downward pressure on the exchange rate. The average real interest rate on the government securities increased to 24.9 %.
9. Privatization of the state economic enterprises. Under this measure, the government would privatize certain SEEs and restructure the others to increase their efficiency.

In order to make this stabilization program successful and sustainable, which was supported by the World Bank and IMF, the IMF signed a $ 720 million stand-by agreement in May 1994.

The April 5th stabilization program partially succeeded to achieve its short-term goals, such as stabilizing the financial markets and the Turkish lira; however, it failed to achieve its long-term goals of decreasing the public deficit and high inflation on a permanent basis.

In August 1998, the Asian financial crisis hit the Turkish economy. Financial crisis, fiscal and current account deficits, the inflation rate, and unemployment rates significantly increased after the Asian crises. These economic developments forced the government to sign a new stand-by agreement with the IMF in 1999. But Turkey did not benefit from this agreement as efficiently and then eventually culminated in another major economic crisis in 2001 (Durgut, 2002).

6 Stability Period (2001–2017)

In 2001; As a result of the increase in interest rates stemming from the November-2000 crisis, the Treasury borrowed at a 67 % interest rate which was more than the year-end inflation rate.

It states that the structural conditions and indicators which that indicate the crisis would occur clearly revealed itself before the crisis of February 2001. In this context, the system that tried to stand up with the artificial capital inflows caused by the banking system and the interest-exchange stalemate, which did not have sufficient foreign exchange surpluses, laid the ground for a new crisis as a result of the increasing insecurity in the markets.

Generally, basis of the February 2001 crisis reasons are:

1) Excessive mobility in exchange rates due to excess foreign exchange demand,
2) The effects of financial crises on the real economy,
3) A lot of noninterest surplus constriction caused by high determination,
4) Increase in external debt stock,
5) The balance of payments was very high, and
6) Uncertain political environment.

After the political crisis in the National Security Council between the Prime Minister and the President resulted a speculative attack, a massive demand for foreign exchange was made on February 19, 2001, and 7.6 billion dollar demand for foreign exchange. CBRT demanded only 1.2 billion dollars. The outflow of foreign investors and the turnover of banks and savings holders to foreign exchange caused an increase at the interest rate and interest rate increased to 1000 %. The overnight repo rate at the Interbank Money Market reached 7500 %, and Treasury borrowing interest rates increased to 144 %. As a result of the economic crisis in 2001, a new structural reform program under the name of Transition to Strong Economy was implemented with the support of the IMF and the World Bank. The program implemented was positive in terms of growth, inflation, and interest rates; but it created negative developments in terms of current account deficit and employment indicators. The main objectives of the program were: eradication of inflation, the failure of unsustainable public domestic debt dynamics, and the elimination of structural problems in the face of growth

The GDP, which was USD 238 billion in 2002 due to the ruling power of governing party Adalet ve Kalkınma Partisi (AKP), increased to USD 863 billion at the end of 14 years. Initially capturing extremely rapid growth with the AKP government, Turkey, following the year 2008, first came to a standstill and then showed a shrinking economic performance. Although the 5 % inflation rate was targeted by the Central Bank, it has not been achieved; the budget deficit has approached to zero. However, while the budget deficit fell, current account deficit and unemployment increased in this process (Sungur, 2015; Eğilmez, 2018b).

7 2018 Exchange Rate Fluctuation

The market analysis for the recent past shows that the exchange rate band for US dollar was 2.5–3.5 Turkish liras between the time period of 2012–2017; including Gezi Park protests (2013), 17–25 December 2013 indictments (2013), 6–7 October riots (2014), ISIS attacks (between 2013 and 2015), and the July 15 coup attempt (2015) occurred. However, the US dollar rate had a dramatic increase last summer, as it can be seen in Tab. 2. Last summer, the US President Donald Trump imposed sanctions against the Turkish economy on the grounds that pastor Andrew Brunson was not released. The Turkish economy, which has already undergone an important fragility for structural reasons, was harshly hit by these sanctions.

The US dollar rate, which had started at 3.79 Turkish liras, increased to 4.79 at July18, when Brunson's request for release was rejected at the trial. On August 1, the US Treasury announced the sanctions for two Turkish ministers, and the US dollar currency passed the 5 Turkish liras threshold. On August 13 when Trump announced that he implemented the second phase of the sanctions decision to increase customs duty on steel and aluminum imports from Turkey, the US dollar rate, the highest point in history, saw 7.21 Turkish liras. This climbing of the exchange rate has had a shocking effect on the Turkish economy. In particular, it was observed that a number of negativities have been chained up to the increase in the balance sheets of the companies which were borrowed in foreign currency or working on imports based on their balance sheets.

Following the release of Brunson by the court on October 12, a normalization in relations with the United States was started, and an improvement in economic indicators began.

Ankara and Washington, which had left behind a problematic year in Turkish-American relations, entered a tense period again since USA was sending strong signals that it would react with sanctions at this step after Turkey's decision to purchase the S-400 systems from Russia. While some analysts call the "new Brunson crisis," diplomatic maneuver space narrows down, Ankara is forced to make a choice between Russia and USA while meeting its long-range air and missile defense needs. In case USA implements defense sanctions, Turkey's defensive/offensive capability may face the risk of damage.

Due to the fact that Brunson's return to his country and the US' decision to withdraw from Syria was welcomed in Ankara in the first place, it was thought

Tab. 2: $/₺ Exchange Rate 2016–2019 (*Investing, 2019*)

that the problems were left behind between Ankara and Washington. However, with the approaching dates of delivery of the S-400s, Washington increased its warnings to Ankara. US officials declared that if Turkey was not giving up the purchase plan of S-400 system, US F 35 fighter aircraft should not be delivered to Turkey. As a result of this tension, the financial market and dollar price was affected (İnan, 2019; Yeni Çağ Gazetesi, 2019).

Conclusion

The process of economic crisis means a dangerous and unstable period for the economies of the country, and it is also referred to as a turning point in economic structure. Dealing with the economic crisis since the 1970s, emerging Turkey has implemented different policies towards crises in every period. But some of the IMF-backed stabilization policies have clashed with the internal dynamics of the country and have not adapted to the changing world order. External developments in the world in the period between 1973 and 1980 affected Turkey in a negative way. In the 1973–1980 period with the impact of external developments in Turkey, foreign debt payments were not made and inflation reached 100 %. Economic growth had fallen to zero, and the country's economy has remained in a big crisis. The first objective of the program, which started to be implemented in January 24, 1980, has been reducing high inflation. Between 1980 and 1983, financial liberalization was targeted. During 1983–1989, free market regulations and structural reforms were taken into consideration.

Increase in exports with exchange rate, interest, and incentive policies during 1980–1988 has shown itself in manufacturing industry products. However, although the Stability Program of January 24 was partially successful in the first years, it was replaced by crises in the following years. In 1989–1994, the annual growth rate of GNP, which had a new crisis, remained below 2 %, while the inflation rate slowed slightly; but it still exceeded 60 %. Public sector deficits increased. With the decisions of April 5, it was aimed primarily to reduce public deficits and then to maintain stability. In exchange with inflation rate in 1994, domestic debt stock increased but external debt stock decreased. Turkish Lira stabilized for a while, and thus domestic borrowing has been closed. However, targets on fiscal policy and taxes have not been met and making changes in macro issues such as privatization has been delayed. Affected by the financial crisis in Russia, Turkey, until the end of the 1999, has tried to overcome the inflation problem with exchange policies by using the tight currency and fiscal policies as well as the foreign exchange as an anchor. The program aims at a new economic program for realization of exchange rate and monetary policy, incomes policy compatible with inflation target, and structural reforms based on reducing inflation. In the early 2000s, the high rate of inflation was expected to lead to a decrease in confidence in the economic program. Due to increase in public deficit, burden of debt, and high interest rates and high inflation; Turkey has again entered an economic crisis. In this crisis, small banks could not compete with big banks. Besides, liquidity crisis emerged.

With regard to the November 2000 crisis, increased share sales of foreigners initiated a fall in the stock market from 20,000 to 9,000. In the aftermath of the crisis, financial markets contracted, and real markets have also stagnated.

Considering the historical process, Turkey was faced with macroeconomic imbalances. As a result, macroeconomic imbalances and capital movements are negatively affected by economies that lack banking regulations.

Economic stability requires a long and very painful process. In Turkey the stabilization programs implemented have achieved partial successes in a short time and have not been successful in a long time. The crises experienced in our country or in any country in the world may cause to lose their power to a large extent but on the other hand to face new opportunities also. Turkey as a player in the globalized world must take part in this change.

Finally, Turkey needs to exit the crisis mood in the fastest way. Relations with international organizations should be developed in the environment of confidence in economic and political stability by increasing production capacity in the economy. To avoid crises and to integrate with the world integration, it is necessary to establish a national economic policy with a social content and to implement these policies with determination in every period.

Bibliography

Alpay, Y. and Alkin, E. (2017), **Olaylarla Türkiye Ekonomisi Yirminci Yüzyıl Türkiye Ekonomi Tarihi**, İstanbul: Humanist.

Arabacı, H. and Çavdar, F. (2015), "Crisis and Development of Financial Structure in Turkey After 1980", **Social Sciences Research Journal**, v.2, pp. 302–207.

Durgut, A. (2002), **The 1994 Economic Crisis in Turkey**, Monterey, CA, USA: Naval Postgraduate School.

Eğilmez, M., (2018a), **Değişim Sürecinde Türkiye**, İstanbul: Remzi.

Eğilmez, M., (2018b), "Kendime Yazılar", http://www.mahfiegilmez.com/2018/11/dolar-kurunun-kararlar-uzerindeki-etkisi.html, (26.11.2018).

Fırat, E. (2009), "Türkiye'de 1980 Sonrası Yaşanan Üç Büyük Kriz ve Sonuçlarının Ekonomi-Politiği", **SÜ İİBF Sosyal ve Ekonomik Araştırmalar Dergisi**, pp. 501–524.

İnan, M. (2019), "S-400'le Tetiklenen Dolar Kritik Seviyeyi Test Etti", https://kriptokoin.com/s-400le-tetiklenen-dolar-kritik-seviyeyi-test-etti/, (03.2019).

Investing.com (2019a), "USD/TRY – US Dollar Turkish Lira", https://www.investing.com/currencies/usd-try (01.03.2019).

Investing.com (2019b), "Investing.com", https://www.investing.com/ (29.03.2019).

Karabıçak, M. (2000), "Türkiye'de Ekonomik İstikrarsızlığın Tarihsel Gelişimi", **Süleyman Demirel Üniversitesi İktisadi ve İdari Bilimler Fakültesi Dergisi**, pp. 49–65.

Keser, M. (2015), **Türkiye'de Finansal Piyasalar**, İstanbul: York University Turkey Representation.

Matriksdata. (2014), "Matriksdata.com", https://www.matriksdata.com/website/finansal-piyasalar.

Morgül, T. (2013), **Türkiye'de Finansal Piyasalar**, Yalova: York University Turkey Representation.

Oktayer, A. (2009), "Türkiye'de Finansal Serbestleşme ve Derinleşme Süreci Üzerine Nitel Bir İnceleme", **Akademik İncelemeler**, v.2, pp. 73–100.

Şahin, İ. and Karanfil, M. (2015), "Türkiye Ekonomisinde 1980–2013 Dönemi Para Arzının Enflasyon", **Business and Economics Research Journal**, pp. 97–113.

Sermaye Piyasası Kurulu, Borsa İstanbul A. Ş., İstanbul Takas ve Saklama Bankası A.Ş. Uzmanları. (2017), **Finansal Piyasalar**, İstanbul: Sermaye Piyasası Lisanslama Sicil ve Eğitim Kuruluşu A.Ş.

Sungur, O. (2015), "2000 Sonrası Türkiye Ekonomisi: Büyüme, Enflasyon, İşsizlik, Borçlanma ve Dış Ticarette Gelişmeler", **Toplum ve Demokrasi**, pp. 243–269.

Turkish State Planning Institute. (2001). **Economic And Social Indicators 1950–1998**, Ankara: Turkish State Planning Institute.

Yeni Çağ Gazetesi. (2019). "Türkiye-ABD arasında ikinci "Brunson krizi" yolda mı?", https://www.yenicaggazetesi.com.tr/turkiye-abd-arasinda-ikinci-brunson-krizi-yolda-mi-226149h.htm (08.03.2019).

Assist. Prof. Dr. Neyir Tekeli

Review on the Development of Tourism Sector in Turkey Before 80S, 80S and Tourism Law: 2634

Abstract: The world tourism industry has developed with great momentum, especially since the second half of the twentieth century. Especially until the 1980s, the face of mass tourism dominated by sea-sun-sand until the 1980s made itself felt seriously. Alternative tourism has arisen due to problems in mass tourism and demand for different tourism products by tourism consumers. Since the second half of the 1980s, alternative tourism developed rapidly in the world and Turkey. Turkey reached to a very important position in the world in tourism industry with the arrangements made since the second half of 1980. The works on diversification of the tourism industry, works of sustainability, and the start of works to spread it to all seasons coincide again to this period. It is observed that Turkey's foreign tourism, with the effect of the globalization phenomenon experienced in this period in the world, has shown significant improvement. It is seen after this period that Turkey becomes a popular tourist attraction for all tourists in the world. In 1983–1989, there was a significant increase in the number of tourists and tourism revenues thanks to the great and significant effect of the "Tourism Promotion Law No. 2634," which was enacted in 1982.

Keywords: Tourism, tourism sector, Tourism Law 2634

Introduction

One of the main economic objectives of developed and developing countries is to minimize the deficits of "balance of payments" and "current transactions balance" which is the most effective account on this balance. In general, the current account deficit is tried to be covered by the tourism sector, which is in the services having the surplus items of the balance of payments. Tourism makes significant contributions to the economies of the countries by means of creating employment for some developing countries, contributing to other sectors, stimulating investments, and generating income.

Tourism sector in terms of structure is taking place in the sectors in which competitive advantage and the variations can be seen. Tourism, the people-oriented sector, which is the most important feature of the service sector, has its advantages, such as being open to development. It is seen as a sector capable of creating an important source of income in the future. Tourism, as an important branch of the service sector as in many other developing countries in Turkey, seizes a significant place in terms of economic contribution. Turkey, which is located on the top row in the world tourism market and accepted as a tourism country, has aimed to evaluate its unique, natural, historical, and cultural assets, especially with the help of outward opining policy and incentives arrangements for the sector in the 1980s, it has achieved a rapid uptrend in tourism sector (Gülbahar, 2008: 154).

It is known that tourism sector in Turkey has reached to its existing potential particularly by means of various policies produced in 1980 and after. Turkey's "Active Foreign Tourism" in particular has started to show a significant improvement from the 1980s, and it has become one of the sources of income making a huge contribution to the national economy (CIMAT and Bahar, 2003:2).

Various legislative arrangements have been produced in order to improve the sector and ensure it to assist in the economic development. In this context, with the "Tourism Encouragement Act" adopted on 12.03.1982 No. 2634 identification of the areas and the centers of tourism regions in Turkey, and on behalf of the opportunities will be provided to potential entrepreneurs in order to develop tourism in these areas are provided. Due to the adoption of this law in Turkey and thanks to the increased globalization and technological development in an inevitable way, the tourism sector has gained great momentum.

1 Development of Tourism Industry in Turkey

Tourism, which is the flue-free industry of Turkey, in the period after 1980, with the targets, policies, and legal regulations set in the direction to developed tourism sector, has become one of Turkey's most foreign currency providing sectors. In parallel with Turkey, the growth rate of this sector in the world is in an increasing trend. The development in Turkey's tourism sector of the republican era is examined in two periods. The first period is the unplanned period between 1923 and 1962, while the second period is the planned period covering after 1962 (Tunç and Saç, 1998:97).

1.1 Tourism of Turkey in the Planned and Unplanned Period

Turkey's development in the planned and preplanned period will be studied in this section.

1.1.1 Tourism of Turkey in the Preplanned Period

In Turkish tourism, in the time period referred as "The Preplanned Period" (1923–1962), showing that as the first organization as a tourism activity was "The

Seyyahi's Society" founded by Rashid Saffet Atabinen and a group of intellectuals. The Society conducted research for 3 years and examined the organizations and activities of peer societies in Europe. Founded in 1923 after these researches, it would become operational in 1926. The biggest goal of the Society was to organize big trips, to introduce historical and touristic works in the important cities such as Istanbul and Bursa to foreigners, and to introduce the world cities to the Turkish citizens. They also carried out studies on the conservation, supervision, and restoration of historical monuments. This society in the future would take place in the Turkish tourism literature as "Turkey Touring Club" and then "Touring and Automobile Club of Turkey."

With the Works of Seyyahi Society of Turkey's first tourism promotions, the first tourism posters and land road maps of Turkey were published. Interpreter and tour guide exams and the initial researches on tourism are also coincided to this period. In the first years of the Republic, with the authority obtained from the Municipality, courses were opened to teach foreign languages and train interpreters, translators were retrained by theoretical and practical courses by the archeological experts of the Association, "badge" was given to deserving ones, and their duties and fees were determined. Important steps were taken to promote "The Image of Turkish" and Turkey particularly in Europe (Kozak et al., 1997:83). The first legal regulations related to Turkey's tourism sector coincide with 1934.

The name of this legal regulation is referred to as 24 Law No. 2450 on the "Organization and Duties of the Ministry of Economy" (Yağcı, 2003:17).

Tourism in Turkey entered the economic program of the State as of 1930. In 1934, works of tourism, propaganda, and publications were included within the tasks of the Ministry of Economy and a unit named "Türkofis" formed in the mandate of the Foreign Trade Chamber within this ministry has been obliged to carry out tourism and propaganda activities. As of 1938, "Tourism Bureau" was established as a branch in Türkofis "Publications and Propaganda Service," and this office was named "Tourism Directorate" during the establishment of the Ministry of Trade in 1939. This department worked under the Ministry of Commerce of the time. In 1940 the Directorate was first named "Press and Public Directorate," in 1943 "General Directorate of Press and Publication," and in 1949 as they were collected under the department of Tourism it was named "General Directorate of Press and Tourism" (Evcin, 2016;14).

In Turkey, the matter of encouragement of investments planned on tourism was handled first by the enactment of the act of "Tourism Organization Incentives Act" in 1950. Again, in the 1950s, a loan fund of $1,000,000 for the tourism incentives has been created in the state-owned bank "Turkey

Tab. 1: Incoming Foreign Tourists to Turkey Between Years 1949 and 1957. **Source:** (Evcin, 2016:11)

1949	19.451
1950	28.625
1951	31.377
1952	38.837
1953	70.055
1954	71.331
1955	79.369
1956	99.414
1957	100.803

Real Estate Credit Bank." In 1953, the Law No. 6086 Promoting the Tourism Industry came into force. By this law, it is ensured that tourism entrepreneurs do not pay taxes for 10 years in order to encourage them to invest in the tourism sector. Although with the Law No. 6086 on the Encouragement of the Tourism Industry enacted in 1953, it was aimed these economic activities were grown and enlarged; until 1982, a development capable of contributing to the external balance of the Turkish economy in this field was unfortunately not achieved. Until in this period until 1982 Tourism Bank was established in 1955. The purpose of the establishment of the tourism bank on that day was to meet the financing needs of the tourism sector (Turkish Grand National Assembly Session Minutes).

In 1957, the General Directorate of Press and Tourism became the Ministry under the name of "Ministry of Press and Tourism" (Tunç and Saç, 1998:98). By the 1960s (especially after the coup d'etat on May 27, 1960), all activities in the field of tourism and all economic inputs and outputs made up until that time were questioned. Many investment projects completed or planned to be completed in the tourism sector were canceled in this period; the loans yield to the investors were stopped (Tab. 1).

In Tab. 1 a steady increase in the number of tourists visiting Turkey between the years 1947 and 1957 is seen.

In Turkey especially after the 1960s, it is seen that tourism was developed. During this period, especially after the Second World War (in the 1940s and 1950s), Greece, the immediate neighbor of Turkey, wishes to raise more revenues from tourism – making its own propaganda, on the one hand, through agencies and distributorships located worldwide and, on the other hand, making negative propaganda against Turkey, the country which it sees as its nearest competitor in the field of tourism.

According to the information given based on the Greek newspapers of the time to change the minds of the tourists who intend to visit Turkey, they spread propagandas such as: in Turkey's water resources typhoid germs are located, the foods in Istanbul were filthy, while the hotels are in poor condition, thief's and pickpockets were harassing tourists, and Turkish police were imprisoning foreigner tourists on trivial accusations. As a result of these propaganda, the number of tourists visiting their capital Athens in the neighboring country in the 1950s extremely exceeded the number of tourists who visited Istanbul (Evcin, 2016:17).

1.1.2 Planned Period and Tourism of Turkey

Tourism policy of Turkey in the planned period differs from the unplanned period. In 1961, together with the 1961 constitution, tourism development plans were started. Turkey's economic development plans outlining its economic goals, although a guideline for the private sector, is imperative for the public sector and has a binding nature. Thanks to these development plans, by determining the current status of Turkey's tourism resources efficient use has been targeted. The concept of policy has a general guideline status leading to decision-making (Yagci, 2007:194).

Tourism policies taking place in the development plans determine the activities for the development of tourism. Thanks to tourism policies, public and private sector duties are determined for the tourism sector (Şahin, 1990:111).

Thus, while the gains from tourism are maximized, the costs are reduced to a minimum (Olalı, 1990: 30). Tourism sector has been included in all ten development plans that have been initiated since 1963 and put forward in the process covering 2018. In all development plans, it is pointed out that the country will be developed by way of industrialization, and tourism activities will accelerate this process (Oktayer et al., 2007:44).

In the period following the 1960s, resource inventories were made by regions, physical planning studies were made, and technical infrastructure investments were made. Tourism investments such as marina and accommodation facilities have been constructed by the State (Acuner, 2006:29).

In the 1963–1990 period, Turkey's tourism policy was shaped as contributing to the Turkish economy, to the balance of payments, to increase foreign exchange revenues of the state, to create new employment areas, and reviving domestic tourism. Again, this is the period when the "Ministry of Tourism" was established.

2 Planned Period and Development of Turkish Tourism

The development of planned period Turkish tourism;

2.1 The First Five-Year Development Plan (1963–1967)

According to the 1963 data of the State Planning Organization, in order to ensure the development of tourism, in Turkey, it was decided that the needed expenditure was made, and propaganda and promotions were carried out. Besides the importance given to accommodation facilities in order to make the most efficient use of the limited resources allocated by the State to tourism; tourism investment was decided to be made in regions suitable for tourism and tourism centers with high attraction. It was decided that importance be given to domestic tourism as well as to foreign tourism, customs and foreign exchange transactions for tourists will be simplified, and priority should be given to opening advisory offices for publicity and advertising. In this planning period, tourism revenues will be ensured to be higher than tourism expenditures (SPO, 1963:425–510). The most important tourism projects can be listed as follows: hotels, holiday villages, and camps capable of developing tourism will be established. *Importance shall be given to natural and historical resources, and national parks suitable for tourism shall be established. *All kinds of transportation opportunities between Balkans, Greece, Italy, Israel, and Turkey will be increased. *Tourism personnel training will be given priority. *Production and sales of food, drinks, and souvenirs that will meet the needs of tourists will be supported and regulated by local efforts in the places where tourist facilities are established (DPT, 1963–1967:467).

2.2 Second Five-Year Development Plan (1968–1972)

This period is the second Five-Year Planning period, and it is a period when tourism was expected to be an important source of income for Turkey.

According to the 1968 data of the State Planning Organization, tourism being a labor-intensive sector will increase the employment level. Increasing tourism revenues, number of foreign tourists, and average consumption are among the objectives of the second five-year development period. Investments planned to be made in the tourism sector will primarily focus on increasing the accommodation facilities and accommodation capacity and bed capacity of these facilities. The main principle of tourism policy in the Second Plan period is the development of " Mass Tourism" which is developing in the world with legal and financial facilities. Accommodation capacity will be established as facilities for mass tourism and in certain regions with high tourism potential. Large capacity holiday sites investments will be particularly supported.

The fundamentals of tourism policy to be followed in the Second Five-Year Development Plan are grouped under the following headings. *Domestic tourism movements will be increased along with foreign tourism revenues. *Touristic promotion and propaganda will be given more importance than previous periods. *In the investment policy in tourism sector, infrastructure facilities and exemplary facilities of the region to be invested will be handled by the public sector, and the private sector will be given the opportunity to make other touristic facilities investments. *Tourism investments will be intensified especially in certain regions (especially Marmara, Aegean, and Antalya regions) with high tourism potential, and accommodation and transportation facilities suitable for mass tourism will be provided. *Environmental health and food controls will be given importance for the development of tourism activities. *Various cooperation opportunities will be sought in the international arena and especially in the promotion of joint tourism with Mediterranean countries. *Priority will be given to the places where the touristic accommodation facilities will be concentrated in the protection, evaluation, and restoration of natural, historical, and archeological values, monuments, and pieces of art during the Second Five-Year Development Plan period (DPT, 1968–1972:299593).

Again, in the early 1970s (1972) at the end of the Second Development period, "Turkey Travel Agencies Union" (TÜRSAB) was founded and thus all travel agents were collected under TÜRSAB roof.

2.3 Third Five-Year Development Plan (1973–1977)

In this period, as an economic recession was experienced in many economic areas of Turkey, depending on the oil crisis; this stagnation was also manifested in the tourism sector.

According to the State Planning Organization 1972 data, many of the objectives of the Third Five-Year Development Plan have not been achieved. Priority regions of accommodation facility investments have been identified; these regions differ from other periods. Mediterranean, Göreme, Uludağ, South Aegean, and partly Marmara regions are among the priority regions. Within the infrastructure investments of the mentioned regions were: airport construction, improvement of highways, construction of water, electricity and sewerage facilities, and construction of marinas.

National park investments and restoration of historical monuments will be accelerated, and private sector will be prominent in tourism investment and management. The investment and management of the public sector will lead to the aim of accompanying leading and exemplary facilities. The shifting of investments in the tourism sector to other regions will be developed in parallel with the tourist flow. In the past, the personnel trained in hotel schools for tourism services has been insufficient in terms of quantity and quality. Not all of the tourism personnel trained in this field ensured to work in the tourism sector. In this context, it is planned to open Hotel Management and Tourism Vocational High Schools in order to train personnel and ensure their employment. In order to improve tourism potential, underground and aboveground historical values will be preserved, credit opportunities of the sector will be increased, and foreign capital investment management will be included (DPT, 1972:614–1003).

3 The 1980s Tourism and Incentive Law No. 2634

In 1980, it is observed that Turkey's active foreign tourism in particular, with the effect of the phenomenon of globalization experienced in the world, showed an important development. Especially after 1980, it is observed that Turkey takes the form of a popular tourist attraction for all tourists around the world. In 1983–1989, there was a significant increase in the number of tourists and tourism revenues thanks to the great and significant effect of the "Tourism Incentive Law No. 2634" which was enacted in 1982. In this period; the essence of this law, which was enacted with the aim of creating the tourist supply that can meet the increasing tourist demand thanks to the effects of global developments, was to direct the investors to tourism and to increase the supply capacity (number of rooms, beds and facilities, etc.) that are not sufficient in the country (Küçükaltan, 2005:92). Yet since the 1980s, the trend of tourism in Turkey's Current Account Balance is related to the implementation of the determined goals and policies. In this respect, the place of tourism in the Development Plans and the regulations made come to the fore. Tourism has become a driving force for economic development since the 1980s and an important part of economic policies (Unur, 2000:10).

The Travel Agencies and Travel Agencies Association Law enacted in 1972 and the Tourism Incentive Law enacted in 1982 reflected both the importance given to the development of Turkish tourism and enabled our country to become a tourism country. It can be said that the 1982 Tourism Incentive Law is a turning point in terms of Turkish tourism.

By the law enacted in 1972, Turkey Travel Agencies Association (TÜRSAB) was created and made legal arrangements regarding travel agents. With the

Tourism Incentive Law, in the direction of encouraging investments for the development of tourism especially in certain regions (such as the Mediterranean region); various tax reductions, tax exemptions, low interest loans, grants, and many other conveniences and innovations have been introduced. The main elements of the Fourth Five-Year Development Plan covering the years 1979–1983 are aimed at increasing tourism revenues, number of tourists, tourist bed capacity, and accommodation facility investments; policies such as highlighting mass tourism, encouraging public and private sector tourism investments, and giving importance to tourism education were adopted (DPT, 1979:429–432). The 1980s, with the encouragement of tourism investment, are the years when the Mediterranean shores of Turkey turned into a major tourist center (Altun & İnceoğlu, 2006:8). Especially after 1985, foreign capital inflows for tourism investments were increased in Turkey. In this year and in subsequent times, by the incentives applied, the number of accommodation establishments, in particular leisure accommodations, had reached the very high figure and bed capacities. During this period, the concept of leisure accommodation (resort) also changed and the concept of relaxation, which has priority, has been replaced by "fun and adventure." Leisure accommodation guests now want to end their holidays or travels with a spirit of excitement and an advanced brain (Altun & Inceoğlu 2006:6).

Law no: 2634 "Tourism Incentive Law" (1982) has been a start, a turning point for Turkey in terms of tourism. Law no: 2634 claimed that the tourism investments in Turkey be directed primarily to areas that will allow the development of Turkish tourism and scarce resources be used effectively.

The 1980s were a period when Turkey gave weight to privatization activities. Through associations and unions such as TÜRSAB, Turkey Hoteliers Association (TÜROB), the Tourism Development Foundation (TUGEV), and the Turkish Tourism Investors Association (TTYD) tourism private sector representatives acquired effective positions.

By the end of the 1980s, in 1989; with the decree numbered 364, it was again separated as the Ministry of Culture and Tourism. Then it was reunited, with the Law No. 4848 on the Organization and Duties of the Ministry of Culture and Tourism, which was published in the Official Gazette no. 25093 dated 2003. Still in the early 1980s, Turkey defined new targets in the tourism industry has developed a new legal framework for the tourism sector by the decision "Tourism Incentive Framework Decision" decision no: 8/1133 and dated 06.20.1980. 'The Tourism Coordination Board' has been established in order to determine the regions where investments will be intensified and to plan these regions, to create new financing sources and methods for the

Tab. 2: Tourism Revenues Between 1980 and 1998. **Source:** Önen, 2000: 31

Years	**Years Revenue (Million $)**	**Years**	**Years Revenue (Million $)**
1980	326	1991	2654
1983	411	1992	3689
1984	840	1993	3959
1985	1482	1994	4321
1986	1215	1995	4957
1987	1721	1996	5962
1988	2355	1997	8088
1989	2556	1998	7088
1990	3525		

tourism sector, to encourage foreign capital in this field, and to consider and regulate the principles for the promotion of tourism investments in general (Uluturk, 1998:164).

In Turkey, structural change and development have accelerated in particular after the 1980s. As a result of economic analysis, the importance of tourism in Turkey and the country's economy is observed. Since the introduction of the Tourism Promotion Law no: 2634 in 1982, the share of the tourism sector in the Turkish economy has increased considerably. Again, with the Law No. 2634, and with tourism and culture center applications the distribution of urban rent are organized from the beginning; it also has caused the commercialization of the house and land sector completely.

With the Law No. 2634, by directing tourism investments primarily to tourism regions that will provide development, some of these resources were used more efficiently and primary planning and coordination activities were realized in this way. With this law, the Ministry of Tourism provided various conveniences by facilitating procedures related to the allocation of state lands. Thus, many new types of tourism in Turkey not implemented before emerged, and these varieties were allowed to be developed.

Still the year 1983 and its continuation (in the transition period to the market economy) were the period when the state withdrew from the superstructure investments and the privatization started.

It was an economic period where the state's investment in these areas decreased considerably, and the economic structure was transformed to a private sector predominantly.

Table 2 shows the foreign exchange revenues obtained from tourism activities between 1980 and 1998. It is observed that tourism revenues generally increased in the period in which the tourism revenues were handled except for 1998. Tourism foreign exchange revenues, which were only 326 million dollars in 1980, increased to 8 billion dollars in 1997. As a result of the effects of the economic crisis in Russia and the Far East in 1998, a slowdown was observed in world tourism foreign exchange revenues in 1998.

The share that Turkey owns between the years 1989 and 1998 in international tourism revenues rose from 3 in thousand to 1.8 %, the number of foreign tourists from 2.8 million to 9.7 million, while tourism revenues rose to $ 7.2 billion from $ 2 billion. After the earthquake disaster in 1999, after the reservation cancellations, the number of tourists was reported as 7.5 million and tourism revenue was $ 5.2 billion (Yağcı, 2003:204).

In the 1980s, decisions that entered into force especially in three areas directly affected the development of the tourism sector (Coşkun, 2010:27):

- Free floating of exchange rates,
- The decision on the foreign capital framework decree, and
- Tourism Promotion Law No. 2634 (1982).

With the entry into force of this law in 1982, the credit facilities to be given to the tourism sector were increased, ease of payment of electricity, coal gas and water fees at the lowest tariff applied in the tourism region invested or to be invested, many advantages were provided in the field of communication, it is allowed to employ foreign personnel not exceeding 10 % of the total personnel employed in tourism enterprises and in order to support tourism investments, a Tourism Development Fund was established within the Ministry (Official Gazette, 16 March 1982).

By the 2634 tourism promotion law in the 1980s with the attempts determining tourism centers in Turkey and allocation of public lands to tourism investors, tourism increase in the tourism investments in Turkey is provided. In 1985–1989, granting the opportunity to benefit from grant-type incentives to tourism investors played an important role in increasing tourism investments (Toker, 2007:83–85).

When analyzed economically, the incentives to be provided for tourism investments between 1983 and 1995, which were periods of intense tourism incentives, contributed positively to the development and growth of the Turkish economy. Rising tourism revenues have also increased its GDP and per capita income of the people of Turkey (Bahar, 2006:18).

Conclusion

Turkey's tourism sector, especially in the 1980s, recorded a rising momentum during the times of Turkey's downturn, economic difficulties tourism has provided a huge foreign currency inflow and even a solution to the employment problem in the country. It served as an important locomotive in balancing the balance of payments. The importance of tourism and its place in Turkey's economy, the situation in the period of planned and unplanned tourism, the 1980s and even the 2684 using both Turkey's economy and important position of Turkey in world tourism, the share of national income, exports, and total investments became more outstanding later than this period.

Developments in tourism sector started in the 1980s; in terms of increasing the number of tourists and tourism revenues, more compatible with the environment, competitive and sustainable policies will lead Turkey in the coming years to take many more shares of international tourism revenues. This will increase the social welfare as soon as possible.

Bibliography

Acuner, Ş.A. (2006), **Alternatif Turizm Türlerinin Doğu Karadeniz Bölgesi Turizm Potansiyelinin Gelişmesine Etkisi**, Ankara: MPM Yay.

Altun, S. and İnceoğlu M. (2006), "Tatil Amaçlı Konaklama Tesislerinde Zamana Bağlı Değişim", **İTÜ Dergisi: Mimarlık Planlama Tasarım**, Vol.5, N.2. p.88.

Bahar, O. (2006), Küreselleşme Sürecinde Türkiye 'de Turizm Sektörüne Sağlanan Teşvikler, Dokuz Eylül Üniversitesi Sosyal Bilimler Enstitüsü Dergisi, Vol.8 .

Coşkun, N. (2010), **Türkiye'de Turizm Politikaları ve Turizm Sektörü Üzerindeki Etkileri (Master's Thesis)**, Ankara: T.C. Kültür ve Turizm Bakanlığı Kütüphaneler ve Yayımlar Genel Müdürlüğü.

Çımat, A. and Bahar, O. (2003), "Turizm Sektörünün Türkiye Ekonomisi İçindeki Yeri ve Önemi Üzerine Bir Değerlendirme", **Akdeniz İ.İ.B.F. Dergisi**, N.6, pp. 1–18.

DPT. (1963–1967). **Birinci Beş Yıllık Kalkınma Planı**, Ankara. http://ekutup.dpt.gov.tr/plan1.pdf (Access Date: 30.04.2016)

DPT. (1968–1972), **İkinci Beş Yıllık Kalkınma Planı,** Ankara. http://ekutup.dpt.gov.tr/plan2.pdf aCC30.04.2016 (Access Date: 01.05.2016)

DPT. (1979–1983), **Dördüncü Beş Yıllık Kalkınma Planı** Yayın No: 1664, Ankara. http://ekutup.dpt.gov.tr/plan4.pdf (Access Date: 01.05.2016)

Evcin, E. (2016), "Türkiye Cumhuriyeti'nin İlk Yıllarında Turizm ve Tanıtma Faaliyetleri", **Ankara Üniversitesi Türk İnkılâp Tarihi En stitüsü Atatürk Yolu Dergisi**, N.55, pp. 68–69.

Gülbahar, O. (2008), "Turizmin Türkiye'de 1980 Sonrası Dönemde Cari İşlemler Dengesine Etkisi", **Journal of Qafqaz University**,Vol.24, pp.154–169.

Küçükaltan, G. (2005), **Turizm Sektöründeki Teşviklerin Çevresel Etkileri**, 1. Çanakkale Turizm Biyenali (5–7 May 2005), Çanakkale: Dünya Turizm Örgütü Yayınları Dairesi.

Kozak, N., Akoğlan, M. and Kozak, M. (1997), **Genel Turizm İlkeler ve Kavramlar**, Ankara: Detay Yayıncılık.

Oktayer, N., Susam, N. and Çak, M. (2007), **Türkiye'de Turizm Ekonomisi**, İstanbul: İTO Yayın.

Önen, O. M. (2000), **Türkiye'nin Turizm Sektöründeki Gelişmeler, Dünya Turizmindeki Yeri ve Türkiye Kalkınma Bankası'nın Rolü**, Ankara: Türkiye Kalkınma Bankası.

Sertoğlu, M. (1950), "Yunanistan'da Turizm Çalışmaları", **Av ve Turizm**, Vol.1, N.2.

Toker, B. (2007), "Türkiye'de Turizm Sektörü Teşviklerinin Değerlendirilmesi", **Yönetim ve Ekonomi**, Vol.14, N.2.

Tunç, A. and Saç, F. (1998), **Genel Turizm**, Ankara: Detay Yayınevi.

Turizm Teşvik Kanunu. (1982, March 16), Resmi gazete, (Karar Sayısı: 2634, Sayı: 17635) retrieved from: http://www. resmigazete.gov.tr/arsiv/17635.pdf. Access Date: 21 Şubat 2017.

Ulutürk, Z. G. (1998), Türkiye'de Turizm Teşvikleri, **21. Yüzyılın Eşiğinde Türkiye Turizmi Sempozyumu Bildiri Kitabı**. Ankara: Başkent Üniversitesi

Unur, K. (2000), "Turizmin Türkiye'nin Ödemeler Dengesine Etkisinin Analizi", **Dokuz Eylül Üniversitesi Sosyal Bilimler Enstitüsü Dergisi**, Vol.2.

Yağcı, Ö. (2003), **Turizm Ekonomisi**, Ankara: Detay Yayınları.

https://www.tbmm.gov.tr/tutanaklar/TUTANAK/TBMM/.../tbmm20028103ss0268.pdf. Access Date:21.09.2019

Assist. Prof. Onur Özdemir

An Assessment of the Relationship Between Economic Freedom and Income Inequality for Turkey

Abstract: This section investigates the long-run relationship between economic freedom and income inequality in the control of several macroeconomic indicators such as economic growth, human development, and total population to reveal that whether the cointegration exists between the series over the 1995–2017 period in Turkey. Unlike the traditional econometric procedures on the cointegration analysis, we use a different type of approach produced by Bayer and Hanck (2013) which combines different cointegration methods in one method. The empirical results suggest that the series are cointegrated. In other words, the estimated models show that there is a long-run relationship between economic freedom and income inequality for the Turkish economy between the period 1995 and 2017.

Keywords: Economic freedom, income distribution, income inequality, distributional conflicts, Turkish economy

1 Introduction

Each definition of freedom in terms of social, political, and economic relations can have differing characteristics which are both affected by the historical components of countries all over the world. This study only focuses on economic freedom by necessarily ignoring the other factors to understand its effect on the distribution of national income. However, the concept of economic freedom needs to deal with multifactorial concepts that income distribution is basically linked to different economic factors. Therefore, the limit of this study will be determined by economic issues which may have a potential effect on economic freedom-income distribution nexus. For instance, one of the major factors is the role or the consequences of economic growth in changing income dispersion among individuals. Kuznets (1955) argued that the initial and the later stages of economic development and thereby the economic growth may have changing effects on income distribution. As economic growth maintains, the initial conditions of income distribution will be worse off which is valid for different countries across the world. However, the later stages of the economic development and growth show that the differences of inequalities in the distribution of income become smaller due to the fact that the long-run dynamics of income distribution provide an efficient market allocation for the benefits of both high- and low-income groups. In this theoretical context, if the economic freedom as a whole fully prevails in the economy, the inequality gap between high- and low-income groups become narrower and the overall level of welfare improves; and thus, the distribution of income is allocated more equally both within and between countries. To sum up, the higher level of economic freedom is beneficial for more equal distribution of income only if the growth rate of income from the lowest segment of income group is higher than that of other groups. In that sense, the major aim of this study is to investigate the long-run relationship between economic freedom and income distribution in Turkey over the 1995–2017 period by considering the other factors such as economic growth, human development index, and total population.

The analysis of the time-series dimension of economic freedom-income distribution nexus is rarely discussed in the literature, especially in terms of the countries from developing economies. Though this problem is very common for each country including different income groups, the other studies on the basis of panel data have no consensus about the relationship between economic freedom and income distribution. Therefore, this study contributes to the examination of this relationship by using almost a new kind of econometric method initiated by Bayer and Hanck (2013) to investigate whether the long-run cointegration exists between the series. First, we approach unit root test produced by Zivot and Andrews (1992) which allows for one endogenous break in time series. Second, we also follow Clemente et al. (1998) model to determine whether the series are stationary by allowing for two structural breaks in case of Additive Outlier (AO) and Innovative Outlier (IO) approaches[1]. Since economic freedom has skyrocketed after the 1980s compared to the previous periods, the Bayer-Hanck method provides clear information for the changing dynamics of income distribution whether the series have a long-run linkage among each other. Therefore, this study will be the first in the literature in which the Bayer-Hanck combined cointegration is used in case of the Turkish economy.

The study is structured as follows. Section 2 focuses on the empirical evidence for the economic freedom-income inequality nexus. Section 3 summarizes the data set and the methodology framework that we use in the following part. Section 4 presents unit root test results considering the structural breaks. Section

1 The details of these models will be discussed in section 3.

5 presents the results for the Bayer-Hanck combined cointegration approach and section 6 concludes.

2 Literature Review

The literature on economic freedom has controversial empirical findings when income inequality is taken into account in the context of differing econometric procedures for both time-series and panel studies. In other words, the distributive mechanisms of a higher level of economic freedom about national income remain ambiguous. While some of these studies find that a higher level of economic freedom leads to a higher degree of equality, the others argue that this positive relationship is conditioned on some major factors; and therefore, the reverse case may be valid for that linkage. In this sense, the major question of this study depends on the fact that which factors critical for the determination of this positive nexus between economic freedom and income distribution should be well-documented. According to Berggren (1999), an increase in equality through a higher level of economic freedom is provided only if the taxes and regulations are reduced to a minimum degree[2]. Additionally, the negative effects of progressiveness in the redistribution system on equality should be stabilized by way of providing a higher level of growth in incomes in which income level of poor people is increased more than that of rich people brought about through more economic liberalization in trade and finance (Berggren, 1999). Grubel (1998) also finds that economic freedom has a significant and positive impact on human well-being indicators such as income level and human development. Therefore, the greater is the economic freedom the higher is the income inequality. The redistributive policies in terms of promoting a higher level of income lead to the reduction of both freedom and human well-being indicators. The same conclusion can be obtained from the empirical evidence of Scully (2002). According to Scully (2002), economic freedom lowers the Gini coefficient but economic growth increases income inequality measured by the Gini data. The author argues that the trade-off between income inequality and economic growth determines the role of economic freedom for a set of advanced and newly industrialized Asian countries. Reuveny and Li (2003) examine the effects of both economic globalization and democracy on income distribution for a pooled sample of 69 countries and argue that these two variables should be jointly taken to obtain robust empirical outcomes about their effects on income

2 Berggren (2003) has an extended survey on the benefits of economic freedom which gives some critical details about the freedom-inequality nexus.

inequality. The results indicate that whereas democracy is negatively linked to income inequality, the proxies for globalization such as foreign direct investment, trade openness, and foreign financial capital inflows have mixed effects on income distribution. Carter (2007) argues that income equality can be provided in two ways: (i) increasing the income-earning opportunities and (ii) promoting redistributive policies towards the poor. In the consideration of these two factors, the second way is the leading one for more equal distribution of income if the level of economic freedom is high. Clark and Lawson (2008) shed some light on the impact of progressive taxation on income inequality. They argue that high top marginal tax rate which is proxied for tax policy leads to an unequal distribution of income. In addition to the tax policy indicator, there are also other factors including private property, sound money, trade liberalization, and the size of government which are correlated with the change in income distribution. Bergh and Nilsson (2010) also find that there is a positive effect of increased economic freedom on within-country income inequality across different country groups. Furthermore, the liberalization indicators studied in Bergh and Nilsson (2010) show no significant effects on income inequality. Bennett and Nikolaev (2017) ascertain that the empirical results are controversial depending on different econometric models and inequality measures.

Ashby and Sobel (2008) examine the relationship between economic freedom and income inequality through the use of cross-sectional data for the US states. According to the authors, the international level and within-country analyses have different impacts on income inequality in terms of economic freedom. In other words, the institutional differences in international level and country-based level are far from each other in case of their effects on income inequality. While the former effect is very intense, the latter have a measurable impact. Furthermore, Ashby and Sobel (2008) find that the level of economic freedom and income inequality are, contrarily, negatively related and the regressions provide generally insignificant results. Bennett and Vedder (2013) also investigate the dynamic link between economic freedom and income equality for the 50 US states over the 1970–2014 period. The empirical outcomes suggest that there is an inverted U-shaped link among these two variables, which supports Apergis's (2015) and Apergis and Cooray's (2017) results. It means that the initial stages of economic freedom benefit relatively more to the upper segments of the society than that of lower segments; and therefore, the level of income inequality increases at low levels of economic freedom. However, at the later stages of economic freedom as the enhancements of it continue, income gains spread out all over the society. On the other hand, Apergis et al. (2013) document that there is a bidirectional Granger-causality both in short- and long-run between economic freedom and income inequality across the US states over the 1981–2004 period. According to these empirical results provided by Granger-causal dynamics for freedom-inequality nexus, a higher level of income inequality leads to the implementation of redistributive policies in states, which, in turn, lead to economic freedom to decline. Pérez-Moreno and Angulo-Guerrero (2016) also note that there is a piece of strong empirical evidence between economic liberalization and income inequality in the EU countries for the 2000s. However, the distribution of income does not associate with the same weight in all areas of economic liberalization. Therefore, the additional indicators should be checked perfectly to obtain robust evidence and to get significant results that the authors suggest. Graafland and Lous (2018) link life satisfaction to the relationship between economic freedom and income inequality and suggest that income inequality is negatively associated with the subjective well-being. In addition, the overall effect of economic freedom in terms of fiscal freedom, free trade, and freedom from government regulation on the level of income inequality is negative. Finally, Sturm and Haan (2015) find that the impact of income redistribution on the level of economic freedom is conditional due to the changes in ethno-linguistic fractionalization.

Given the panel and cross-sectional data results on economic freedom-income distribution nexus, in the following sections that relate to the empirical background of this study, we provide empirical evidence by approaching Bayer-Hanck combined cointegration test to reveal whether the long-run relationship exists or not in the presence of other variables such as economic growth, human development index, and total population. Our results suggest that there is no long-run cointegration between economic freedom and income inequality.

3 Data and Methodology

3.1 Data

The data for the empirical part is collected from different sources but the major variable which measures the economic freedom is obtained from the database of Heritage Foundation. Though this is not the only source for the measure of economic freedom, the others are limited with either because of nonavailability for a long-term period in the time series or unbalanced characteristics of the series. For instance, while the Economic Freedom Index of Gwartney et al. (2006) is available for 1970 and so on, the period between 1970 and 2000 is structured as five-year panels. The rest of the data series is comprised of income inequality, economic growth, human development index, and the logarithm of population which are collected from Solt (2016), World Indicator Database, UNDP

Tab. 1: List of Variables and Definitions

Variable	Definition	Measurement	Source
EFI	Economic Freedom Index	The overall score of the following indicators: property rights, government integrity, judicial effectiveness, tax burden, government spending, fiscal health, business freedom, labor freedom, monetary freedom, trade freedom, investment freedom, financial freedom	The Heritage Database
GINI	Gini coefficient	Gini coefficients based on the index of inequality in equivalized household disposable (i.e., post-tax and post-transfer) income	Solt (2016)
GRW	Economic Growth	Annual percentage growth rate of GDP at market prices based on constant local currency	World Bank, World Development Indicators Database
HDI	Human Development Index	A summary measure of average achievement in key dimensions of human development: a long and healthy life, being knowledgeable, and having a decent standard of living	UNDP Database
LOGPOP	Total Population	Logarithm of the total population	IMF, World Economic Outlook October 2018 Database

Database, and World Economic Outlook 2018 Database, respectively. Table 1 shows the definitions and sources on the list of variables.

To understand the details of the variables, we can focus on some major characteristics of the series. First, the Gini coefficient (GINI), proxying for income inequality is one of the major variables using in the analysis. The GINI ranges between 0 and 100. The value 0 shows perfect income equality and 100 shows perfect income inequality. Second, the Economic Freedom Index (EFI) captures different subfactors from the whole economic structure and thus reflects important facts about the changing dynamics of the Turkish economy to a certain point in time. The following main components of EFI are the basis of the whole data and the overall score is the weighted average of them: (1) Property Rights, (2) Government Integrity, (3) Judicial Effectiveness, (4) Tax Burden,

Fig. 1: Economic Freedom in Turkey, 1995–2015. **Source:** Heritage Database

(5) Government Spending, (6) Fiscal Health, (7) Business Freedom, (8) Labor Freedom, (9) Monetary Freedom, (10) Trade Freedom, (11) Investment Freedom, and (12) Financial Freedom. Each component is ranged from 0 to 100. Similar to the methodological context of Gini coefficient, for the case of the overall score, 0 indicates no economic freedom and 100 indicates full economic freedom. The EFI and the other indices are constructed on a somehow familiar theoretical framework. Therefore, the exchange for more regulatory economic environment instead of personal and economic liberties is rapidly reflected as a change in the overall score of EFI. For instance, Gwartney and Lawson (2002) point out that if there is a substitution for personal preference, voluntary exchange, and market coordination instead of the higher level of taxes, government expenditures, and regulations, the overall score of economic freedom increases or vice versa. In the empirical results, we ignore the inclusion of these subcomponents of EFI as an additional series due to the fact that further studies will consider this issue with a panel of other countries by using different econometric procedures. On the contrary, we examine the effects of macroeconomic and social components on the economic freedom-income distribution nexus in Turkey, which may have different dynamics that are critical for changing the inequality level. These components include economic growth (GRW), human development index (HDI), and the logarithm of total population (LOGPOP).

While the series for these additional variables are available for the 1970s at least, the annual observation for the EFI database starts only by 1995. Therefore,

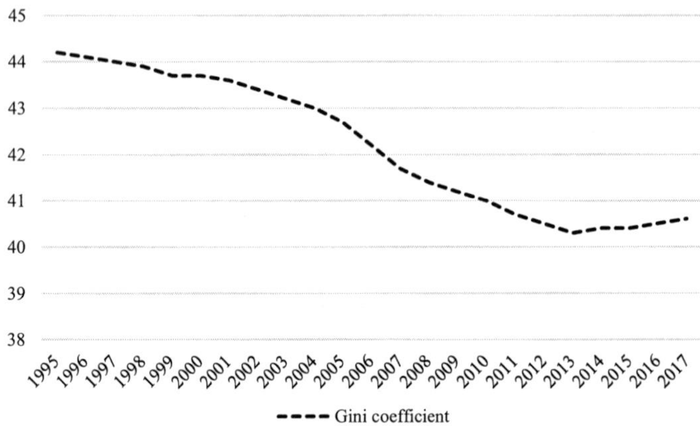

Fig. 2: Income Inequality in Turkey, 1995–2015. **Source:** Solt, 2016

this study covers the period between 1995 and 2017. Figure 1 shows the historical movements of economic freedom in Turkey over the 1995–2017 period. In particular, the increasing trend of this variable is very clear across this time span. This trend for the overall score of economic freedom also implies the downgrading of the regulatory structure of the Turkish economy. However, the subcomponents may have different trends due to their weights in an aggregate economic framework. In addition, Fig. 2 shows the changing dynamics of income inequality over the same period. It is clear that the degree of income inequality has decreased since 1995. However, the reasons behind this upturn in income distribution among individuals are several and hence should be analyzed by considering the other factors from the political, social, and historical spheres. Finally, Tab. 2 provides descriptive statistics for the series in detail, including variance, skewness, and kurtosis.

3.2 Methodology

This subsection gives an information on the methodological background for an investigation of the economic freedom-income distribution nexus in Turkey. As mentioned in the introduction, the empirical foundation of this study is based on the combined cointegration approach produced by Bayer and Hanck (2013). While the cointegration is analyzed by different econometric procedures in the time-series method, few of them elaborate the critical importance of the presence of the structural breaks in the series, which may result in producing biased

Tab. 2: Descriptive Statistics

	EFI_t	$GINI_t$	GRW_t	HDI_t	$LOGPOP_t$
Mean	59.7	42.2	5.05	0.70	7.84
Median	60.8	42.2	6.43	0.70	7.84
Maximum	65.2	44.2	11.1	0.79	7.91
Minimum	50.6	40.3	-5.96	0.61	7.78
Std. Dev.	4.24	1.47	4.52	0.06	0.04
Variance	18.0	2.16	20.4	0.01	0.01
Skewness	-0.73	0.01	-1.22	0.03	-0.00
Kurtosis	2.49	1.34	3.62	1.79	1.83

estimators. Therefore, the initial stages of Bayer-Hanck method need unit root tests considering the potential structural breaks that may occur over time in order to gauge whether the series are stationary or not.

The standard unit root test produced by Dickey and Fuller (1981) is further developed by Perron (1990) to solve biased estimation results which may emerge due to the presence of a structural break in the trend function. Whereas the traditional methods for testing the unit roots ignore the potentiality of any structural break in the series and thus treat them as a random walk process, the extended unit root tests emphasize that the only way to make series stationary is to take their first differences. According to Altuzarra (2015: 118), the structural breaks occur due to several reasons such as economic crises, changes in real interest rates, labor reform measures, or the changes in other policies including both social and political factors. Saatcioğlu and Korap (2007: 111) argue that the selection of the actual date of structural break is determined as a priori. The selection bias of the actual data and the exogenously chosen date should be removed. Therefore, the new methods are allowed for an endogenous determination of the structural breakpoints. For instance, Zivot and Andrews (1992) developed this kind of method which allows for one endogenous break to test the stationary of the time series. Additionally, we use the method proposed by Clemente et al. (1998) which captures two structural breaks in the series. The two models, which are called Additive Outlier (AO) and Innovative Outlier (IO), capture sudden and gradual changes in means, respectively (Glynn et al., 2007).

The method provided by Zivot and Andrews (1992) considers three different kinds of models in case of the presence of one structural break in the series. While Model A and Model B include a shift in the intercept and a change in the slope, respectively, Model C deals with both intercept and slope. Equation

(1) shows the simple time series form y_t to test the Zivot-Andrews method that is used to measure the abovementioned three models:

$$y = \mu + y_{t-1} + \varepsilon_t$$

The null hypothesis, α=0, is based on the fact that time series are integrated irrespective from the exogenous structural break. However, the alternative hypothesis, α≠0, takes into consideration of the exogenous structural break. According to the null hypothesis, trend-stationary *I(0)* process with a break arising in an unknown period of time is possible under some conditions. In this sense, Zivot and Andrews (1992) conduct their unit root tests on the basis of selection of the point of a structural break as the minimum *t*-value on the autoregressive y_t variable. It occurs at time 1 < TB < T. In addition, three potential models are estimated by ordinary least squares with the break fraction, λ = TB/T. By considering these details on unit root tests, Zivot and Andrews (1992: 254) provide augmented regressions in Eqs (2), (3), and (4) as follows:

Model A:

$$y_t = \hat{\mu}^A + \hat{\theta}^A DU_t\left(\hat{\lambda}\right) + \hat{\beta}^A t + \hat{\alpha}^A y_{t-1} + \sum_{j=1}^{k} \hat{c}_j^A + \Delta y_{t-j} + \hat{\varepsilon}_t$$

Model B:

$$y_t = \hat{\mu}^B + \hat{\gamma}^B DT_t^*\left(\hat{\lambda}\right) + \hat{\beta}^B t + \hat{\alpha}^B y_{t-1} + \sum_{j=1}^{k} \hat{c}_j^B + \Delta y_{t-j} + \hat{\varepsilon}_t$$

Model C:

$$y_t = \hat{\mu}^C + \hat{\theta}^C DU_t\left(\hat{\lambda}\right) + \hat{\gamma}^C DT_t^*\left(\hat{\lambda}\right) + \hat{\beta}^C t + \hat{\alpha}^C y_{t-1} + \sum_{j=1}^{k} \hat{c}_j^C + \Delta y_{t-j} + \hat{\varepsilon}_t$$

where DU_t is an indicator dummy variable for a mean shift occurring at each potential breakpoint and DT_t is a corresponding trend shift variable (Waheed et al., 2006: 5). Formally, DU_t (λ) = 1 if 1 is greater than $T\lambda$, 0 otherwise; DT_t^* (λ) = $t - T\lambda$ if t is greater than $T\lambda$, 0 otherwise. In these regressions, Δ shows the difference operator and k shows the number of lags corresponding to each potential structural break. ε is the error term. One of the most crucial point of the Zivot-Andrews method is the likelihood of any specific time denoting as a potential break date. Therefore, each regression is sequentially conducted on the basis of estimating the presence of every possible break date.

The actual date is determined by way of minimizing the one-sided t-statistics for testing $\hat{\alpha} = 1$ where the t-statistic with a highest significant rate is selected for α[3]. Additionally, the major role of Δy_{t-j} is to remove the autocorrelation issue occurring in the models. The smallest t-statistics for α indicates the actual structural breakpoint. Though structural breakpoints are determined in case of these contexts, the Zivot-Andrews method also considers the presence of end points to minimize the problems occurring due to asymptotic distribution of the statistics to diverge towards infinity. Therefore, the exact region for the determination of an actual structural breakpoint is obtained by ignoring some potential end points of the sample.

Besides the Zivot-Andrews method to test the stationary of the sample in case of one potential endogenous break which is allowed for, Clemente et al. (1998) offer an extended version of this initial method allowing for two endogenous breaks through two models, IO and AO. In the IO approach, the shifts suddenly occur in the mean; and thus, two potential breaks belong to the innovational outliner. Equation (5) estimates the IO approach as follows:

$$y_t = \mu + \rho y_{t-1} + \delta_1 DTB_{1t} + \delta_2 DTB_{2t} + d_1 DU_{1t} + d_2 DU_{2t} + \sum_{i=1}^{k} c_i \Delta y_{t-i} + \varepsilon_t$$

Moreover, the stationary hypothesis of the time series can be determined by way of additive outliners. In the AO approach, the shifts gradually occur in the mean; and thus, the primary way to do is to eliminate the deterministic coefficient produced in Eq. (5). In that vein, Eq. (6) estimates the AO approach as follows:

$$y_t = \mu + d_1 DU_{1t} + d_2 DU_{2t} + \tilde{y}_t$$

All in all, Eq. (7) implements the test in consideration of taking the minimal t-statistics for the hypothesis conducted on $\rho = 1$ as follows:

$$y_t = \sum_{i=0}^{k} \omega_{1i} DTB_{1t-i} + \sum_{i=0}^{k} \omega_{2i} DTB_{2t-i} + \rho \tilde{y}_{t-1} + \sum_{i=1}^{k} c_i \Delta \tilde{y}_{t-i} + \varepsilon_t$$

where DTB_{it} is a pulse variable and DU_t is an indicator dummy variable for a mean shift occurring at each potential breakpoint. $DTB_{it} = 1$ if $t = TB_i + 1$ ($i = 1, 2$), and 0 otherwise; $DU_{it} = 1$ if $t > TB_i$ ($i = 1, 2$), and 0 otherwise. TB_1

3 For more technical information, please see Waheed et al. (2006: 5).

Tab. 3: Lag Length Selection

Lag	LogL	LR	FPE	AIC	HQIC	SBIC
VAR lag order selection criteria						
0	2.39007		8.8e-07	0.248565	0.302538	0.497261
1	161.232	317.68	2.8e-12	-12.4982	-12.1744	-11.0061*
2	197.553	72.644*	1.6e-12*	-13.5765*	-12.9828*	-10.8409

Notes: * indicates lag order selected by the criterion. LR: sequential modified LR test statistic, FPE: final prediction error, AIC: Akaike information criteria, HQIC: Hannan and Quinn information criteria, SBIC: Schwarz's Bayesian information criteria.

and TB_2 indicate the dates in which the shifts in the mean occur over the sample period.

Finally, the models proposed by Clemente et al. (1998) point that the potential breakpoint of the series follow a first-order autoregressive process, AR(1) where the hypotheses are based on this AR(1) process. The null (H_0) hypothesis is conducted on the following model as shown in Eq. (8):

$$H_0 : y_t = y_{t-1} + \delta_1 DTB_{1t} + \delta_2 DTB_{2t} + \varepsilon_t$$

The alternative (H_1) hypothesis, on the other hand, is conducted on the following model as shown in Eq. (9):

$$H_1 : y_t = \mu + d_1 DU_{1t} + d_2 DTB_{2t} + \varepsilon_t$$

The next section shows the results of the unit root tests produced by Zivot and Andrews (1992) and Clemente et al. (1998). In the consideration of these results, we will proceed by implementing the combined cointegration approach developed by Bayer and Hanck (2013) in the subsequent section.

4 Unit Root Tests Results

In this part, we present the unit root tests results for methods of both Zivot and Andrews (1992) and Clemente et al. (1998). However, in the first step, we determine the optimum lag length which is a basic point of unit root tests. In that sense, Tab. 3 shows the selection-order criteria. According to these results, we employ AIC for the determination of the maximum lag length.

In consideration of the selection-order criteria, Tab. 4 gives the Zivot-Andrews unit root test results. It allows for the endogenous breaks in the series. Each estimation result indicates that the nonstationary characteristics of the series are not valid allowing for intercept, trend, and both. The unit root test of Zivot-Andrews

Tab. 4: Zivot-Andrews Unit Root Test Results

Variable	Intercept			Trend			Both		
	k	min-t	T_B	k	min-t	T_B	k	min-t	T_B
EFI	0	-4.084	2002	0	-2.838	2004	0	-3.959	2002
GINI	1	-2.411	2006	1	-2.745	2013	1	-2.388	2011
GRW	0	-4.479	1998	0	-4.416	1999	0	-4.933	2002
HDI	1	-3.564	2011	1	-2.641	2008	1	-3.449	2013
LogPOP	1	-3.568	2013	1	-3.327	2007	1	-3.424	2013

Notes: In all models, the trim value is accepted as 0.05. Lag length is determined by Akaike-Schwarz information criteria (AIC). min-t is the minimum t-statistic measured. The critical values of t-statistics are as follows: intercept: -5.34 (1 %), -4.80 (5 %), -4.58 (%10); trend: -4.93 (1 %), -4.42 (5 %), -4.11 (10 %); both: -5.57 (1 %), -5.08 (5 %), -4.82 (10 %).

Tab. 5: Additive Outlier Model

Variable	T_B	min-t	du_1	t-stat (du_1)	du_2	t-stat (du_2)
EFI	2002, 2007	-3.396	-5.34	-3.852***	9.09	6.831***
GINI	2003, 2008	-3.665	-1.56	-6.806***	-1.58	-6.904***
GRW	1999, 2007	-5.229	1.09	0.404	-0.35	-0.156
HDI	2003, 2011	-2.995	0.07	6.552***	0.07	5.650***
LogPOP	2002, 2010	-2.810	0.05	6.491***	0.04	6.096***

Notes: ***, **, and * denote significance at the 1 %, 5 %, and 10 % levels, respectively. T_B denotes the estimated breakpoints. The 5 % critical value of t-statistics with two breaks is -5.490. The coefficients (du_i) are also reported in the Table. T-statistics for du_i are given in parentheses.

method shows that the series are difference-stationary in *I(1)*. In other words, the null hypothesis is not rejected due to the fact that the min-*t* values are smaller than the critical values in absolute terms. In that sense, the unit root test results in first-differences of the series should be stationary. All outputs imply that the series become stationary in their first-differences. Therefore, it means all series are integrated at *I(1)*.

While the Zivot-Andrews method allows for only one endogenous structural break in the series, Clemente et al. (1998) present an extended case of this unit root test by way of allowing for double mean shifts of the series in case of AO and IO models. Table 5 and Tab. 6 present the unit root tests produced by Clemente et al. (1998) for AO and IO models, respectively. First, Tab. 5 denotes the "additive outlier" model which stands for a sudden change

Tab. 6: Innovative Outlier Model

Variable	T_B	min-t	du_1	t-stat (du_1)	du_2	t-stat (du_2)
EFI	2000, 2004	-4.410	-5.52	-3.904***	6.60	4.904***
GINI	2000, 2004	-6.812	-0.24	3.396***	-0.52	-5.237***
GRW	2000, 2008	-6.037	2.14	1.071	0.61	0.344
HDI	1998, 2008	-4.672	0.01	2.678**	0.01	4.702***
LogPOP	2007, 2011	-6.109	0.00	6.721***	0.00	0.351

Notes: ***, **, and * denote significance at the 1 %, 5 %, and 10 % levels, respectively. T_B denotes the estimated breakpoints. The 5 % critical value of t-statistics with two breaks is -5.490. The coefficients (du_i) are also reported in the Table. T-statistics for du_i are given in parentheses.

in the mean of the series. The results show that break date is not limited to any year. For each variable, the break date differs subject to several economic factors influencing from the changes in the Turkish economy over the 1995–2017 period. Both of these two breaks also differ irrespective of the factors affecting the series.

Second, Tab. 6 shows the "innovative outlier" model results in which the series have a gradual change. According to the outcomes of the model, the first breakpoint starts in 1999 and the last breakpoint emerges in 2011. Therefore, the empirical results show that the inner dynamics of the Turkish economy are substantially affected by different sources emerging in the societal structure.

5 Bayer-Hanck Combined Cointegration Test Results

The econometric side of the cointegration analyses is not specific to any model. Therefore, each model has its own assumptions and theoretical structure. The pioneer of these models can go back to the cointegration approach developed by Engle and Granger (1987). The major way to estimate the long-run relationship between the series in terms of the cointegration analysis grounds on the regression provided by ordinary least squares (OLS) method. In the context of the OLS method, the cointegration test is also based on the derivation of the residuals and then uses these residuals to detect whether the series are stationary. Furthermore, Granger (1988) developed a bivariate system analysis. According to this extended approach, in case of existing two series such as x_t and y_t, the true forecast value of x_{t+1} is obtained only by the presence of the same order integration of x_t and y_t and of full information about the y_t. If this is the case, one can suppose that there is a Granger causality from y_t to x_t.

However, both Engle and Granger (1987) and Granger (1988) ignored the spurious causality relationship between the time series. In that sense, Johansen (1988) developed a new model to eliminate this problem emerging in the series in which they are stationary in *I(1)* by taking the first-differences of the variables. Boswijk (1994) also investigates the cointegrating series in consideration of single-equation and simultaneous models to detect whether the series have a long-run linkage among each other by way of the conditional error correction model with Wald tests. Finally, Banerjee et al. (1998) consider the cointegration analysis in which the variables are assumed to be highly oriented to the weak exogenous. All these different cointegration tests lead to the emergence of a new type of joint approach developed Bayer and Hanck (2013) to test whether the series are cointegrated in the long run.

According to Bayer and Hanck (2013), both of these tests provide mixed results. Therefore, the empirical framework of these tests is controversial. Though each estimation result has its own interpretation, the p-values provided by these cointegration tests are not perfectly correlated (Gregory et al., 2004). In that sense, there is no exact choice of which approach gives the true estimation results.

All these issues lead Bayer and Hanck (2013) to develop a new and generalized type of method which is the so-called combined cointegration approach. According to this newly emerged method, the most efficient estimators are selected through the elimination of inconvenient multiple testing procedures (Rafindadi, 2015: 188). Therefore, Bayer and Hanck (2013) follow a joint test decision proposed by Fisher (1932) to combine the other testing methods.

The theoretical background of this joint test decisions is provided in Eqs. (10) and (11) as follows:

$$EG - JOH = -2[\ln(PBG) + \ln(PJOH)]$$

and

$$EG - JOH - BO - BDM = -2[ln\,(P_{BG}) + ln\,(P_{JOH}) + ln\,(P_{BO}) + ln\,(P_{BDM})]$$

where P_{BG}, P_{JOH}, P_{BO}, and P_{BDM} present the p-values of the cointegration test developed by Engle and Granger (1987), Johansen (1988), Boswijk (1994), and Banerjee et al. (1998), respectively. Contrary to these cointegration tests, Bayer and Hanck (2013) benefit from the Fisher statistics to get a significant result for estimating the condition of cointegration. In particular, Eq. (11) has two different test statistics.

In the case of Bayer-Hanck approach, the null hypothesis is conducted on the assumption that the cointegration is rejected if the estimated Fisher statistics are

Tab. 7: The Results of Bayer and Hanck Cointegration

Estimated Models	EG–JOH	EG–JOH–BO–BDM	Cointegration
$EFI_t = f(GINI_t, GRW_t, HDI_t, LogPOP_t)$	55.305	110.567	Yes
$GINI_t = f(EFI_t, GRW_t, HDI_t, LogPOP_t)$	55.276	165.800	Yes
$GRW_t = f(EFI_t, GINI_t, HDI_t, LogPOP_t)$	56.943	167.467	Yes
$HDI_t = f(EFI_t, GINI_t, GRW_t, LogPOP_t)$	56.672	167.196	Yes
$LogPOP_t = f(EFI_t, GINI_t, GRW_t, HDI_t)$	56.472	111.734	Yes
Significance Level	Critical Values	Critical Values	
1 % Level	15.845	30.774	
5 % Level	10.576	20.143	
10 % Level	8.301	15.938	

higher than the critical value. However, the lag length should be well-established due to the fact it changes the p-values of the estimated models. Therefore, the optimal lag length is selected as three according to the VAR lag order criteria.

Table 7 presents the Bayer-Hanck combined cointegration test results. The empirical outcomes show that both of these two test statistics are greater than the critical values. In other words, the null hypothesis of no cointegration between the series is rejected for all estimated models.

Our empirical findings on the basis of cointegration analysis developed by Bayer and Hanck (2013) show that there is a long-run relationship between economic freedom and income inequality over the 1995–2017 period in Turkey. Though we add additional variables into the models such as economic growth rate, human development index, and the logarithm of total population, the Fisher-statistics are higher than the critical values for %1, %5, and %10 significance levels. Therefore, we can conclude that the long-run relationship in terms of these models exists for that period in Turkey.

6 Concluding Remarks

The debate on the relationship between economic freedom and income distribution is still one of the major areas in which many scholars investigate the factors that change the dynamics of this nexus. While some of the studies argue that more economic freedom means a lower level of income inequality, the others suggest the reverse case is true mainly due to unequal distribution of available resources in the society which is affected from both policy changes and economic differences across countries. To the best of our knowledge, this study is the first for the case of Turkey in which the long-run linkage between economic freedom and income inequality is examined to reveal that whether there is a cointegration or not between the series over the 1995–2017 period through the use of Bayer-Hanck combined cointegration approach.

The primary issue to implement the Bayer-Hanck combined cointegration approach was to test the stationary of the series. Therefore, we applied the Zivot-Andrews unit root test allowing for one endogenous break in the time series. The estimation results showed that there is no change in the nonstationary features of the variables. It means that the series are difference-stationary in *I(1)* in which the null hypothesis is not rejected. In the first differences of the variables, both series became stationary. The second issue was the determination of the stationary condition of the variables in two endogenous breakpoints. Hence, we used the unit root test produced by Clemente et al. (1998) allowing for double mean shifts of the series for both AO and IO models. The results provided by AO and IO models showed that the first and second breaks do not depend on a specific year. In that sense, the series were also not stationary in levels but the reverse held in the first differences of the series.

Finally, the Bayer-Hanck combined cointegration tests illustrated that there is a long-run relationship between economic freedom and income inequality over the 1995–2017 period in Turkey. This empirical evidence was also supported in the presence of other control variables such as economic growth, human development index, and the population level. In a technical context, the results pointed out that the Fisher-statistics are greater than the critical values which indicate that both tests statistically reject the null hypothesis of no cointegration between the series. In other words, our finding showed that there is cointegration between EFI_t, $GINI_t$, GRW_t, HDI_t, and $LOGPOP_t$. This implied that the long-run relationship is prevailing between economic freedom, income inequality, economic growth, human development, and population level over the 1995–2017 period in Turkey.

Bibliography

Altuzarra, A. (2015), "Measuring Unemployment Persistence by Age and Gender", **Journal of Economic Forecasting**, Vol.4, pp. 110–133.

Apergis, N. (2015), "Economic Freedom and Income Inequality: Further Evidence from 58 Countries in the Long-Run", **Financial Theory and Practice**, Vol.39, N. 4, pp. 349–370.

Apergis, N., and Cooray, A. (2017). "Economic Freedom and Income Inequality: Evidence from a Panel of Global Economies-A Linear and a

Non-Linear Long-Run Analysis", **The Manchester School**, Vol.85, N.1, pp.88–105.

Apergis, N., Dincer, O., and Payne, J. (2013), "Economic Freedom and Income Inequality Revisited: Evidence from a Panel Error Correction Model", **Contemporary Economic Policy**, V.32, N.1, pp. 67–75.

Ashby, N., and Sobel, R. (2008), "Income Inequality and Economic Freedom in the U.S. States", **Public Choice**, Vol.134, N.3–4, pp. 329–346.

Banerjee, A., Dolado, J., and Mestre, R. (1998), "Error-Correction Mechanism Tests for Cointegration in a Single-Equation Framework", **Journal of Time Series Analysis**, Vol.19, N.3, pp. 267–283.

Bayer, C., and Hanck, C. (2013), "Combining Non-cointegration Tests", **Journal of Time Series Analysis**, Vol.34, pp. 83–95.

Bennett, D. L., and Nikolaev, B. (2017), "On the Ambiguous Economic Freedom-Inequality Relationship", **Empirical Economics**, Vol.53, N.2, pp.717–754.

Bennett, D. L., and Vedder, R. K. (2013), "A Dynamic Analysis of Economic Freedom and Income Inequality in the 50 U.S. States: Empirical Evidence of a Parabolic Relationship", **Journal of Regional Analysis & Policy**, Vol.43, N.1, pp. 42–55.

Berggren, N. (1999), "Economic Freedom and Equality: Friends or Foes?" **Public Choice**, Vol.100, N.3–4, pp. 203–223.

Berggren, N. (2003), "The Benefits of Economic Freedom: A Survey", **The Independent Review**, Vol.8, N.2, pp. 193–211.

Bergh, A., and Nilsson, T. (2010), "Do Liberalization and Globalization Increase Income Inequality?", **European Journal of Political Economy**, Vol.26, N.4, pp. 488–505.

Boswijk, P. H. (1994), "Testing for an Unstable Root in Conditional and Structural Error Correction Models", **Journal of Econometrics**, Vol.63, N.1, pp. 37–60.

Carter, J. R. (2007), "An Empirical Note on Economic Freedom and Income Inequality", **Public Choice**, Vol.130, N.1/2, pp. 163–177.

Clark, J. R., and Lawson, R. A. (2008), "The Impact of Economic Growth, Tax Policy and Economic Freedom on Income Inequality", **Journal of Private Enterprise**, Vol.24, pp. 23–31.

Clemente, J., Montañés, A., and Reyes, M. (1998), "Testing for a Unit Root in Variables with a Double Change in the Mean", **Economic Letters**, Vol.59, N.2, pp.175–182.

Dickey, D. A., and Fuller, W. A. (1981), "Likelihood Ratio Statistics for Autoregressive Time Series with a Unit Root", **Econometrica**, Vol.49, N.4, pp. 1057–1072.

Engle, R. F. and Granger, C. W. J. (1987), "Co-integration and Error Correction: Representation, Estimation, and Testing", **Econometrica**, Vol.55, N.2, pp. 251–276.

Fisher, R. A. (1932), Statistical Methods for Research Workers, 4th edition, Edinburg: Oliver & Boyd.

Glynn, J., Perrera, N., and Verma, R. (2007), "Unit Root Tests and Structural Breaks: A Survey with Applications", **Journal of Quantitative Methods for Economics and Business Administration**, Vol.3, N1, pp. 63–79.

Graafland, J., and Lous, B. (2018), "Economic Freedom, Income Inequality and Life Satisfaction in OECD Countries", **Journal of Happiness Studies**, Vol.19, N.7, pp. 2071–2093.

Granger, C. W. J. (1988), "Some Recent Development in a Concept of Causality", **Journal of Econometrics**, Vol.39, N.1–2, pp. 199–211.

Gregory, A. W., Haug, A. A., and Lomuto, N. (2004), "Mixed Signals Among Tests for Cointegration", **Journal of Applied Econometrics**, Vol.19, N.1, pp. 89–98.

Grubel, H. G. (1998), "Economic Freedom and Human Welfare: Some Empirical Findings", **Cato Journal**, Vol.18, N.2, pp. 287–304.

Gwartney, J., and Lawson, R. (2002), **Economic Freedom of the World 2002 Annual Report**, Vancouver: The Fraser Institute.

Gwartney, J., Holcombe, R., and Lawson, R. (2006), "Institutions and the Impact of Investment on Growth", **Kyklos**, Vol.59, N.2, pp. 255–273.

Johansen, S. (1988), "Statistical Analysis of Cointegration Vectors", **Journal of Economic Dynamics and Control**, Vol.12, N.2–3, pp. 231–254.

Kuznets, S. (1955), "Economic Growth and Income Inequality", **American Economic Review**, Vol.45, N.1, pp. 1–28.

Pérez-Moreno, S., and Angulo-Guerrero, M. (2016), "Does Economic Freedom Increase Income Inequality? Evidence from the EU Countries", **Journal of Economic Policy Reform**, Vol.19, N.4, pp. 327–347.

Perron, P. (1990), "Testing for a Unit Root in a Time Series With a Changing Mean", **Journal of Business & Economic Statistics**, Vol.8, N.2, pp. 153–162.

Rafindadi, A. A. (2015), "Econometric Prediction on the Effects of Financial Development and Trade Openness on the German Energy Consumption: A Startling Revelation from the Data Set", **International Journal of Energy Economics and Policy**, Vol.5, N.1, pp. 182–196.

Reuveny, R., and Li, Q. (2003), "Economic Openness, Democracy, and Income Inequality: An Empirical Analysis", **Comparative Political Studies**, Vol.36, N.5, pp. 575–601.

Saatcioğlu, C., and Korap, L. (2007), "Turkish Money Demand, Revisited: Some Implications for Inflation and Currency Substitution Under Structural Breaks", **Boğaziçi Journal**, Vol. 21, N.1–2, pp. 107–124.

Scully, G. (2002), "Economic Freedom, Government Policy, and the Trade-Of Between Equity and Economic Growth", **Public Choice**, Vol.113, N.1/2, pp. 77–96.

Solt, F. (2016), "The Standardized World Income Inequality Database", **Social Science Quarterly**, Vol.97, N.5, pp. 1267–1281.

Sturm, J.-E., and Haan, D. J. (2015), "Income Inequality, Capitalism and Ethno-Linguistic Fractionalization", **American Economic Review**, Vol.105, N.5, pp. 593–597.

Waheed, M., Alam, T., and Ghauri, S. P. (2006), "Structural Breaks and Unit Root: Evidence from Pakistani Macroeconomic Time Series", **Munich Personal RePEc Archive (MPRA),** Paper No. 1797.

Zivot, E., and Andrews, D. W. K. (1992), "Further Evidence on the Great Crash, the Oil-Price Shock, and the Unit-Root Hypothesis", **Journal of Business & Economic Statistics**, Vol.10, N.3, pp. 251–270.

Dr. Sezgi Gedik

International Tourism and the Importance of Tourism in the Turkish Economy (2008–2019)

Abstract: After the 2000s, with the development of technology, people's leisure time has increased, transportations have developed, access to information has become easier, globalization has accelerated and the borders have disappeared. These developments have allowed people to devote more time to their different needs such as traveling-seeing, eating-drinking, having fun, resting, learning, health, religion, and sports. Thus, people started to travel more and tourism became a necessity instead of being a luxury. While the number of people participating in tourism in 1950 was 25 million, this number reached 1400 million in 2018 and still increasing.

Keywords: Tourism, Tourism Economy, Turkey

Tourism is intertwined with the economy, and it is an important sector that has a positive impact on both national and international economies. The tourism sector is a branch of activity that contributes to the socioeconomic development levels of the countries in various aspects. Tourism, especially for developing countries, is very important in providing employment, a high multiplier effect, positive effects on the balance of payments, and economic growth. In addition to providing needed foreign exchange, providing modern living conditions to people, tourism appears to be a sector that stimulates investments in the general economy, increases personal income and public revenues, and balances income distribution and regional development level (İçöz, 2005:182; Yağcı, 2007:164). Furthermore, tourism, which has become a competitive strategy of the countries, is one of the largest sectors in the world and continues to grow rapidly.

Especially for developing countries such as Turkey, tourism has many advantages such as developing infrastructure and subsectors related to tourism, providing technology transfer and encouraging foreign capital investments. Touristic infrastructure and superstructure investments also attract direct domestic and foreign investments to the region. Multinational companies in foreign investors create positive contributions to the regions where they invest by creating employment, increasing foreign exchange income of countries, and transferring advanced knowledge and business methods they have (Dinçer, 1993:90–91). In a region, the opening of new business areas together with tourism investments increases the income of employees, positively affecting

Tab. 1: International Tourist Arrivals by Subregion (2008–2018). **Source:** (World Tourism Organization (UNWTO) Tourism Highlights 2010–2018)

International Tourist Arrivals 2008–2018 (Million)											
Years	2008	2009	2010	2011	2012	2013	2014	2015	2016	2017	2018
Europe	485.2	461.7	474.8	516.4	534.4	563	584	609	615	671	710
Asia and Pacific	184.1	181.1	204.4	218.2	233.5	248	263	278	309	324	348
Americas	147.8	141.7	150.7	156.0	162.7	169	182	191	200	207	216
Africa	44.4	45.9	49.7	49.4	52.9	56	56	53	58	63	67
Middle East	55.2	52.8	60.3	54.9	51.7	52	50	54	54	58	60
World	917	883	940	995	1.035	1.087	1.134	1.195	1.235	1.323	1451

income distribution (Çeken, 2003:147). Tourism is also a sector that makes significant economic contributions to the services sectors such as transportation and accommodation (Bahar and Kozak, 2006:144).

International Tourism

Every year, a very high proportion of the world's population travels outside the borders of their country. However, when the distribution of international tourism among the countries is examined, although some countries have a huge income from international tourism, the income of some countries constitutes a very small share. Today, most of the international tourism is in the hands of European and Asia and Pacific countries. However, in recent years, there has been a considerable increase in the African and Middle East regions, and their share in tourism has been increasing.

International tourist arrivals (overnight visitors) in the world increased by 5 % to 1.4 million in 2018 based on the data reported by destinations around the world. International tourist arrivals increased by 5 % in the Middle East (60 Million), 7 % in Africa (67 Million), 7 % in Asia and Pacific (348 Million), 5 % in Europe (710 Million), and 2% in America (216 Million) (Tab. 1).

When the changes in tourist arrivals are examined over the years, 174 % between 1950 and 1959, 139 % between 1960 and 1969, 73 % between 1970 and 1979, 56 % between 1980 and 1989, 44 % between 1990 and 1999, 25 % between 2000 and 2007, and in the last decade 52.9 % (2008–2018) increase was observed (UNWTO, 2012; Bahar and Kozak, 2012:111–112). Although the rates of tourist arrivals change over time, there is generally a continuous increase.

Tab. 2: International Tourist Arrivals Top 10 (2018 **Source:** (World Tourism Organization (UNWTO) Tourism Highlights 2010–2019)

Rank	Destinations	International Tourist Arrivals (Million)		Change (%)
		(2018)	(2008)	
1	France	89	79.2	12
2	Spain	83	57.2	45
3	USA	80	57.9	38
4	China	63	53.0	18
5	Italy	62	42.7	45
6	Turkey	46	25.0	84
7	Mexico	46	22.6	82
8	Germany	39	24.9	57
9	Thailand	38	---	---
10	United Kingdom	36	30.1	20

* Provisional figure or data

The data reported above suggest that the expected growth was realized 2 years before the long-term forecasts in 2010, and the tourist arrivals expected to be 1.360 million in 2020 reached 1.4 million according to the 2018 forecast data.

In 2017, 1.323 million people participated in the world tourism arrivals, and it is increased by 5 % to 1.451 million people in 2018. Table 2 lists the most traveled countries in the world published by the World Tourism Organization. France ranks first with 89 million visitors, followed by Spain with 83 million visitors, and the USA with 80 million visitors. Turkey was ranked 6th in the ranking with 46 million visitors, according to the 2018 data.

International tourism receipts for 2018 increased by 5.4 % to 1.401 billion (US $) (Tab. 3). The increase in the changes in international tourism receipts by regions is 5 % in Europe, 7 % in Asia and Pacific, 0 % in America, 4 % in the Middle East, and 2 % in Africa.

When the changes in international tourism receipts are examined over the years, 223.8 % between 1950 and 1959, 163.2 % between 1960 and 1969, 471.5 % between 1970 and 1979, 162.9 % between 1980 and 1989, 51 % between 1990 and 1999, 37 % between 2000 and 2007 and the last decade 43 % (2007–2017) increase is observed (UNWTO, 2012; Bahar and Kozak, 2012:111–112).

When the economic effects of tourism are subjected to an intercountry comparison, developed economies have higher values than developing countries. The

Tab. 3: International Tourist Receipts by Subregion (2008–2018). **Source:** (World Tourism Organization (UNWTO) Tourism Highlights 2010–2018)

International Tourist Receipts (Billion) (US$)											
Years	2008	2009	2010	2011	2012	2013	2014	2015	2016	2017	2018
Europe	473.7	410.9	409.3	466.7	454.0	491.7	513.7	449.6	468.1	519.2	570
Asia and Pacific	208.9	203.1	255.3	298.6	329.1	360.7	359.0	349.4	370.8	389.6	435
Americas	188.1	166.2	180.7	197.9	212.9	264.2	288.9	305.6	313.7	326.2	334
Africa	30.2	28.8	30.4	32.7	34.3	35.5	36.5	32.8	33.0	37.3	38
Middle East	39.9	42.0	51.7	46.4	47.5	45.2	53.6	57.6	59.0	67.7	73
World	941	851	927	1.042	1.078	1.197	1.252	1.196	1.245	1.340	1401

* Provisional figure or data

Tab. 4: International Tourism Receipts Top 10 (2018 **Source**: (World Tourism Organization (UNWTO) Tourism Highlights 2008-2019)

Rank	**Destinations**	**International Tourism Receipts Top 10 (US$ Billion)**		**Change (%)**
			2008	
1	**USA**	214	110.0	94.5
2	**Spain**	74	61.6	20
3	**France**	67	56.6	18
4	**Thailand**	63	–	–
5	**United Kingdom**	52	36.0	45
6	**Italy**	49	45.7	7
7	**Australia**	45	24.8	81
8	**Germany**	43	40.0	- 7
9	**Japan**	41	–	–
10	**China**	40	–	–

foreign exchange income provided by the developed countries from the tourism event is much higher than the foreign exchange income provided by the developing countries from the tourism event (Bahar and Kozak, 2013:61).

According to the UNWTO in Tab. 4, USA has grown by 94.5 % in the last 10 years and achieved the highest revenue in international tourism movements in 2018 (214 US$ Billion). In addition, Australia grew by 81 % and the UK by

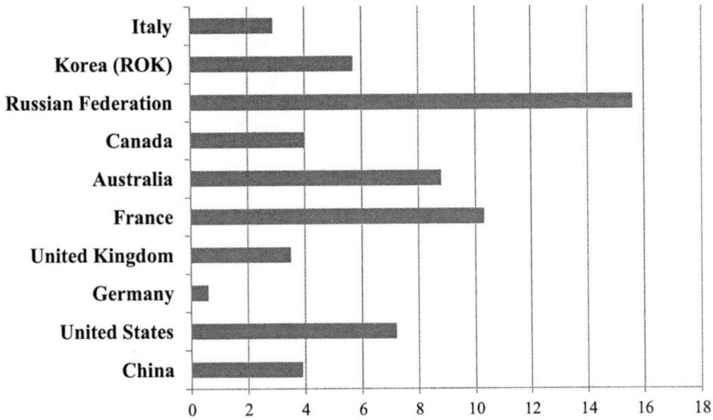

Chart 1: International Tourism Expenditure, 2018 YTD World's Top 10 Expenders (Real % Change over Same Period of Previous Year). **Source:** (World Tourism Organization (UNWTO) Provisional Data for the First 9 to 11 Months)

45 %. Italy (7%) and Germany 7 %) have achieved the same growth in the last decade. Spain has followed the US with 74 billion dollars and France 67 billion dollars. While Turkey ranked 9th in 2008 with 22.0 billion dollars, in 2018, Turkey ranked 14th.

In addition, Thailand and Japan, which were not included in the ranking in 2008, are among the top 10 concerning international tourism receives in 2018.

Among the world's top ten spenders, the Russian Federation (+16 %), France (+10 %), and Australia (+9 %) reported the strongest increase in outbound expenditure in the first nine to eleven months of 2018. The United States (+7 %) and the Republic of Korea (+6 %) also recorded solid spending figures, all of them fueling inbound growth in their respective regions and beyond (Chart 1).

While the arrival of tourists is expected to be 1.809 million in 2030, between 2010 and 2030 Europe will take first place in world tourist arrivals. However, Asia and the Pacific will continue to grow rapidly and remain second. This shows that the competition between Europe and Asia/Pacific will continue (Tab. 5).

In 2008, travel for leisure, recreation, and holidays accounted for half of all international tourist arrivals (51 % or a total of 467 million arrivals); in 2018, this rate increased to 56 %. Some 15 % of international tourists reported traveling for business and professional purposes; in 2018, this rate decreased to 13 %. In 2008 another 27 % traveled for other reasons, such as visiting friends and relatives (VFR), religious reasons/pilgrimages and health treatment. The purpose of the visit for the remaining 7 % of arrivals was not specified. These rates

Tab. 5: UNWTO Tourism Towards 2030: International Tourism by Region of Destination.
Source: (World Tourism Organization (UNWTO) Tourism Highlights 2012)

Destinations	International Tourist Arrivals Received (Million)				Share (%)	
	2010	Projections				
		2020	2030	2010–2030, of which	2010	2030
Africa	50.3	85	134	5.0	5.3	7.4
Americas	149.7	199	248	2.6	15.9	13.7
Asia and Pacific	204.0	355	535	4.9	21.7	29.6
Europe	475.3	620	744	2.3	50.6	41.1
Middle East	60.9	101	149	4.6	6.5	8.2
World	940	1.360	1.809	3.3	100	100

did not change in 2018. Between 2008 and 2018, there were no major changes in the purpose of the travel of tourists (UNWTO).

The Importance of Tourism in the Turkish Economy

For many developing countries such as Turkey, a certain amount of tourism income obtained from tourism has an important place concerning the economic growth and development of those countries. When evaluated from this perspective, the economic benefits and effects of tourism in many underdeveloped countries, which are not developed countries and which are agricultural countries, may be much higher than those of developed countries (Bahar and Kozak, 2013:61).

During the period under review Turkey's tourism revenue was 7.6 billion dollars in 2000, in 2010 it increased to 25 billion dollars, while in 2015 it increased to 31.4 billion dollars. When Tables. 6 and 7 are analyzed, it is seen that there has been an increase in the number of tourists and tourism expenditures from the last 10 years until 2015, but a significant decrease especially in 2016.

In 2015, tourism revenues declined as a result of various events that took place on the international arena, particularly for economic reasons. Turkey in the world ranking moved down an estimated four places following the security incidents and failed coup in 2015. Concerning of receipts, Turkey moved down five places to the 17th position (Chart 2). In 2016, there was a significant decrease in the number of international tourists due to terrorist attacks. Due to these developments, tourism revenues for 2016 were well below expectations (22

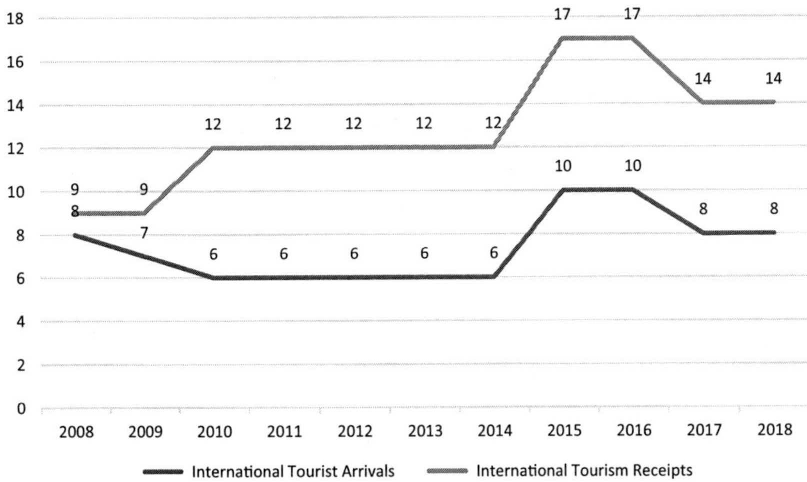

Chart 2: Turkey's Position in the World Ranking (International Tourist Arrivals and Tourism Receipts by Turkey). **Source:** (World Tourism Organization (UNWTO) Tourism Highlights 2010–2018)

Tab. 6: Tourist Arrivals by Turkey (2009–2018). Source: Republic of Turkey Ministry of Culture and Tourism and Turkey Statistical Institute Data Was Compiled

Years	**Tourist Arrivals by Turkey (2009–2018)**
2009	31759816
2010	32997308
2011	36769039
2012	37715225
2013	39860771
2014	41627246
2015	41114069
2016	30906680
2017	37969824
2018	46112592

Tab. 7: Tourist Receipts and Expenses by Turkey (2008–2017) (1000 $). **Source:** (Akın, 2018:9–14; Worldbank, Republic of Turkey Ministry of Culture and Tourism, 2018; Turkey Statistical Institute and Central Bank Data Was Compiled.)

Years	**Tourist Receipts 1**	**Export 2**	% 1/2	**Tourism Expenses 3**	**Import 4**	*% 3/4*	*GDP*	*(%) 1/5*
2008	25 415 067	140.906	18	4 266	193.823	2.2	703.796	3,6
2009	25 064 482	109.732	22.8	5 090	134.494	3.8	669.831	3,7
2010	24 930 997	120.992	20.6	5 875	177.317	3.3	731.168	3,4
2011	28 115 692	142.392	19.7	5 531	231.552	2.3	795.311	3,5
2012	29 007 003	161.948	18.0	4 593	227.315	2.0	812.231	3,5
2013	32 308 991	161.789	20.0	5 254	241.706	2.1	846.284	3,8
2014	34 305 903	168.926	20.3	5 470	232.523	2.3	871.843	4.0
2015	31 464 777	151.970	20.7	5 698	200.127	2.8	1.087.550	2.9
2016	22 107 440	150.161	14.7	5 050	191.020	2.6	1.118.833	2,0
2017	26 283 656	166.161	15.8	5 137	225.117	2.3	1.205.786	2.2.

107 440 billion dollars). However, tourism revenues, which started to rise again in 2017, became 29.5 billion dollars in 2018. According to world tourism data, Turkey remained 8th in arrivals and 14th in receipts in 2018.

The growth in the tourism sector is more volatile than the GDP growth of the country. It is observed that the tourism sector experiences higher peaks in good times and sharper decreases in bad times. During the period under review, except for 2009, 2015 and 2016, the tourism sector has grown continuously in the country. Even after the 2009 global crisis, in which the country's GDP shrank too much and was adversely affected, the tourism sector showed a positive development. It is possible to say that the tourism sector is a key sector that will enable the country's economy to emerge from the troubled period (Akın, 2018:11).

Turkey has given particular importance to the tourism sector in the national economy after the 2000s; tourism investments in the economic and social development process have improved to some extent and also increased. In parallel with the increasing number of tourists in recent years, tourism investments have increased and there has been a positive development in tourism revenues.

Conclusions

Turkey, cultural, historical, and natural value have very vibrant tourism potential; and Turkey cannot use enough tourism potential. According to UNWTO data, the number of tourists visiting Turkey has demonstrated a significant increase until 2015 and shows that it takes place in the first ten countries. However, tourism revenues could not increase at the same rate. Which indicates lower spending by tourists visiting Turkey.

As of 2018 indicating the tourist arrives and tourism receips grew again in Turkey has begun to increase their investments in tourism. Suggestions to ensure more effective use of tourism potential in Turkey are as follows:

- Turkey's new tourism strategy to identify,
- Developing international marketing and promotion strategies,
- Increasing public and private sector cooperation,
- Increasing tourism diversity and investing more in tourism types with high income-generating effects such as health tourism and congress tourism,
- Increasing the number of Middle East tourists as well as North-East and European tourists,
- Employing a trained workforce (continuous development strategy),
- Increasing tourism investments, and
- Maintaining warm relations with neighboring countries in particular.

Bibliography

Akın, A. (2018), "Türk Turizminin Makroekonomik Göstergeler Üzerindeki Etkileri", **Journal of Tourism and Gastronomy Studies**, V.6, N.3, pp. 3–23.

Bahar, O. and Kozak, M. (2006), **Turizm Ekonomisi**, Ankara: Detay Yayıncılık.

Bahar, O. and Kozak, M. (2012), **Turizm ve Rekabet**, Ankara: Detay Yayıncılık.

Bahar, O. and Kozak, M. (2013), **Turizm Ekonomisi**, Ankara: Detay Yayıncılık.

Central Bank of the Republic of Turkey, https://www.tcmb.gov.tr/wps/wcm/connect/TR/TCMB+TR/Main+Menu/Istatistikler, (20.05.2019).

Çeken, H. (2003). Küreselleşme, Yabancı Sermaye ve Türkiye Turizmi, İstanbul: Değişim Yayınları.

Dinçer, M. Z. (1993), **Turizm Ekonomisi ve Türkiye Ekonomisinde Turizm**, İstanbul: Filiz Kitabevi.

İçöz, O. (2005), **Turizm Ekonomisi**, Ankara: Turhan Kitabevi.

Republic of Turkey Ministry of Culture and Tourism, Directorate General of Investments and Enterprises, http://yigm.kulturturizm.gov.tr/TR-201116/turizm-gelirleri-ve-giderleri.html, (20.05.2019).

The World Bank (2018), www.worldbank.org, (15.06.2018).

Turkish Statistical Institute, http://www.tuik.gov.tr/UstMenu.do?metod=temelist, (20.05.2019).

UNWTO. "Tourism Highlights-2009", https://www.e-unwto.org/doi/book/10.18111/9789284413591, (22.05.2019).

UNWTO. "Tourism Highlights-2010", https://www.e-unwto.org/doi/pdf/10.18111/9789284413720, (22.05.2019).

UNWTO. "Tourism Highlights-2011", https://www.e-unwto.org/doi/book/10.18111/9789284413935, (22.05.2019).

UNWTO. "Tourism Highlights-2012", https://www.e-unwto.org/doi/pdf/10.18111/9789284414666, (22.05.2019).

UNWTO. "Tourism Highlights-2013", https://www.e-unwto.org/doi/book/10.18111/9789284415427, (22.05.2019).

UNWTO. "Tourism Highlights-2014", https://www.e-unwto.org/doi/pdf/10.18111/9789284416226, (22.05.2019).

UNWTO. "Tourism Highlights-2015", https://www.e-unwto.org/doi/pdf/10.18111/9789284416899, (22.05.2019).

UNWTO. "Tourism Highlights-2016", https://www.e-unwto.org/doi/pdf/10.18111/9789284418145, (22.05.2019).

UNWTO. "Tourism Highlights-2017", http://www2.unwto.org/publication/unwto-tourism-highlights, (22.05.2019).

UNWTO. "Tourism Highlights-2018", http://www2.unwto.org/publication/unwto-tourism-highlights, (22.05.2019).

UNWTO. "Tourism Highlights-2019", http://www2.unwto.org/publication/unwto-tourism-highlights, (18.12.2019).

UNWTO. "International Tourism Results 2018 and Outlook 2019", http://cf.cdn.unw to.org/sites/all/files/pdf/unwto_barome ter_ jan19 _ presen tation _en.pdf, (22.05.2019).

Worldbank. (2018), "www.worldbank.org", (15.06.2018).

Yağcı, Ö. (2007), Turizm Ekonomisi, Ankara: Detay Yayıncılık.

Assist. Prof. Dr. Suna Muğan Ertuğral

The Effects of Employment in Turkey Tourism Investment

Abstract: The tourism sector is an important source of employment for Turkey. Turkey's tourism employment amount has been increasing on a yearly basis, and this has positive effects on the country's development. These positive effects are caused by the start of tourism investments. Especially, the employment of tourism has positive effects on economic development. As the tourism sector grows employment opportunities increase. Especially, tourism investment and management directly and indirectly or induced substantially provide employment. Owing to tourism the employment levels of underdeveloped regions in a country are increased considerably thus helping to reduce the differences in regional development. Therefore, the tourism sector is very important.

Keywords: Tourism Sector, Employment, Tourism İnvestment, Economic Development

1 Economic Impact of Tourism Investments

Tourism is of tremendous economic importance worldwide. Tourism is a huge sector of both goods and service exports. For this reason, tourism sector has many economic effects.

Tourism has positive economic effects such as effect on balance of payments, income effect, domestic import effect, labor multiplier effect, regulating effect of export and income distribution, employment increase and creation of new job opportunities, economic development and foreign exchange income generation, development of small-scale enterprises, and improvement of life standard and quality (Arabacı, 2018: 104).

One of the biggest problems in developing countries is finding solution to the unemployment problem. The rapid population growth in these countries brings with the problem of unemployment reaching significant levels. Tourism plays, especially for developing countries in terms of providing foreign exchange earnings, increasing employment opportunities, and economic development, a very important role.

Tourism sector has a labor capital sector. For this reason, the tourism sector provides employment for more employees. The tourism sector is an important source of Turkish economy because tourism has played an important role in the development of the economy. Especially, as the tourism sector develops employment opportunities increase as well. With the development of tourism the revival of other sectors of the economy emerges as the multiplier effect of tourism and its employment creation feature influences other sectors.

Employment effects of tourism revenues were frequently conducted. The employment impact of tourism investments and expenditures is very important, but the employment impact studies are limited (Muğan, 1988: 133). The economic impact of tourism is the measurement of the balance between gains and expenditures (Özğüç, 1984: 95). Investments in tourism sector have many economic effects. Tourism provides foreign currency gain. Tourism has an effect on the balance of payment positively.

1.1 Direct and Indirect Economic Effects of Tourism Investments

Tourism is a major economic factor for the developing country and its surrounding regions. Tourism contributes directly or indirectly-endoced to employment and economic growth in the region through the ongoing operations and activities of different firms that serve tourists.
The tourism sector contributes directly or indirectly to employment and economic growth by touristic enterprises.

In numerous economic sectors; including accommodations, food and beverage, retail, recreation, entertainment, and transportation; tourism has both direct and indirect or induced effects on production, jobs, wages, and taxes (Fig. 1) (Clark, 2014: 1).

The three major components of economic impact are classified as direct, indirect, and induced impacts. Collectively, these impacts measure the role of tourism industry on the broader economy at a local, provincial, and/or national level (InterVISTAS, 2017:6).

Tourism and hospitality industries create many employment opportunities in different areas like accommodations, transportation, and attractions sites (Aynalem et al., 2016: 5). Tourism's role in the economy is often perceived as being limited to the hospitality industry (cafes, hotels, and restaurants) and outbound and inbound travel agencies and carriers, which form the leading service sector in many countries. However, the economic impact of tourism is much greater, since many inputs are needed in order to produce tourism and leisure services, spanning the whole range of farm, agrifood, and industrial production, including the production of capital goods as well as construction and public works (Vellas, 2011: 3). Front offices in hotels, restaurants, travel agencies, tourism information offices, aircrafts, cruise lines, resorts, or shopping outlets provide direct employment because their employees are in contact with tourists and cater for tourist demand (UNWTO, 2014: 24). Tourism's economic impacts

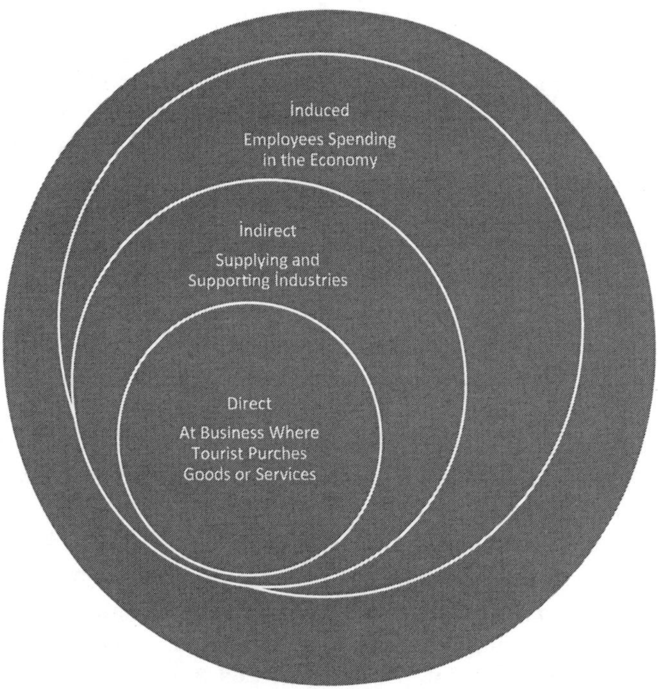

Fig. 1: Economic Impact of the Tourism Industry. **Sources:** InterVISTAS, 2017

are an important consideration in state, regional, and community planning and economic development.

2 The Effects of Tourism Investments on Employment

The labor-intensive character of the tourism sector plays an important role for preventing of unemployment by increasing employment. The employment contributions of tourism sector in Turkey are very important.

There are three types of employment in the tourism sector. Tourism sector is directly or indirectly or induced substantially providing employment (Olalı and Timur, 1988:147). The employment in the facilities located in the tourism sector constitutes direct employment. Industries involved in the supply of touristic goods and services benefit from spending made by tourists, and this constitutes indirect employment. "Induced Impacts, Represents the wider contribution of tourism through the expenditures of those who are directly or indirectly employed by the tourism sector" (Lemma, 2014: 2).

Formally, regional economists distinguish direct, indirect, and induced economic effects. Indirect and induced effects are sometimes collectively called secondary effects. The total economic impact of tourism is the sum of direct, indirect, and induced effects within a region. Any of these impacts may be measured as gross output or sales, income, employment, or value added (Stynes, 1999: 5–6). Measuring the indirect and induced workforce can be tricky but these effects are important. Therefore, the employment effect of tourism is increasing.

There are employment impacts of tourism investments both in the investment phase and the operation phase. A completed touristic investment creates a direct and indirect employment effect at the national and regional stage. The products of the tourism sector that are subject to foreign sales are zero-cost products such as sun, sea, fresh air, and sand. These products include low-cost products such as fruit, vegetables, and fish. For this reason, it is possible to provide higher benefits. As demand increases, other sectors are growing. Touristic activities accelerate the economic impacts. The tourism sector consists of many different tourism companies. For this reason, the tourism sector provides employment to qualified, unqualified, or semiqualified work force (Muğan, 1988: 137–139). However, the employment of qualified labor force is important when tourism sector develops. The tourism sector, which is based on labor-capital weight production techniques in particular, requires a certain level of education, knowledge, and skill, depending on the nature of the job. Tourism in developing countries such as Turkey is an undeniable dimension in economic development. The training of human capital in Turkey's tourism industry and the development of knowledge and skills is of great importance in terms of economic development and increasing the level of competition (Muğan Ertuğral and Gedik, 2018: 80). Therefore, especially in developing countries with high population density, the development of human capital is crucial in ensuring economic development.

Tourism investments also have large-scale investment. Therefore, the investment phase is also important to provide employment. Especially tourism investment provides employment in the construction sector and other sectors of the supplier.

2.1 Tourism Investment and Employment Relations in Turkey

Comparing tourism and industrial sectors on solving unemployment problem, features of employment created by tourism sector are important that tourism sector has less capital for employment.

Tab. 1: Employment Opportunity Provision of Power Sector in Turkey. **Source:** Olalı and Timur, 1986:112

Investment subject (other sectors)	**The amount of investment required to provide a job (million TL)**
Crude Oil Production	240.8
Chemical fertilizers	91.6
Energy	65.0
Iron and Steel	45.0
Cement	40.8
Flour and Bakery Products	20.8
Fruit and Vegetable Processing	20.5
Nonalcoholic Beverages Industry	12.9
Motor Vehicles	12.6.
Weaving	12.1.
Power Tools	9.9
Shoe Industry	3.3
Tourism (Hospitality) Industry	1.5

According to the work of DPT, in 1984 prices, comparing tourism and other sectors on solving unemployment problem, the amount of employment created by sectors are analyzed.

As shown by the study in Tab. 1, tourism sector provides more employment with less capital.

This work was renewed as of 2007–2010. Due to the labor-intensive feature of tourism, one person is used less amount of investment for the job (Tab. 2).

The amount of investment required to provide a job (million TL) is low in the tourism sector. The amount of capital required for employment varies depending on the size of the hotel.

Turkish tourism sector, which was operating in a motionless way for long years, has entered in a rapid growth trend since No. 2634 Tourism Incentive Law came into force in 1983, and by the support of the government. This law is a milestone for the tourism sector. No. 2634 Tourism Incentive Law was the dawn of a policy change for tourism development in Turkey. In the early 1980s, the investment expenditures for touristic investments were done. Especially

Tab. 2: Incentive Certificated Fixed Investment Costs in Turkey – Employment Relations (2007–2010). **Sources:** Hazine Yatırım Teşvik Belgeleri, 2010:7; Ünlüönen and Sahin, 2011:5

Sectors	The amount of investment required to provide a job (million TL) for Person	Index value (tourism = 100 TL)
Education	89,4	60,2
Leather – Leather sole	112.0	75.4
Construction	133,4	89,8
Tourism	148,6	100,0
Seafood	169,1	113,8
Health	180,4	121,4
Mining	188,4	126,8
Farming	203,1	136,7
Weaving – Clothing	221,5	149,1
Iron and Steel	271,3	182,5
Chemistry	308,5	207,6
Infrastructure	459,4	309,1
Transportation	2454,0	1650,9
Energy	2941,0	1985,9

the investments of accommodation enterprises accelerated. Tourism sector started to develop by the 1980s in Turkey. In this way, the number of incoming tourists and tourism revenue of Turkey reached to 39 million 488 thousand 401 million tourists and $ 29,513 billion dollars. million at 2018, while it was 1,625 million tourists and $411 million at 1983. Therefore, tourism is one of the indispensable sectors for Turkey. According to the data of tourism sector, between the years of 1980 and 2018, tourism sector was very important (Tabs. 3 and 4).

These numbers indicate a significant development in tourism sector: increasing accommodation capacity, increasing employment, and increasing value added of tourism in domestic output in Turkey over the years. Between 1993 and 2010 both the direct employment and total employment increased consistently.

Tourism investments that started in the 1980s increased the capacity of accommodation facilities. Increases in accommodation capacity imply direct employment are increasing in the tourism industry. The results of the studies started in the 1980s were taken as positive in the following years. The number of accommodation establishments and the number of employees increased by years (Tab. 5).

Tab. 3: Share of Tourism in Employment, (%). **Source:** Zengin, 2010:11

Years	**Tourism direct employment**	**Change rate%**	**Share of direct employment in total%**	**Turkey total employment**
1993	662.081		3.5	18.600.000
1997	891.334		4.3	20.900.000
1998	975.399		4.6	21.374.000
1999	1.012.152		4.6	21.860.000
2000	1.009.211		4.8	20.934.000
2001	1.007.793	**Change rate%** 1993–2001 %52	5.1	19.742.000
-	-	**Change rate%** 2001–2008		
2008	1.807.890	% 79	8.7	21.736.000

Tab. 4: Tourism Sector Employment Data in the World and Turkey. **Source:** WTTC, 2014

	Turkey				**World**			
Years	**Direct**		**Total employment**		**Direct**		**Total employment**	
	(000 person)	**%**	**(000 person)**	**% ratio**	**(000 person)**	**%**	**(000 person)**	**% ratio**
2004	521,5	2,4	1853,7	8,5	94246,3	3,3	254790,0	9,5
2005	474,0	2,1	1794,2	8,1	95307,4	3,5	256508,0	9,4
2006	495,4	2,2	1747,3	7,9	98473,9	3,5	263553,0	9,5
2007	441,4	2,1	1710,3	8,2	97794,0	3,4	271805,0	9,6
2008	461,1	2,1	1756,0	8,3	97527,6	3,4	260838,0	9,1
2009	459,1	2,1	1773,5	8,3	95260,1	3,3	252720,0	8,8
2010	477,3	2,1	1833,9	8,1	96130,5	3,3	250565,0	8,6
2021*	658,0	2,5	2216,0	8,3	120427,0	3,6	323826,0	9,7

*Estimated Data

In Turkey, tourism provides jobs for more than 1 million people. As well as accommodation sector, when the other related sectors examined from the table,it is seen that in 153.608 workplaces, 1.175,864 people are works. In the accommodation sector, there are 19.529 workplaces and it provides job for 388.961 people.

Tab. 5: Employment in Tourism Industry. **Source:** The Association of Turkish Travel Agencies, 2008 (Transfer; Akal, 2010)

Employment area	1993	1997	1999	2000	2001
Accommodation	79864	140119	146 201	151 320	161 207
Restaurants, Bars	72117	120119	119603	125997	172732
Transportation, tour operators	510100	631096	746348	731894	673854
Total direct employment	662081	891334	1012152	1009211	1007793
% Change yearly1		17.14	3.77	-0.29	-0.14
Indirect mp=(direct emp)*1.5	993122	1337000	1518227	1513816	1511689
Direct + indirect employment	1655203	2228334	2530379	2523026	2519481
Total employment (DIE)	-	20900000	21860000	20934000	19742000
Direct employment share in total	3.56	4.26	4.63	4.82	5.10
Indirect employment share in total	8.90	10.66	11.58	12.05	12.76

(1) Note: Direct employment percentage change from 1993 to 2001 equals 52.22 %.

The tourism sector is the largest job-providing sector in total employment in the country. In addition to direct employment, employment in tourism indirectly creates one and half times as much employment in other sectors. Thus employment in the tourism sector contributes significantly to reduce overall unemployment in Turkey.

The public and private sector decision-makers see tourism development as a major source of jobs and have, as a result, been supportive of tourism since the 1980s. Tourism has recently become a key sector in the world, since it contributes to economic growth and employment. Tourism supports employment through creating new jobs. Tourism is an opportunity for Turkey as a developing country to speed up its economic development. At the present time, tourism is no longer just for sea-sand-sun tourism; it is diversified as historical, green nature, health, thermal, sports, cultural, congress tourism, etc. Therefore, the employment effect of tourism is increasing. Promoting tourism as a priority sector in the 1980s was a very important development. Turkey has seen large-scale development in tourism within a span of 40 years.

As the 10th most popular tourist destination in the world and attracting more than 38.6 million tourists in 2017, Turkey continues to present vast investment opportunities in both the established and newly developing subsectors of the tourism industry (Invest Tourism, 2019). This will increase employment opportunities. The tourism sector accompanied by the change of sectoral structure in Turkey is the main element which determines economic growth and employment problem.

Governments should accelerate tourism investments to create employment areas. As the number of employees increases, the level of development between regions will be minimized. As a result, the tourism sector may also reduce regional disparities in terms of labor. Thus, everyone will have the opportunity to work in their own region and the labor demand will be equal.

Bibliography

Arabacı, H., (2018), "Turizm Sektörünün Ekonomik Büyümeye Etkisi Üzerine Teorik Bir İnceleme", **Balkan and Near Eastern Journal of Social Science**, Vol.4, N.3, pp. 104–109.

Aynalem, S., Birhanu, K., and Tesefay, S. (2016), "Employment Opportunities and Challenges in Tourism and Hospitality Sectors", **Journal of Tourism & Hospitality**, Vol.5, N.6, pp. 1–5.

Clark, N. (2014), **The Economic Impact of Tourism Development**, Retrieved from http://www.solimarinternational.com/resourcespage/blog/item/146-the-economic-impact-of-tourism-development, 06 October 2014, (39.03.2019).

Hazine Yatırım Teşvik Belgeleri. (2010), **2007–2010; TÜROFED Turizm Raporu.**

InterVISTAS. (2017), **Economic Impact of Tourism in Kelowna and the Greater Kelowna Area, B.C.**, Final Report, 1 March 2017, p.5.

Invest Tourism. (2019), **Tourism**, Retrieved from http://www.invest.gov.tr/en-US/sectors/Pages/WellnessAndTourism.aspx, (27.03.2019).

Lemma, A. F. (2014). Tourism Impacts- Evidence of Impacts on **Employment, Gender, Income**, ECONOMIC AND PRIVATE SECTOR, 22, U.K.: Overseas Development Institute.

Muğan, S., (1988), **Turizm Yatırımlarının İstihdama Olan Etkisi** (Yüksek Lisans Tezi), İstanbul Üniversitesi, İstanbul.

Muğan Ertuğral, S., and Gedik, S. (2018), "Türkiye'de Beşeri Sermaye ve Turizm İlişkisi", **IV. Uluslararsı Sosyal Bilimlerde Yeni Yönelimler Sempozyumu**

(SOBY), 06–07 Temmuz 2018 Talinn Abstract Book, (Zehra Göre and Zafer Gölen, Eds.), 1. Baskı, Gece Kitaplığı, Ankara.

Olalı, H., and Timur, A. (1986), **Turizmin Türk Ekonomisindeki Yeri**, İzmir: Ofis Matbaaacılık.

Olalı, H., and Timur, A. (1988), **Turizm Ekonomisi**, İzmir: Ofis Matbaacılık.

Özgüç, N. (1984), **Turizm Coğrafyası**, İstanbul: Güryay Matbaaası.

Stynes, D. J. (1999), **Economic Impacts of Tourism**, http://web4.canr.msu.edu/mgm2/econ/pdf/ecimpvol1.pdf, (27.03.2019).

The Association of Turkish Travel Agencies. (2008), Retrieved from http://www.tursab.org.tr (05.01.2019). Transfer; Akal, M. 2010, "Economic Implications of International Tourism on the Turkish Economy" **Tourismos: An International Multidisciplinary Journal of Tourism**, Vol. 5 N.1, pp. 131–152.

Ünlüönen, K., and Sahin, S. Z. (2011), "Turizmde İstihdam", **Elektronik Sosyal Bilimler Dergisi**, Vol.10, N.37, pp.1–25.

UNWTO – World Travel & Tourism Council. (2014), **Measuring Employment in the Tourism Industries**, UNWTO Publication, World Tourism Organization (UNWTO) and International Labour Organization (ILO), Retrieved from https://www.e-unwto.org/doi/pdf/10.18111/9789284416158, (05.01.2019).

Vellas, F. (2011), **The Indirect Impact of Tourism: An Economic Analysis**, Paris: Third Meeting of T20 Tourism Ministers.

WTTC – World Travel & Tourism Council – (2014), **Tourism Economic Research**, Retrieved from www.wttc.org, (15.02.2014).

Zengin, B. (2010), "Turizm sektörünün Türkiye ekonomisine reel ve moneter etkileri", **Akademik İncelemeler Dergisi**, Vol.5, N1, pp. 102–126.

Dr. Yeliz Sevimli Saitoğlu

"Examination of Turkey's Employment Diversities Between the Years 2004 and 2018 Based on Region Using Classification and Regression Trees (CART) Method"

Abstract: In this study to examine the labor market and its properties in Turkey and to examine the economic indicators of unemployment, there was focus on demographic characteristics of those who are employed and the unemployed. Secondly, it was aimed to assess the differences in the employment structure based on regions in Turkey. For this purpose a classification tree was formed by CART method. In the model each region is considered to be a class. A tree structure was obtained for the assignment of observations to each class i.e. region. Employment rates in agriculture, industry and service sectors were found to be the most important variables in determining the differences in employment structure by regions. In this case, while looking at employment profile by regions, the rate of employment in economic activity branch is the most important variable, while gender seems to be the least significant variable. From this point of view, it has been concluded that the employment rate in the economic activity of the regions exhibits a parallel appearance with the development level of the regions.

Keywords: Labor Force Statistics, Regions of Turkey, Classification and Regression Tree (CART)

1 Introduction

Since unemployment is one of the most important macroeconomic problems of countries, the objective of ensuring full employment is an important part of economic policies. In this study to examine the labor market and its properties in Turkey and to examine the economic indicators of unemployment, there was focus on demographic characteristics of those who are employed and unemployed. In particular, in the demographic study it was examined how the employed and the unemployed have changed over time according to various indicators such as gender, age group, education level and economic activity. To this end, it was benefited from the Household Labor Force Survey conducted by the Turkey Statistical Institute containing data that have been collected regularly since 1988 and providing information about the characteristics of the labor market in the country. By means of the data obtained from these surveys, the analysis was conducted on how different the participation to labor force of those employed and the unemployed, based on gender and regions in Turkey.

There are many statistical methods developed to analyze the data and reveal the hidden information within it. In this study Classification and Regression Trees (CART) method is used. CART is a nonparametric statistical method that uses decision trees while solving the classification and regression problems using both categorical and continuous variables. If the dependent variable is categorical, the method is called a classification tree. If the dependent variable is continuous the method is called a regression tree.

In this study, it was aimed to assess the differences in the employment structure based on regions in Turkey. For this purpose, a classification tree was formed by CART method. Twelve regions of Turkey formed by Turkish Statistical Institute (TurkStat) according to Statistical Regions (Level 1) Classification were included in the model as dependent variable. These regions are Istanbul, West Marmara, Aegean, East Marmara, West Anatolia, Mediterranean, Central Anatolia, West Black Sea, East Black Sea, Northeast Anatolia, Middle East Anatolia and Southeast Anatolia, respectively. For this purpose, labor statistics of Turkey formed between 2004 and 2018 according to regions are used. The rates of unemployment for each region based on gender and education, gender-based employment rates according to economic activity branches, gender-based rates of labor force participation, gender-based job search times (shorter than one year/longer than one year) and the gender-based rates of those who have no hope of finding a job were included in the model as independent variables. Thus, the profile of Turkey was revealed based on both the regions and the structure of employment of men and women.

2 Labor Market in Turkey

A portion of the total population in a country over the age of 15, except for those living in places such as barracks, prisons, nursing homes and hospitals, is called the noninstitutional working age population.

This population is divided into three basic groups based on labor force: as employed, unemployed and nonlabor force. The group of nonlabor force includes unemployed people who do not seek employment for various reasons such as housework, education and retirement. The labor force includes the population of the unemployed and the employed (TurkStat, 2018). Those mentioned above can be summarized as follows:

$$\text{Labor force} = \text{Employed} + \text{Unemployed}$$

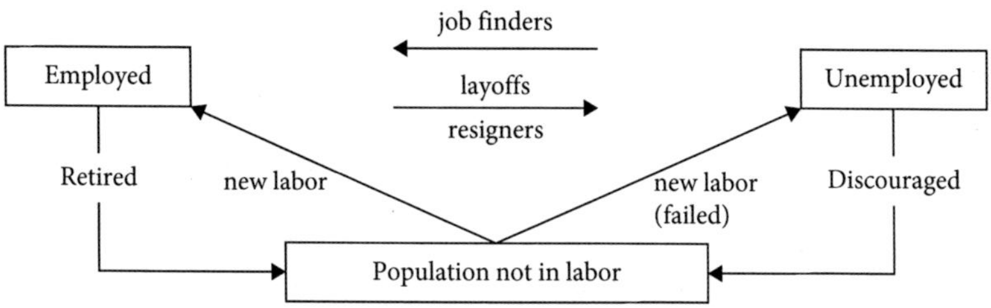

Fig. 1: Movements in Non-Institutional Civilian Population. **Source:** Ünsal, 2013

Noninstitutional Working Age Population = Labor force + Nonlabor force Accordingly, the noninstitutional population in working age consists of employed, unemployed and nonlabor force. There is a constant movement within this population. Fig.1 shows this flow.

As it can be understood from the examination of Fig. 1, some of the nonlabor force participate in the new labor force. These new participants (new graduates from the university, new recruits, etc.) have either become employed finding a job or become unemployed failing to find a job. On the other hand, some of the employees become nonlabor force by being retired, while others hold the status of unemployed by being fired or leaving their jobs. Some of the unemployed become employed by finding a job. Some of them losing their hopes to find a job (discouraged workers) become nonlaborers (Ünsal, 2013: 106).

Employment of a country depends on the country's level of development, population, natural resources, technological innovations, education and economic conditions. If all of the production factors in an economy work and participate in production, it means that there is a "full employment" situation (Yahşi, 2007: 22).

There are various definitions about who should be considered unemployed in an economy. According to the generally accepted definition,; anyone who seek a job at the current wage level and cannot find, should be considered unemployed. For example, a student should not be in this group if he/she is not seeking a job (Çepni, 2014: 106). Accordingly, the unemployment rate is the ratio of the unemployed population to the labor force.

$$Unemployment\ rate = \frac{Unemployed\ population}{Labor\ force}$$

Tab. 1: Turkish Labor force Status of Noninstitutional Population, 2014–2018. **Source:** The Table Is Generated by Benefiting from the Labor Statistics of Turkish Statistical Institute

Thousand Person	**2014**	**2015**	**2016**	**2017**	**2018**
Population	77,696	78,741	79,815	80,810	82,004
Population 15 years and over	56,986	57,854	58,720	59,894	60,654
Labor Force	28,786	29,678	30,535	31,643	32,274
Labor force participation rate (%)	50.5	51.3	52.0	52.8	53.2
Employed	25,933	26,621	27,205	28,189	28,738
Employment rate (%)	45.5	46.0	46.3	47.1	47.4
Unemployed	2,803	3,057	3,330	3,454	3,537
Unemployed rate (%)	9.9	10.3	10.9	10.9	11.0
Not in labor force	28,200	28,176	28,185	28,251	28,380

On the other hand, the employment rate is the ratio of employed to the noninstitutional working age population.

$$Employment\ rate = \frac{Employed}{Non-institutional\ working\ age\ population}$$

The labor force participation rate is the ratio of the labor force to the noninstitutional working age population.

$$labor\ force\ participation\ rate = \frac{Labor\ force}{Non-institutional\ working\ age\ population}$$

When the developments in the labor market in Turkey between the years of 2014 and 2018 examined in Tab. 1, Turkey's population which was around 77.7 million in 2014, increased by 5.5 % in the last 5 years and reached 82 million in 2018. The population over the age of 15 reached 60.6 million with a 6.4 % increase in the last 5 years. Accordingly, the population growth rate over the age 15 years seems to be higher than the overall growth rate of the population in Turkey. These figures show that there has been an increase in labor force and employment in parallel with the increase in population and especially in the working age population above 15 years of age. There has also been an increase in the number of unemployed and unemployment rates. The unemployment rate, which was 9.9 % in 2014, reached 11 % in 2018, and the unemployment rate significantly increased by 11.1 % in the last 5 years. Therefore, unemployment stands before us as the most serious problem of the labor market at first glance.

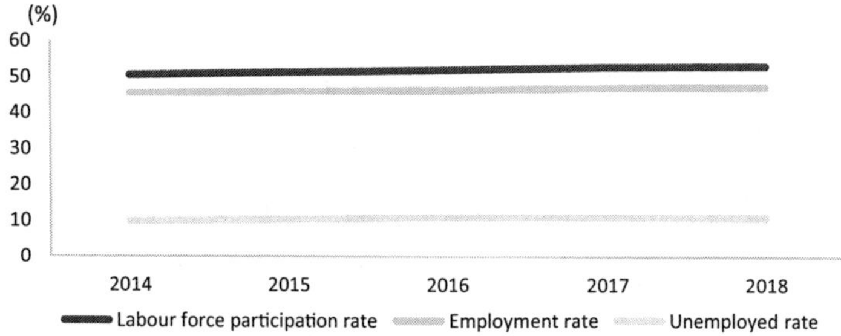

Fig. 2: Basic Labor Force Indicators, 2014–2018

Tab. 2: Employed Persons by Branch of Economic Activities and Gender, 2014–2018. **Source:** The Table Is Generated by Benefiting from the Labor Statistics of Turkish Statistical Institute

	2014		2015		2016		2017		2018	
	Thousand person	(%)	Thousand person	(%)	Thousand person	(%)	Thousand person	(%)	Thousand person	(%)
Male										
Agriculture	2,937	16.1	2,956	15.9	2,920	15.5	2,993	15.4	2,943	14.9
Industry	5,912	32.4	5,944	32.0	5,961	31.6	6,118	31.4	6,222	31.6
Service	9,394	51.5	9,662	52.1	10,011	53.0	10,349	53.2	10,554	53.5
Female										
Agriculture	2,533	32.9	2,527	31.4	2,384	28.7	2,471	28.3	2,353	26.1
Industry	1,315	17.1	1,302	16.2	1,322	15.9	1,360	15.6	1,444	16.0
Service	3,841	50.0	4,230	52.5	4,606	55.4	4,897	56.1	5,220	57.9

When the graphs of basic labor force indicators, unemployment, employment and labor force participation rates are examined, it is seen that the current problem is in an increasing trend structure due to the addition of new unemployed people to the labor market over time (Fig. 2).

When the distribution of employed persons by economic activities in Turkey was examined in Tab. 2 between 2014 and 2018, it reveals that the highest employment rates of men and women is in the service sector. In agriculture, employment rate declines with time. Agricultural employment decreased by 26 % in women and by 7.5 % in men in the last 5 years. Parallel to the decline in agricultural employment among women, there was an increase in the employment rate in service branch and in service, which was 50 % in 2014, increased to 57.9 % with a 15 % increase in 2018. When it comes to men, the employment rate, which was 51.5 % in 2014, rose to 53.5 % in 2018 with an increase of 3.8 %. Accordingly, it is observed that the employment rate of women in the service sector is higher than men. But in the industry, it is seen that the employment rate of men is higher, and the number of employees increases with time.

2.1 Change of Employment and Unemployment in Turkey over Time

The official data on the labor market in Turkey is based on the Household Labor Force Survey, which is made by TurkStat keeping into consideration the norms and standards of International Labor Organization (ILO) and European Community Statistical Office (Eurostat) in this regard (Sapancalı, 2008:8). Household Labor Force Survey is applied since 1988 on regular basis by the Turkey Statistical Institute. This survey is applied in order to compile information on economic activity, occupation, job status and working time, job search time occupation they seek and similar characteristics of the unemployed, and is an important source of information about the characteristics of the labor market in the country (TurkStat, 2018).

Labor market refers to a structure where various dynamics such as gender, age group, education level, marital status and economic activity branch of the employed and unemployed are included (Çondur and Bölükbaş, 2014:81). Accordingly, in determining the structure of the labor market, it is useful to examine the demographic characteristics of the employed and unemployed individuals.

In Tab. 3, when it was examined the reasons for noninclusion to labor force of those not included in the labor force, in Turkey between the years 2014 and 2018, it is seen that the population not included in the labor force is 20 million in women and 8 million in men, and there is a difference of approximately 12 million. This difference is stemming from the fact that women are engaged in housework, and the number of women engaged in housework is about 11 million. The number of people who have no hope of finding a job is generally increased in females, but decreased in males.

The existence of well-trained skilled labor force, the ratio of this labor force in the total and the use of the knowledge and skills of this resource play an important role in the development of countries. When we look at the developed countries, it is seen that the proportion of skilled and educated labor force is higher (Taş and Bozkaya, 2012: 158).

When unemployment rates by education level in Turkey between the years 2014 and 2018 is examined in Tab. 4, it is observed that the lowest unemployment rates in women is in illiterate segment while the highest rate is observed in those having

Tab. 3: Reasons of Noninclusion to Labor Force by Years and Gender, 2014–2018. **Source:** The Table Is Generated by Benefiting from the Labor Statistics of Turkish Statistical Institute

		Reason							
Years	**Population not in labour force**	**Not seeking a job, but available to start**		**Working seasonally**	**Housewife**	**Education/ Training**	**Retired**	**Disabled, old ill etc.**	**Other**
		Discouraged	**Other**						
Male									
2014	8,089	370	614	27	-	2,220	3,003	1,410	445
2015	8,120	416	582	26	-	2,211	3,156	1,351	377
2016	8,133	406	584	24	-	2,220	3,201	1,351	345
2017	8,166	370	535	28	-	2,204	3,322	1,317	390
2018	8,206	311	512	55	-	2,148	3,406	1,344	429
Female									
2014	20,112	246	1,255	67	11,589	2,250	824	2,512	1,368
2015	20,056	260	1,144	68	11,498	2,275	926	2,527	1,359
2016	20,052	252	1,177	64	11,098	2,320	958	2,685	1,498
2017	20,085	267	1,092	58	11,133	2,263	1,045	2,692	1,535
2018	20,174	236	1,112	100	11,061	2,324	1,130	2,696	1,515

Tab. 4: Unemployed Persons by Educational Status and Gender, 2014–2018. **Source:** The Table Is Generated by Benefiting from the Labor Statistics of Turkish Statistical Institute

	2014 (%)	2015 (%)	2016 (%)	2017 (%)	2018 (%)
Male					
Illiterate	13.6	11.3	11.8	11.2	11.7
Less than high school	9.5	10.0	9.8	9.6	9.8
High and vocational high school	8.7	8.6	9.6	9.6	9.2
Higher education	7.6	7.6	8.8	8.7	9.1
Female					
Illiterate	3.0	2.9	3.2	3.6	3.4
Less than high school	9.3	10.1	11.0	10.5	10.9
High and vocational high school	19.2	19.3	20.8	20.9	20.4
Higher education	15.5	16.3	16.9	18.4	17.1

high school education. In males, unemployment rates are different from females according to education. It is observed that the highest unemployment rate is in the illiterate segment and the least unemployment rate is in higher education segment.

In Tab. 5 job search time by gender in Turkey between the years 2014 and 2018 is given. The extent of long-term unemployment and hence the constantly winning unemployment (hysteresis) have an important place in the investigation of the unemployment structure. Among the types of unemployment, the longest-term unemployment is the most damaging to the individual and society. OECD has defined long-term unemployment as unemployment for 1 year or more (Durak and Kaya, 2014: 64). When long-term unemployment is examined, there has been a significant increase in both men and women in the last 5 years.

When the unemployment rate of the 15–24 age group in Turkey between the years 2014 and 2018 is examined in Tab. 6, it is observed that the youth unemployment rate is higher in women than men. In 2014, the unemployment rate was 16.6 % in men, amounting to the level of 17.6 % in 2018 increased by 6 % in the last 5 years. In women, the unemployment rate raising from 20.4 % in 2014 to 25.3 % in 2018 significantly increased by 24 % in the last 5 years. In total, the unemployment rate was 17.9 % in 2014, amounting to 20.3 % in 2018, drastically increased by 13.4 % in the last 5 years.

3 Classification and Regression Trees

Use of trees in regression dates back to the AID (Automatic Interaction Detection) program developed by Morgan and Sonquist in the early 1960s. The

Tab. 5: Unemployed Persons by Job Search Time and Gender, 2014–2018. **Source:** The Table Is Generated by Benefiting from the Labor Statistics of Turkish Statistical Institute

Thousand person							
Years							
Male	1–2 months	3–5 months	6–8 months	9–11 months	1–2 years	2–3 years	over 3 years
2014	843	433	176	51	206	68	36
2015	857	448	191	62	236	69	28
2016	924	476	192	66	246	62	39
2017	923	467	208	71	247	69	39
2018	974	465	191	78	260	72	43
Female	1–2 months	3–5 months	6–8 months	9–11 months	1–2 years	2–3 years	over 3 years
2014	353	260	110	38	202	58	19
2015	408	261	136	49	226	63	23
2016	456	317	161	51	246	62	31
2017	459	326	182	63	287	81	33
2018	489	315	168	65	286	87	44

Tab. 6: Unemployed Persons by Age (15–24) and Gender, 2014–2018. **Source:** The Table Is Generated by Benefiting from the Labor Statistics of Turkish Statistical Institute

Thousand person						
Years	**Unemployed**			**Unemployed rate (%)**		
	Male	Female	Total	Male	Female	Total
2014	527	331	858	16.6	20.4	17.9
2015	529	390	919	16.5	22.2	18.5
2016	562	424	985	17.4	23.7	19.6
2017	593	476	1,069	17.8	26.1	20.8
2018	593	459	1,052	17.6	25.3	20.3

study on trees began in 1973 by Breiman and Friedman independently of each other and began to use tree methods in classification. Later, they joined forces and were joined in turn by Stone, who contributed significantly to the methodological development. Olshen was an early user of tree methods in medical applications and contributed to their theoretical development (Breiman et al., 1993: ix)

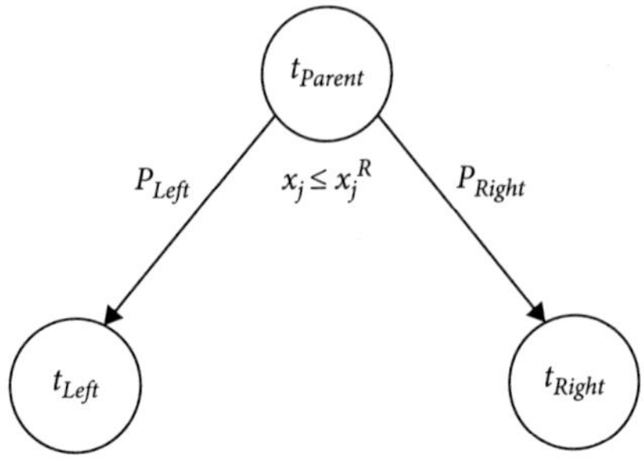

Fig. 3: Splitting Algorithm of CART. **Source:** Timofeev, 2004

CART is a nonparametric statistical methodology developed for analyzing classification issues either from categorical or continuous dependent variables. If the dependent variable is categorical, CART produces a classification tree. When the dependent variable is continuous, it produces a regression tree. CART partitions the data into two subsets so that the records within each subset are more homogeneous than in the previous subset. The construction of a CART classification rule consists of three parts. These are the sample splitting rule, the goodness of split criteria and the criteria for choosing an optimal or final tree for analysis. CART splits a sample into binary subsamples based on the response to a very simple question requiring only a yes/no answer (Yohannes, Webb, 1999). Here is an example of splitting algorithm of CART (Fig. 3).

In the classification trees, the formation of the binary tree structure begins with the separation of the initial dataset X into two homogeneous subset. A learning sample consists of data $(\mathbf{x}_1, j_1)$, …, $(\mathbf{x}_N, j_N)$ on N cases where $\mathbf{x}_n \in \mathbf{X}$ and $j_n \in \{1,2,\ldots,J\}$, $n = 1,\ldots,N$. The learning sample is denoted by $L = \{(\mathbf{x}_1, j_1), \ldots, (\mathbf{x}_N, j_N)\}$. According to this binary tree structured classifiers are constructed by repeated splits of subsets of **X** into two descendant subsets, beginning with **X** itself. This process for a hypothetical six-class tree is pictured in Fig 4. In Fig. 4, X_2 and X_3 are disjoint, with $X = X_2 \cup X_3$. Similarly X_4 and X_5 are disjoint, with $X_4 \cup X_5 = X_2$, and $X_6 \cup X_7 = X_3$. Those subsets which are not split, in this case X_6, X_8, X_{10}, X_{11}, X_{12}, X_{14}, X_{15}, X_{16}, and X_{17} are called terminal subsets. These are indicated in Fig. 4, by a rectangular box; nonterminal subsets are indicated by circles. There may be two or more terminal subsets with the same class label (Breiman et al., 1993. As it is seen in Fig. 4, X_{10} and X_{16} are assigned to the same class, which is the third class.

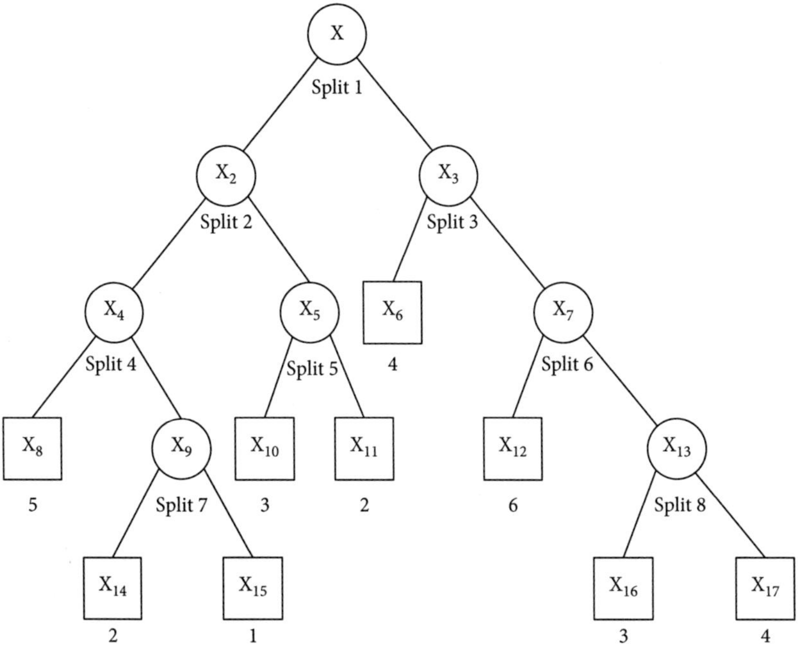

Fig. 4: Binary Tree Structured Classifiers. **Source:** Breiman et al., 1993

The splitting procedure is very important in CART. Gini index is one of the most popular split selection methods, and it is often the default option for the impurity measure and goodness-of-fit measure in classification problems. The basic gini index is defined as:

$$i(t) = \sum_{j \neq i} p(j/t)\, p(i/t)$$

where i and j are categories of target variable, and $p(j/t)$is the estimated probability that an observation belonging to group j given that it is in node t, $p(j/t) = p(j,t)/p(t)$; and $p(j,t)$ is the estimated probability that an observation being in group j and at node t, $p(j,t) = \pi(j)N_j(t)/N_j$; $p(t)$ is the estimated probability that an observation is at node t, $p(t) = N_t/N$; $\pi(j)$ is the prior probability for group j; $\pi(j) = N_j/N$ and $N_j(t)$ is the number of group j members at node t and $N_j$is the sizes of group j (Liu et al., 2011:556).

Thus the split selection procedure can be thought of as a repeated attempt to minimize overall tree impurity. When the records in a node are evenly distributed across the categories, the gini index takes its maximum value. It reaches its minimum (zero) when all records in the node belong to the same category (SPSS Modeler 15 Algorithms Guide, 2012).

4 Method

In this study, using the method of CART it was aimed to determine the factors that affect the unemployment rate in Turkey. Twelve regions of Turkey formed by Turkey Statistical Institute according to Statistical Regions (Level 1) classification were included in the model as dependent variable. These regions are Istanbul, West Marmara, Aegean, East Marmara, West Anatolia, Mediterranean, Central Anatolia, West Black Sea, East Black Sea, Northeast Anatolia, Middle East Anatolia and Southeast Anatolia, respectively. For this purpose, labor statistics of Turkey formed between 2004 and 2018 according to regions are used. The rates of unemployment for each region based on gender and education (illiterate, less than high school, high and vocational high school, higher education), gender-based employment rates according to economic activity branches (service, agriculture, industry), gender-based rates of labor force participation, gender-based job search times (shorter than one year/longer than one year) and the gender-based rates of those who have no hope of finding a job (discouraged workers) were included in the model as independent variables. The related analyses were performed by SPM 8.3 (Salford Predictive Modeler) data mining program.

5 Results

Turkey's statistically classified 12 region's gender-based labor force data set obtained between 2004 and 2018 consists of 360 observations. Some of these observations are used to form the tree and they are called the learning data set. The rest of them are used to test the formed tree and it is called test data. The results of the learning and test data set in the model formed with CART are shown in Tab. 7.

In the classification tree formed by means of CART, all independent variables included in the model are determined according to their level of importance. The results of the independent variables, which are the most important in revealing the differences in the employment structure based on regions, are given in Tab. 8.

Employment rates in agriculture, industry and service sectors, respectively, were found to be the most important variables in determining the differences in employment structure by regions. These variables were followed by other variables in order of importance. As far as the unemployment rates are concerned

Tab. 7: Ratio of Learning and Test Data

				N: Number of observations
Regions	**Learning Data (N)**	**(%)**	**Test Data (N)**	**(%)**
Istanbul	23	76.6	7	23,4
West Marmara	25	83.3	5	16.7
Aegean	20	66.7	10	33.3
East Marmara	25	83.3	5	16.7
West Anatolia	21	70.0	9	30.0
Mediterranean	21	70.0	9	30.0
Central Anatolia	21	70.0	9	30.0
West Black Sea	23	76.6	7	23.3
East Black Sea	23	76.6	7	23.3
Northeast Anatolia	20	66.7	10	33.3
Middle East Anatolia	24	80.0	6	20.0
Southeast Anatolia	26	86.7	4	13.3
Total	272	75.6	88	24.4

based on education level, it is seen that the importance of the education below the high school level is higher than the other education levels. In this case, while looking at employment profile by regions, in classification of regions it was seen that the effect of the unemployment rate on those who had under-high school education was higher than the effect of other education levels. Gender is determined to be the least important variable.

The total true classification ratio of the decision tree composed by using the learning data set is 73.5 % and is given in the table below. The most successful regions in the classification process of the tree were determined as Istanbul and Western Anatolia regions with the true classification rate of 100 %. These regions were followed by the Mediterranean, East Marmara, East Black Sea, Western Black Sea and West Marmara regions, respectively. The most unsuccessful regions in the classification of the tree were observed to be Aegean, Northeast Anatolia, Middle East Anatolia and Southeast Anatolia. Accordingly, the ratio of the true classification of the tree was found to be successful (Tab. 9).

Table 10 shows the results of the test data consisting of 88 observations. Accordingly, the total true classification ratio of the tree was found to be 88.6 %. The most successful part of the tree classification is the Istanbul region with a true classification rate of 100 %. These regions were followed by the Mediterranean,

Tab. 8: Variables Importance

<table>
<tr><th>Variables</th><th>Score</th><th></th></tr>
<tr><td>Employment rate in agriculture</td><td>100.00</td><td>||||||||||||||||||||||||||||||||||||||
||||||||||</td></tr>
<tr><td>Employment rate in industry</td><td>67.79</td><td>||||||||||||||||||||||||||||||||</td></tr>
<tr><td>Employment rate in service</td><td>52.54</td><td>|||||||||||||||||||||||||</td></tr>
<tr><td>Rate of discouraged workers</td><td>44.37</td><td>|||||||||||||||||||||</td></tr>
<tr><td>Rate of job search times (shorter than one year)</td><td>34.96</td><td>||||||||||||||||</td></tr>
<tr><td>Unemployment rate according to education level (less than high school)</td><td>34.47</td><td>||||||||||||||||</td></tr>
<tr><td>Labor force participation rate</td><td>34.39</td><td>||||||||||||||||</td></tr>
<tr><td>Rate of job search times (longer than one year)</td><td>29.63</td><td>||||||||||||||</td></tr>
<tr><td>Unemployment rate according to education level (illiterate)</td><td>27.71</td><td>|||||||||||||</td></tr>
<tr><td>Unemployment rate according to education level (higher education)</td><td>18.07</td><td>||||||||</td></tr>
<tr><td>Unemployment rate according to education level (high and vocational high school)</td><td>14.86</td><td>|||||||</td></tr>
<tr><td>Gender</td><td>2.96</td><td>|</td></tr>
</table>

East Marmara, West Marmara and Western Black Sea and regions, respectively. When composing the tree, it was observed that the most unsuccessful regions in classification were Central Anatolia, Northeast Anatolia and East Black Sea. According to this, when we retested with the tree test data, the percentage of the total true classification of the tree was found to be quite successful.

As seen in Fig. 5, the formed tree has 14 terminal nodes. The rules given in Tab. 11 are established when making assignment to each terminal node. The tree that draws a flow as a result of these rules is as follows: As shown in the figure, the nodes indicated by red are the terminal nodes and in these nodes assignments are made to the classes, i.e., to the regions.

Assignment rules to terminal nodes in the CART model are shown in the table below:

6 Conclusion and Discussion

In this study examining the labor market and its properties in Turkey, examining the economic indicators of unemployment it was focused on demographic characteristics of those who are employed and the unemployed. In particular,

Tab. 9: True Classification Ratio of Learning Sample

Class	Cases (N)	True-classed	True classification ratio (%)
Istanbul	23	23	100.0
West Marmara	25	20	80.0
Aegean	20	7	35.0
East Marmara	25	22	88.0
West Anatolia	21	21	100.0
Mediterranean	21	19	90.4
Central Anatolia	21	13	61.9
West Black Sea	23	19	82.6
East Black Sea	23	20	86.9
Northeast Anatolia	20	11	55.0
Middle East Anatolia	24	12	50.0
Southeast Anatolia	26	13	50.0
Total	272	200	73.5

Tab. 10: True Classification Ratio of Test Sample

Class	Cases (N)	True-classed	True classification ratio (%)
Istanbul	7	7	100.0
West Marmara	5	4	80.0
Aegean	10	5	50.0
East Marmara	5	4	80.0
West Anatolia	9	9	100.0
Mediterranean	9	8	89.0
Central Anatolia	9	4	44.4
West Black Sea	7	5	71.4
East Black Sea	7	3	42.8
Northeast Anatolia	10	4	40.0
Middle East Anatolia	6	3	50.0
Southeast Anatolia	4	2	50.0
Total	88	78	88.6

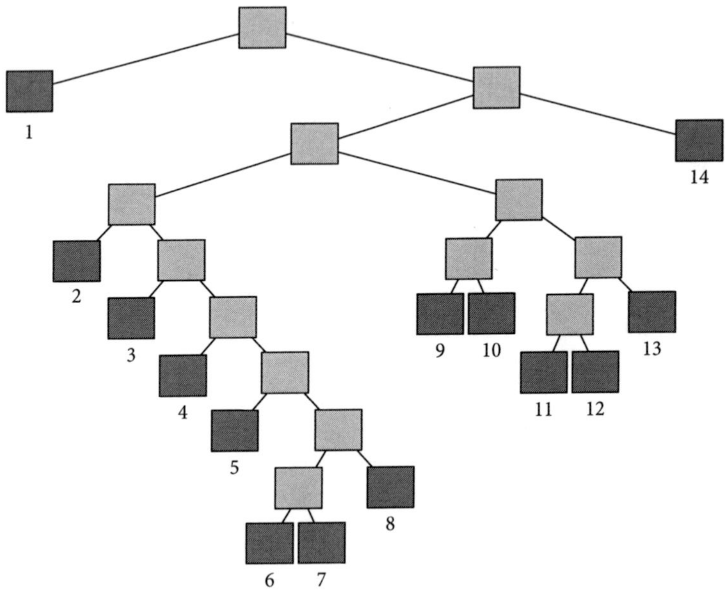

Fig. 5: Classification Tree Topology

in the demographic study it was examined how the employed and the unemployed have changed over time according to various indicators such as gender, age group, education level and type of economic activity. When the distribution of employed persons by economic activities in Turkey was examined between 2014 and 2018, it reveals that the highest employment rates of men and women is in the service sector. When the unemployment rate of the 15–24 age group in Turkey between the years 2014 and 2018 is examined, it is observed that the youth unemployment rate is higher in women than men. In 2014, the unemployment rate was 16.6 % in men, amounting to the level of 17.6 % in 2018 increased by 6 % in the last 5 years. In women, the unemployment rate raising from 20.4 % in 2014 to 25.3 % in 2018 significantly increased by 24 % in the last 5 years. In total, the unemployment rate was 17.9 % in 2014, amounting to 20.3 % in 2018, drastically increased by 13.4 % in the last 5 years.

Secondly, it was aimed to assess the differences in the employment structure based on regions in Turkey. For this purpose, a classification tree was formed by CART method. Twelve regions of Turkey formed by Turkey Statistical Institute according to Statistical Regions (Level 1) Classification were included in the

Tab. 11: Rules for Terminal Node

Terminal Node	Rule	Class	Class Probability
1	if employment rate in agriculture < 4.7	Istanbul	1.0
2	if employment rate in agriculture > 4.7 and employment rate in service<=58.65 and unemployment rate according to education (less than high school)<=7.95 and rates of job search times (shorter than one year)<=1.8	Northeast Anatolia	0.85
3	if employment rate in agriculture > 4.7 and employment rate in service <=58.65 and unemployment rate according to education (less than high school)<=7.95 and rates of job search times (less than one year)>1.8 and labor force participation rate<=29.65	Central Anatolia	0.35
4	if employment rate in service <=58.65 and unemployment rate according to education (less than high school)<=7.95 and rates of job search times (less than one year)>1.8 and labor force participation rate>29.65 and employment rate in agriculture>4.7 and employment rate in agriculture<=29.3	West Marmara	0.67
5	if employment rate in service <=58.65 and unemployment rate according to education (less than high school)<=7.95 and rates of job search times (less than one year)>1.8 and labor force participation rate>29.65 and employment rate in agriculture>29.3 and employment rate in industry<=5.45	East Black Sea	0.78
6	if employment rate in service <=58.65 and unemployment rate according to education (less than high school)<=7.95 and rates of job search times (less than one year)>1.8 and employment rate in agriculture>29.3 and employment rate in industry>5.45 and rates of discouraged workers>29.65 and rates of discouraged workers<=3.78 labor force participation rate>29.65 and labor force participation rate<=34.7	West Marmara	0.73
7	if employment rate in service <=58.65 and unemployment rate according to education (less than high school)<=7.95 and rates of job search times (less than one year)>1.8 and employment rate in agriculture>29.3 and employment rate in industry>5.45 and rates of discouraged workers<=3.78 labor force participation rate>34.7	West Black Sea	0.90

(*continued on next page*)

Tab. 11: (continued)

Terminal Node	Rule	Class	Class Probability
8	if employment rate in service <=58.65 and unemployment rate according to education (less than high school)<=7.95 and rates of job search times (less than one year)>1.8 and labor force participation rate>29.65 and employment rate in agriculture>29.3 and employment rate in industry>5.45 and rates of discouraged workers>3.78	East Black Sea	0.69
9	if employment rate in agriculture>4.7 and employment rate in service <=58.65 and unemployment rate according to education (less than high school)>7.95 and rates of discouraged workers<=1.96 and rate of employment in industry<=23.5	Aegean	0.33
10	if employment in rate agriculture>4.7 and employment rate in service <=58.65 and unemployment rate according to education (less than high school)>7.95 and rates of discouraged workers<=1.96 and rate of employment in industry>23.5	East Marmara	0.78
11	if employment rate in agriculture>4.7 and employment rate in service <=58.65 and unemployment rate according to education (less than high school)>7.95 and rates of discouraged workers>1.96 and rates of discouraged workers<=8.62 and rates of job search times (less than one year)<=13.5	Central Anatolia	0.31
12	if employment rate in agriculture>4.7 and employment rate in service <=58.65 and unemployment rate according to education (less than high school)>7.95 and rates of discouraged workers>1.96 and rates of discouraged workers<=8.62 and rates of job search times (less than one year)>13.5	Mediterr-anean	0.76
13	if employment rate in agriculture>4.7 and employment rate in service <=58.65 and unemployment rate according to education (less than high school)>7.95 and rates of discouraged workers>8.61	Southeast Anatolia	0.54
14	if employment rate in agriculture>4.7 and employment rate in service >58.65	West Anatolia	0.95

model as dependent variable. In the model each region is considered to be a class. A tree structure was obtained for the assignment of observations to each class i.e. region. Employment rates in agriculture, industry and service sectors were found to be the most important variables in determining the differences in employment structure by regions. In this case, while looking at employment profile by regions, the rate of employment in economic activity branch is the most important variable, while gender seems to be the least significant variable. Accordingly, the fact that the employment rate of Istanbul, taking place in the first node with 100 % of probability rate, in the agricultural sector was below 4.7 % was the most important criterion in distinguishing it from other regions. When the employment profile of the West Marmara region was assessed, which is at the fourth node with the rate of 67 % probability and at the sixth node with the rate of 73 %, the fact that the employment rate in the service sector is equal to and lower than the rate of 58.65 % and the unemployment rate is lower than the rate of 7.9 % and that the rate of job seekers for less than a year was higher than 1.8 % have been the most basic indicators. The employment profile of the Western Black Sea region, which is on the seventh node with 90 % of probability rate, differs from the West Marmara region by the fact that the labor force participation rate is higher than 34.7 %. The Aegean and West Marmara regions differ according to the employment rate in the industrial sector. The Central Anatolia and Mediterranean regions differ according to the job search period of the unemployed. When the employment profile in West Anatolia region, which is in the fourteenth node with a probability of 95 %, is examined, it is observed that the employment rate in the agricultural sector is over 4.7 % and the employment rate in the service sector is higher than 58.65 %.

In conclusion, differences in the employment profile in Turkey have been tried to be determined by means of a classification tree formed by CART method. It has been observed that the employment rates in the fields of economic activity have the most significant effect on the differentiation of the regions. From this point of view, it has been concluded that the employment rate in the economic activity of the regions exhibits a parallel appearance with the development level of the regions.

Bibliography

Çepni, E. (2014), **Ekonomik Göstergeler ve İstatistikler Rehberi**, Ankara: Seçkin.

Çondur, F., and Bölükbaş, M. (2014), "Türkiye'de İşgücü Piyasası ve Genç İşsizlik-Büyüme İlişkisi Üzerine Bir İnceleme", **Amme İdaresi Dergisi**, Vol.47, N.2, pp.77–93.

Durak, Ş., and Kaya, V. (2014), "Türkiye'de İşsizlik ve İşsizliği Azaltmaya Yönelik Politikalar: Tarihsel Bir Bakış", **Atatürk Üniversitesi İktisadi ve İdari Bilimler Dergisi**, Vol.28, N.2, pp.55–73.

IBM SPSS Modeler 15 Algorithms Guide. (2012), **C&RT Algorithms**, Retrieved from http://public.dhe.ibm.com/software/analytics/spss/documentation/modeler/15.0/en/AlgorithmsGuide.pdf (01.05.2019).

Breiman, L., Friedman, J.H., Olshen, A.R., and Stone, J.C. (1993), **Classification and Regression Trees**, New York: Chapman & Hall.

Liu, Y., Yang, M., Ramsay, M., Li, X., and Coid, J.W. (2011), "A Comparison of Logistic Regression, Classification and Regression Tree and Neural Networks Models in Predicting Violent Re-Offending", **Journal of Quantitative Criminology**, Vol.27, pp. 547–573.

Sapancali, F. (2008), "Türkiye'de İşgücü Piyasası, Sorunlar ve Politikalar", **TÜHİS İş Hukuku ve İktisat Dergisi**, Vol.21, N.2–3, pp.8–30.

Taş, S., and Bozkaya, G. (2012), "Avrupa Birliğine Uyum sürecinde Türkiye'de Uygulanan İstihdam Politikaları", **Kahramanmaraş Sütçü İmam Üniversitesi İİBF Dergisi**, Vol.1, pp.151–176.

Timofeev, R. (2004), **Classification and Regression Trees (CART) Theory and Applications**, Humbolt University, Center of Applied Statistics and Economics.

Ünsal, E.M. (2013), **Makro İktisat**, Ankara: İmaj Yayıncılık.

Yahşi, F. (2007), **Küreselleşme ve istihdam** (Yüksek Lisans Tezi), Çukurova Üniversitesi, Adana.

Yohannes, Y., and Webb, P. (1999), **Classification and Regression Trees: A User Manual for Identifying Indicators of Vulnerability to Famine and Chronic Food Insecurity**, Washington, D.C. Mimeo: International Food Policy Research Institute.

Salford Predictive Modeler. (2018), **Introducing CART**, Retrieved from http://media.salford-systems.com/pdf/spm8/IntroCART.pdf (01.05.2019).

Turkish Statistical Institute. (2018), **Labour Force Statistics (2014 and after)**, Retrieved from https://biruni.tuik.gov.tr/medas/?kn=72&locale=en (01.05.2019).

List of Figures

List of Tables